Frank Parsons

**Rational Money**

Frank Parsons

**Rational Money**

ISBN/EAN: 9783337365707

Printed in Europe, USA, Canada, Australia, Japan

Cover: Foto ©Suzi / pixelio.de

More available books at **www.hansebooks.com**

A

# National Currency

INTELLIGENTLY REGULATED IN REFERENCE

TO THE

# Multiple Standard.

BY

## FRANK PARSONS

LECTURER IN BOSTON UNIVERSITY LAW SCHOOL; PROFESSOR OF HISTORY AND POLITI-
CAL SCIENCE IN KANSAS S. A. COLLEGE; PRESIDENT OF THE NATIONAL LEAGUE
FOR PROMOTING THE PUBLIC OWNERSHIP OF MONOPOLIES; AUTHOR OF
"THE WORLD'S BEST BOOKS," "THE PHILOSOPHY OF MUTUAL-
ISM," "THE TELEGRAPH MONOPOLY," ETC.; MEMBER OF
THE BOSTON BAR, AND AUTHOR OF "PARSONS'
EDITION OF MORSE ON BANKS AND
BANKING," ETC., ETC.

PUBLISHED BY

## C. F. TAYLOR

1520 CHESTNUT STREET, PHILADELPHIA, PA.

1898

# PREFACTORY NOTE.

In the early spring of 1897, after the subsidence of the remarkable "battle of the standards" of the campaign of 1896, I realized the need of two things:

First—A presentation of the historical instances of success with paper money; also the reasons for the failures that are so often cited by the partially informed as final arguments against paper money.

Second—A further development of, and a strong presentation of the Multiple Standard, which is the only true and rational standard for money—the only thing that will give us a *normal dollar* at all times instead of the abnormal gold standard dollar, or the somewhat less abnormal bi-metalic dollar.

I outlined my plan for such a book and communicated the same to my friend, Prof. Frank Parsons, of Boston University, whose studies had already led him to take advanced views upon the money question in his Arena articles of October and November, 1896. Being myself too busy to undertake the work, I was fortunate (and it was fortunate for the work) in securing the services of so eminent and able a scholar as he, who combines in a phenomenal degree the qualities of investigator, analyst, logician and original thinker.

By the ability and thoroness with which Professor Parsons has done the work, he has placed not only myself, but our country and the cause of economics under lasting obligations to him.

The idea has here-to-fore been quite prevalent that paper money has been a failure in history. This book conclusively shows that many of the popularly considered failures have been successes in the main, and that paper money has succeeded or failed according as the correct principles have been followed or violated. In this respect it is just like the grocery business, brick making, farming, or any other business undertaking; it will succeed when correctly managed and fail when badly managed.

Paper money is the money of civilization. It is here to stay. Its history and principles should be known.

Gold and silver money was evolved by a natural process. The first paper money consisted of promises to pay gold and silver. The idea is still prevalent that paper money is only "representative" money, and that it can "represent" only gold and silver. Why can it not "represent" any kind of wealth, or all kinds of wealth, averaged, as well as gold and silver? The purpose of this book is to solve this question.

Money has been defined as "an instrument of association." Perhaps a better definition is *an instrument of co-operation*. As such it should be made as perfect as possible, and not be allowed to degenerate into an instrument of oppression. An instrument by which all classes exchange products and services with all other classes should be just to all.

It is my pleasure to announce that Professor Parsons is preparing a companion work to this on the transportation question. In this day of steam and electricity the transportation question has become of scarcely less importance than the money question. Other works on pressing public questions will follow.

Philadelphia, August, 1898.   C. F. TAYLOR.

## AUTHOR'S PREFACE.

1. The rise and fall of general prices is one of the greatest evils that can afflict a commercial nation. Industry is apt to be unduly intensified by rising prices, and so obstructed by their fall that depression and panic result. The movement of prices changes the distribution of wealth—alters the shares that go to labor, capital and management, makes hoarded money more or less valuable, and lightens or intensifies the burden of debt. A buys a farm for $4,000 and borrows $2,000 to help pay for it. In a few years the fall of prices brings his land down to a value of $2,000. But the debt has not shrunk and the creditor takes the whole farm for a loan that was worth but half the farm at the time it was made. At the same rate the creditor class, loaning thruout the country, would acquire the United States in return for loans amounting to half its value. It is estimated according to a careful writer, the Hon. Henry Winn, that the fall of prices since 1873 has given the creditor classes of the world, at the expense of debtors, an unearned increment of $3,000,000,000 per annum, equal in eight years to the whole assessed valuation of the United States by the last census, and aggregating, in the quarter of a century covered by the estimate, a sum exceeding the full value of all the property in the country; and this vast value has been paid by debtors in addition to the principal and interest they agreed to pay. No wonder that the creditor classes are anxious to control the money system through which the movement of prices may be governed. And no wonder the debtor classes are anxious to try their hand at managing the machinery of finance. In justice, the money system ought not to be controlled in the interest of any class, but in the interest of the whole people.

The movement of the price average is chiefly influenced by the movements of money-volume, credits, and production. The easiest of these to control is the money-volume, and the control of this confers the power to govern the movement of prices because the influence of any change in credits or production can be overcome by sufficient increase or diminution of the money volume. The movement of the money volume is the vital monetary fact, the key to the financial situation. Through the control of this movement prices may be made to rise or fall or remain substantially steady. This means control of justice or injustice, prosperity or panic, wealth diffusion or congestion.

Power to control the money-volume is power to do justice or injustice between debtor and creditor, laborer and employer, buyer and seller, landlord and tenant, interest receiver and entrepreneur, power to increase the weight and value of every debt, public or private, power to produce panic or prosperity, power to regulate industry and determine the distribution of wealth,—such power is an attribute of sovereignty and ought to belong to none but the sovereign people. Such a control should only be exercised with judgment and intelligence in the interests of the whole people, in order that justice and *not* injustice, fair diffusion and *not* congestion, prosperity and *not* panic, may result. At present this vital matter is left almost entirely to chance and private management. Banks and the vicissitudes of mining and speculations determine the movements of money. It is even possible for foreign influences to exert large control over our money and credits, and put new slopes and notches in our price line. This is all wrong. No chance or private monopoly or foreign power should be permitted to manage our money or draw a price curve for us. The movement of the money-volume is a public affair, and the machinery for controlling it should belong to the public and be operated by and for the public. A matter of such incalculable moment to the nation, and in relation to which private interest is frequently antagonistic to public interest, should not be left to private control, but should be subject to constant, careful, intelligent public regulation. This is the most important lesson that emerges from the fact and philosophy contained in the following pages.[1] A few related thoughts demand some mention here.

2. Given intelligent public control of the money-volume, with a view to regulating the movement of general prices, what is to be the aim? Shall the price line be made a gradual upward slope to afford a moderate stimulus to industry, till the unemployed are reabsorbed and debtors are eased of the overweight of past obligations, or shall the line be level from the start? Much may be said in favor of a temporary upward slope, but on the whole it would seem better to make the line level, and accomplish the other purposes referred to, moderate stimulation of industry, provision for the unemployed, etc., through the establishment of public works, making good roads, planting forests, digging canals, building ships, establishing schools, etc. Meantime providing funds and aiding wealth diffusion by means of progressive income and inheritance taxes. The ideal dollar is one that will not mulct either the debtor or creditor, nor encourage speculation, nor depress industry —a dollar of constant purchasing power, commanding the same average amount of commodities and services from year to year and

---

[1] (For the *method* of public control see Chapter III.) The fundamental doctrine of the importance of controlling the movement of the money volume in the public interest, may be accepted by all, whatsoever their views about the demonetization of silver, metallic redemption, paper money, intrinsic value and other monetary questions. A couple of concrete instances of the utility of even a rough control of the money movement may be of advantage here. First, The way to prevent a speculative disaster or shrinkage of credit, etc., from developing into the wide-spread distress we call panic, is to expand the money volume by easy loans or otherwise. That expansion is the proper medicine for the prevention and cure of panics is recognized by the Bullion Committee, Bagehot, Wm. G. Sumner, Pres. Walker, and all the other financial doctors so far as I know. But our private banks refuse to administer the prescription, because it is dangerous to them. For an ordinary bank to increase its loans in the face of panic would be to risk its existence. But the nation is big enough and strong enough to do the work. It can loan money to merchants and business men in times of stringency, with the certainty of averting loss from itself, instead of the danger of bringing ruin upon itself. Second. A moderate increase of the money volume in the fall of the year when the movement of crops, etc., creates a special pressure on monetary facilities, would be a step toward justice to agriculture.

age to age—an ethical, impartial, democratic dollar, a dollar that will act as a fly wheel to keep the national engine working smoothly all the time, instead of producing or aggravating industrial disaster and explosion. The price line must become a safe horizontal instead of the dangerous zigzag of a bolt of lightning.

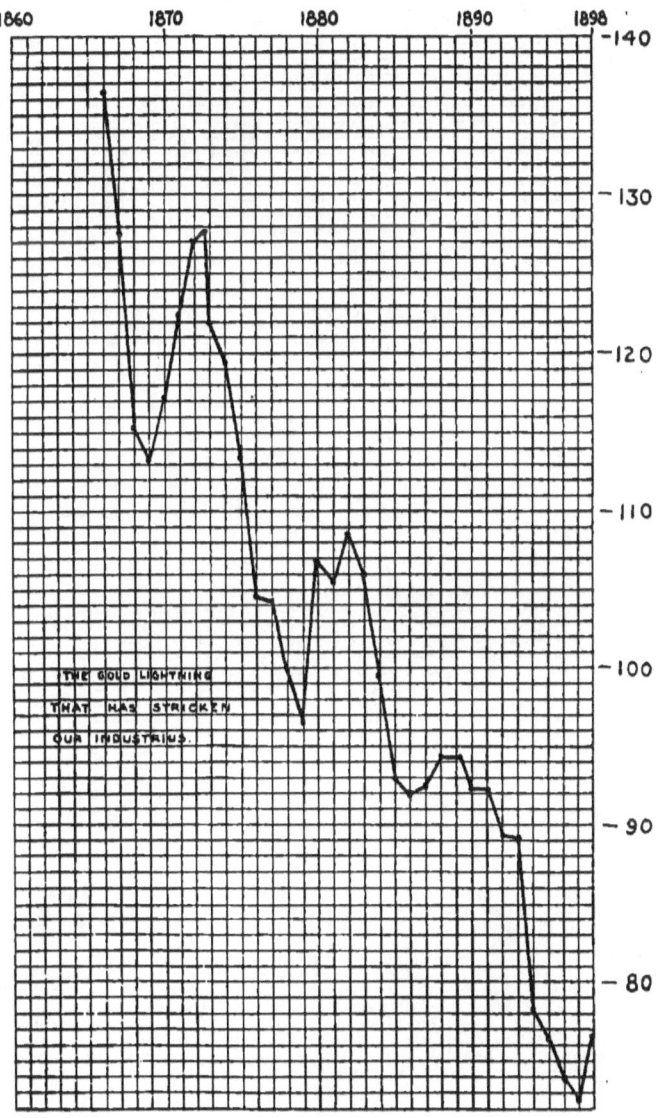

PRICE LINE 1866-1898 - GOLD PRICES
ALDRICH DATA 1866-1891 "AMERICAN" DATA 1891-8.

THE GOLD LIGHTNING THAT HAS STRICKEN OUR INDUSTRIES.

## AUTHOR'S PREFACE.

Since 1873 the chain lightning of prices has been golden (see cut on page V), before that time it was bimetallic (as shown in this cut). Neither of these monetary thunderbolts appear to have much affection for the safe and honest horizontal.

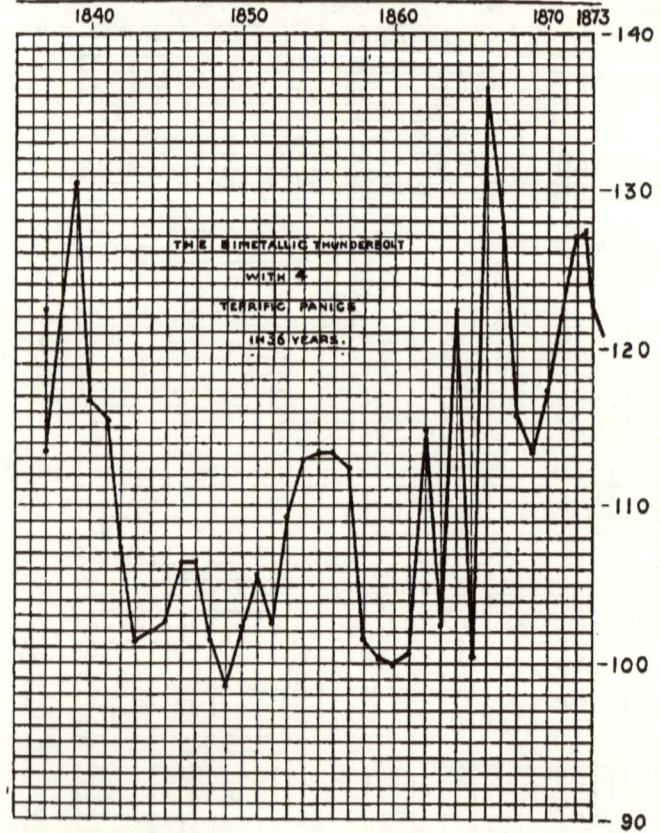

PRICE LINE 1837-1873   BIMETALLIC PRICES
ALDRICH DATA 1840-1873.—1837-1840 BROAD ESTIMATE FROM DATA OF W<sup>m</sup> G. SUMNER & MULHALL'S CITATIONS.

THE BIMETALLIC THUNDERBOLT WITH 4 TERRIFIC PANICS IN 36 YEARS.

If the weekly or even the quarterly variations had been noted, the lines in both of these diagrams would have been full of saw teeth. If the maximum and minimum price levels had been marked instead of the yearly average, the extremes would have been far greater than those shown—the drop in a panic being sometimes more than double that shown by the yearly averages (see p. 57). If *actual* prices had been taken (instead of metallic prices), we should have found that during the war period of unregulated issue of imperfect legal tender paper, the price line would have soared 76 points above the top of the diagram. Altogether these diagrams, full of ruin and injustice as they are, are yet mild representatives of the present money system. They tell part of its evils, but by no means all, nor do they give full emphasis to what they do tell.

# AUTHOR'S PREFACE.

Our prime financial duty is the intelligent public regulation of the money-volume so as to give the dollar a constant purchasing power, yielding the creditor the same average command over commodities and services that he gave, curtailing reckless speculation, preventing panic, and exercising a beneficent and impartial influence upon wealth production and distribution.[1]

3. In performing this duty, what sort of money may be used, and what sort should be used? The answer seems to be that gold or silver or both *may* be used[2] with paper, redeemable or irredeemable—monometalism, bimetalism, co-metalism or greenbacks pure and simple. The latter would seem to be the most perfect plan. It is useless to dig gold to do what regulated paper will do as well or better, and the immediate profit to the government on paper issues to replace the metals (over 1,000 millions), would probably pay for the Spanish War several times over. The best money all round, appears to be, not coin or paper on a metallic base, nor currency on a paper base, but paper money on a com-

---

[1] (See Chapters II and III.) This second doctrine also, that the dollar should be constant in its purchasing power, may be held along with diverse views about gold and silver, paper money, intrinsic value, etc., and is in fact held by men of such widely different opinions as Pres. Andrews, Professor Marshall, Pres. Will, Wm. J. Bryan, Fonda, Walker, Mill, Ricardo, Henry Winn, Prof. Bemis, Prof. J. Allen Smith, Prof. Laughlin, etc., etc.

[2] The metals could not be used as the standard of course. General prices cannot be kept steady in that way. Only the multiple standard can keep the price line level or the purchasing power of the dollar constant. But gold and silver could be used as money of circulation and redemption *provided* the whole currency, metallic and all were regulated in accordance with the multiple base.

The multiple standard steady money plan outlined in President E. B. Andrews' "Honest Dollar," edition of 1889, p. 36 to 42, contemplates the continuance of gold and silver redemption, but the metals cease to be the real standard or regulating base of the currency. The fact that the notes issued were redeemable in metal even at a fixed weight would not prevent the exercise of considerable control over prices by means of injecting notes into the circulation or withdrawing them therefrom. There is a good deal of friction and inertia about metallic redemption in practice. And to a considerable extent the volume of circulation can be changed by the issue or withdrawal of notes. Prices may be influenced in this way and the value of gold itself altered. One of the plans described by Professor Marshall in the Contemporary Review, Vol. 51, also involves metallic redemption by such weight of bullion as is equal in value to the standard multiple unit, at the market price of bullion at the time of redemption. Careful consideration, however, has led me to the conclusion that metallic redemption is not needful, service redemption being entirely sufficient. (See note in Professor Marshall's article just referred to, and Chapter II of this book.) Fixed weight-redemption could only be worked within limits. It would be liable to serious disturbance from foreign influence and from speculation, etc., a promise to redeem in a fixed amount of any commodity puts a premium on cornering that commodity.

Variable redemption in bullion at its market value in the standard multiple unit would be free from the dangers of fixed weight redemption, but it does not seem necessary or wise to pick out any one or two commodities for redemption purposes under the multiple standard. A bill is redeemed every time it buys any commodity or service or pays any debt or tax. When the government gives a bill the legal tender quality, it promises that the bill shall be redeemed in any desired commodities or services at their market value and that is all the redemption requisite. Such redemption and a regulation of volume to keep the price line steady by the multiple standard will give us the ideal money.

Once establish a system of public money under reasonable regulations, and there is little doubt it will be honestly and efficiently administered. The Treasury Department has a reputation for accuracy, honesty, and efficiency, that is above reproach in respect to all matters wherein its duties have been clearly and definitely prescribed. The maintenance of a uniform price level is a matter so clear and simple and the processes would be so easily watched and checked, that there is little likelihood of administrative difficulty. (See Chapter III.)

modity base. While it is true, however, that gold or silver or both, may be used for money and redemption under a steady money plan, yet it must be carefully noted that they cannot be used as *standards*. The only possible constant in exchange is the commodity base or multiple standard, and if money is to be kept steady the gold or silver coins or paper bills or whatever else is used as money must be regulated in reference to the multiple standard, and kept in harmony with it. This constant base cannot be represented by any one or two commodities, especially those so prone to irruptions, spasms, heart-failures, and booms as gold and silver appear to be, and subject at bottom to the law of diminishing return. Men have tied justice and prosperity to a golden kite dreaming it was the solid rock. A change in the value of iron or copper may cause disturbance but does not throw the whole industrial system out of gear. A private monopoly of coal mines or iron or copper mines is bad enough, but a monopoly of the money base is infinitely worse. A change in the value of gold throws the wealth of those who own the products and property of the country into the hands of those who own the dollars, or vice versa; varies the share of production that goes to labor, and alters the value of every debt. Platinum doubled in value recently without producing any commercial disturbance. A true money system would be as little affected by flights of gold as by flights of platinum.

The question of a wholesale replacement of metals by irredeemable paper, important though it is, is nevertheless of minor moment compared to the larger question of regulating the money-volume. Give us public management of the money movement, aiming to keep the dollar steady and the price line level, and the main object will be accomplished. Yet it appears quite clear that when gold has lost its importance, as it would under such regulation,—when fortunes are no longer to be made by its changes of value, it would lose the support of those who defend it now, and it would be seen that a currency consisting entirely of irredeemable paper and subsidiary coin is more economical and more secure from disturbance by changes in mining product or foreign monetary policy, or other cause of variance.

During the greenback movement years ago, I read a speech by Wendell Phillips, in which he took strong ground in favor of an irredeemable paper money. I had a very high opinion of the famous anti-slavery orator, but this pamphlet considerably injured his reputation so far as I was concerned. I said, "A man who imagines that the government can make something out of nothing, or give enormous value to bits of paper by stamping some words on them, is evidently subject to such delusion that it will not do to rely very much on his mental processes." And yet, a few years later, on making a more thorough study of the financial question, I came to see that this judgment of mine was based upon absence of information. I found that substantially all the standard economists agreed with Phillips that government *could* give exchange value to bits of paper by stamping words upon them, making them legal tender for all debts, public and private, and limiting their volume, whether they were redeemable or not; that the sole essentials of sound money are receivability and limitation of volume, "intrinsic value," or value for other purposes than those pertaining to money not being requisite to money, which is not desired for any "intrinsic" utility, but as a means of obtaining commodities and services, a method of accounting like checks and bank books, a title to property like deeds and mortgages,—functions it will perfectly perform if generally receivable and limited in volume, whether it be made of gold or silver or paper. I found that history confirmed the conclusions of the economists, and Phillips became to me once more the sage and prophet I had thought him in my boywood.

4. I still think, however, that the Greenback movement was a mistake. Greenbacks unregulated might be worse than present monies, and the Greenbackers offered no plan for efficient, intelligent regulation.

5. The free silver movement, I think, is another mistake. It is wasting the time and thought of the people on a comparatively unimportant matter. Even if all its supporters claim for it is true, it would amount to very little—a mere temporary palliative, soon exhausting its predicted power to raise prices, not attaining justice, not preventing panics, not achieving any intelligent regulation in the interests of the public, not reaching the sources of financial difficulty.

6. There is another movement more to be regretted than either of those just named. I mean the movement to retire the national notes and give the whole money field to the banks.[4]

The people are asked to retire completely from the money ques-

---

[4] The reasons given for this movement are chiefly two: 1. The need of an *elastic* currency, the bond basis necessary for National Bank notes having gradually failed as the National debt has diminished. 2. The advisability of putting a stop to the working of "the endless chain." As for elasticity, the kind secured is not the kind desired. A money that expands when there is already too much in the field, and contracts when there is too little, is indeed elastic, but not commendable. The kind of elasticity to be sought in money is one that will lead it to expand on notice of stringency, and to contract on notice of surplusage. The first, or reprehensible sort of elasticity, is what the bank note schemes will give us. The second, or desirable elasticity is the kind that will belong to a National Multiple Standard Money.

As for the endless chain, the proper way to get rid of its burdens would be to adopt irredeemable National paper, which, with reasonable regulation, would possess all the valuable monetary qualities that belong to gold, without its weight, or its wobbles, its speculative tendencies, bond proclivities, or foreign affinities.

The scheme of retiring the Greenbacks and giving the banks the power to issue redeemable notes of their own would still subject the Government to endless chain processes so far as the Government stood behind the notes, and if the Government did not guarantee them, their security would be defective,—a substitution of bank promises for Government promises,—a substitution of private paper imperfectly secured and without the legal tender quality necessary to independent circulatory power, in place of public money with the best possible security, the *National guarantee* of full legal tender in its own right, or of redemption in coin legal tenders, or both. So far as the Government is behind the bills you have the endless chain possibility, and so far as the Government is not behind them you have the wild cat principle of private, non-legal tender bills, issued on private security.

Whether the notes are secured wholly by the individual bank issuing

tion, and hand over to the banks even that part of the currency which now belongs to the Nation. This is fundamentally wrong. The powers of private banks should be diminished rather than increased. Indeed it may be confidently affirmed that if the people are to realize the fullest benefits of a wise monetary system, the banks must become public as well as the management of the money-volume. It is not absolutely essential to control credits in order to control prices, for the expansion, and contraction of credits can be conteracted and overcome by a sufficient change in the money volume. But it would be of great advantage to the people if loans and credits were managed in the public interest as well as the money volume.[5]

them, or are secured, to a certain extent, by a two per cent. or ten per cent. bank note redemption fund, to which all the banks contribute, the principle is the same, a resort to defective security. The little margin of reserves and redemption funds of one bank or any group of banks, or all the banks, may be easily swept away in a crisis, and though there may be assets left on which outstanding notes are a lien, the uncertainty, difficulty, and delay of collection, will bring again the complex calculations of the old wild cat days, and merchants may have to spend their days ciphering out the value of bank notes presented to them or paid out by them. The very possibility of trouble with bills left out too long in time of panic would make men run for gold on slight intimation of financial embarrassment. No one bank nor group of banks, nor all the banks can offer security approaching the solidity of National security. The Government must guard the notes or else it must issue them itself with its legal tender stamp upon them.

However the plans for redeemable notes are varied, the substance is always the same. It's a choice between wild cat and endless chain. The bank notes not being legal tender, must rest on redemption in something that is legal tender and therefore will not be thoroughly reliable money unless the Government guarantees their payment on demand. If the Government is to be behind the notes it might as well own them. It is folly for the nation to guarantee bills (as in the Gage plan) and then let the banks issue them for their private profit. And if the Government does not guarantee them, the bills are merely private paper, and in times of panic, when reliable money is most needful, no one could tell whether the bank notes were worth anything or not, They would have no legal tender quality to give them an independent value of their own, and a speculative crash, or fall of prices, with a panic run for redemption, might exhaust the redemption fund and gold reserves of the bank, and the whole margin of security, leaving the outstanding notes redemptionless. And when a thing has no legal tender or general receivability in its own right, and can not be redeemed in something that has such legal tender or receivability, it is not good money. We do not want either wild cat bank notes or suction pipes from the public vaults to Wall Street and Europe. The escape from both lies in a National currency divorced from coin, carefully regulated in volume, and enforced in the courts as a full legal tender.

(⁶) Our Government already does a large business in money transfers, and there is no reason why it should not receive deposits and make loans. Nearly all the civilized nations except the United States have postal banks, the powers of which will inevitably be gradually enlarged until they include the whole range of ordinary banking functions. The question is simply this: Shall we be content with private banks run for the benefit of a few or shall we have public banks run for the benefit of all?

Postal banks will make the people's money absolutely safe, will make the habit of saving more general, will help to secure financial independence for wage-workers, will bring hoarded money into circulation, increase the actual capital of the country, and reduce the current rate of interest. If the Government controls credit as well as money volume, it will not have to contend with the accidents and schemes of expansion and contraction of credits incident to private control. Credit changes will naturally be less than now because the multiple money system will do away with some of the chief causes of credit change. And, on the other hand, if the nation through its banks directly controls the movement of credit as well as the money volume, it will simplify the problem of keeping the dollar in harmony with the multiple standard. To omit the banks and their credits from the National Money System is to leave outside a powerful disturbing influence to be continually watched in order to make the proper adjustment of the money volume to counteract the movements of credit. There appears to be a powerful sentiment in favor of postals savings banks. Still greater good will be accomplished by establishing postal banks with full functions instead of dividing the banking powers.

Our banks are organized for private profit, not for the public weal. In times of rising prices they naturally issue notes and extend credit to the extent of their power, thereby increasing the "boom."

In times of falling prices they naturally withdraw their notes and credits in self protection, thereby producing or intensifying depression and panic. They aid the rise of speculative excitement, and then in times of danger and collapse they withdraw their assistance from the people just when they need it most. To diminish public money and government action, and increase bank money and bank action, is to increase the instability of the money system, intensifying both speculation and panic, emphasize the evils of rising and falling prices, and place the entire control where it will be used for private gain and not for the public good. The whole machinery and management of money and credit constitute a most vital national interest, and should be put into the hands of trained public servants, acting under careful regulations for the people's benefit. Even an ordinary government system would make loans and discounts more difficult or contract them in times of speculative tendency, and in case of stringency would extend their loans instead of calling them in. In England and France the great quasi public banks have adopted this policy to some extent with most beneficent results.

A solid National credit, regulated in the public interest, is much safer and better for depositors and business interests than the private credit of any bank or group of banks managed for private gain; as much safer and better as National money is safer and better than bank checks or drafts or any other private money; as much safer and better as a National army is safer and better than a motley herd of corporation vassals. Deposits would be absolutely safe so long as the United States endures. National credits would not shrink under threat of danger, thereby changing the threat into reality, and changing perplexity into panic, nor would they expand to boom dimensions under the stimulus of rising prices, or rich prospects for investments. Neither would there be any difficulty in making discounts. Official bonds, deductions from incomes, and other forms of personal responsibility would make cashiers as careful in the conduct of public as of private banking, more careful, perhaps, because the temptations of speculative gain would be absent.

Under a system planned to secure the utmost benefits to the people, we should have Postal Banks and a National Money, intelligently regulated in the interests of justice and stability. In this way the Government would directly control not only the movement of money proper, but of credits also. The jagged form of our plunging price line would become a smooth and solid path that commerce could follow with steady certainty. There would be no panics, no cheating of debtors or creditors, no banking aristocracy, no "Invisible Empire" scheming to control the money of the country for private aggrandizement, but a steady, just, reliable dollar, and a democratic financial system, and the profit on loans and monetary transfers, including the unearned increment or excess above reasonable interest and payment for services rendered, would be abolished or converted into the public treasury.

Speculation, private monopoly, foreign policy, and the varying values of gold, would no longer be able to use the money system as a means of disturbing the fair distribution of wealth, diverting to one class the wealth that belongs to another, and jeopardizing the National prosperity by slowing or stopping the wheels of industry or driving them at breakneck speed.

For a summary of the benefits to be derived from National money and scientific finance, the reader is referred to the closing portions of the second and third chapters of this book.

FRANK PARSONS.

Boston, Mass.

# CONTENTS.

## Chapter I.

### PAPER MONEY VINDICATED BY HISTORY.

Sixty millions of Demand Notes.
Silver Certificates.
The Crisis of 1857.
County Scrip.
The Continental Money.
Leather Money.
Indian Money.
North Carolina.
Connecticut.
New York, New Jersey and Pennsylvania.
Pennsylvania Paper Money.
England.
France and Germany.
The Allied Powers.
Russia.
Austria.
Brazil.
Bank of Venice.
Fall of Rome.
The Dark Ages.
Discovery of America
A Metal Base a Builder of Debt and an Ally of Gamblers.
Coin a Coquette.
A Metal Base a Cause of Industrial Crises
Coin a Coward.
Conclusions.

## Chapter II.

### THE BEST MONEY.

Purposes of Money.
Measuring Values.
Storing the Power of Purchase.
Standard of Payment.
Attributes of Money.
Intrinsic Value.
The Only Essential Attributes.
    General Receivability.
    Limitation of Volume.
Steadiness of Value.
Movement of the Money Volume.
What Money should be Adopted.

CONTENTS.

## Chapter III.

## THE MULTIPLE STANDARD.

Its Nature and Operation.
Massachusetts Multiple Standard.
Objections.
Advantages.

## Chapter IV.

## THE AUTHORITIES.

President Frances A. Walker.
President E. B. Andrews.
Professor Alfred Marshall.
    "  W. Stanley Jevons.
    "  Simon Newcomb.
David Ricardo.
Peter Cooper.
United States Supreme Court.
William Jennings Bryan.
Wendell Phillips.
Benjamin Franklin.
Thomas Jefferson.
Abraham Lincoln.
For other authorities see Chapters I, II and III.

Appendix A.
Appendix B.

# CHAPTER I.

### PAPER MONEY VINDICATED BY HISTORY.

Paper money may be based on gold or silver or both, or may rest on the whole body of commodities and values without any specific metallic base. In either case the accuracy with which it conforms itself to its base depends upon the management of its volume and its legal tender qualities. Paper that is, upon demand, exchangeable for metal at a rate specified by law is said to be "redeemable;" and paper not exchangeable for gold or silver, at a rate established by law, and at the option of the holder in the exercise of a legal right of demand upon the issuer, is said to be "irredeemable." It is more scientific to call the first convertible and the second inconvertible, or to call the first dependent and the second independent, for both are really redeemable in any proper sense of the word. Whenever a bill is taken in payment for goods, taxes, or service of any sort it is redeemed as truly as when it is exchanged for gold or silver. There is a popular impression that paper money is unreliable unless it is exchangeable for gold or silver at the option of the holder. Bills that are not redeemable are clearly worthless; and the word redeemable being confined by previous classification to bills that are exchangeable for coin upon demand, it follows that bills independent of coin are lacking in the essentials of value. By reasoning based on such unconscious monetary puns the people are misled. Bills that are not redeemable (in goods or service) are clearly worthless, but they may be irredeemable in gold or silver and yet redeemable in goods and services to such extent that they will be as valuable or even more valuable than coin.

The truth appears to be that men do not accept money for goods and services with a view of converting the money into gold; they accept money for goods and services because they know that other men will accept that same money for other goods and services, and that it will pay debts and taxes. Gold itself is received as money, not as an end but as a means; not because the receiver desires to make use of the gold as such, but simply because it is by law and custom redeemable in goods and services, at a value determined by the limitation of its quantity and the monetary demand. Law and custom impart the fundamental money quality of general receivability in exchange and payment, and have at other times bestowed a money value on bullets, skewers, nails, shells, skins, feathers, beads, notched sticks, etc. If then, by law and custom our bills possess the qualities that give the metals a money value, if they are redeemable in goods and services and are limited in quantity—they will have a money value of their own whether exchangeable for coin upon demand or not.[1]

All great economists[2] emphatically declare that convertibility into coin or bullion is not required to maintain the value of paper money, and that legal tender paper "irredeemable" in coin may be kept at any required value simply by the regulation of its volume. The only use claimed by any scientist for metallic convertibility is to regulate the volume of the circulating medium, and for this purpose there are much more perfect methods, as will appear hereafter.

To reason and authority we add the force of fact. The history of England, France, Russia, Austria, Venice, Brazil and the United States most clearly proves that independent paper money, issued as a full legal tender under a stable government and limited in volume to the needs of business, will not depreciate, but forms a far more reliable and equitable medium of exchange than coin or paper on a metal base, the value of which is governed by chance or private manipulation, and is therefore open to ruinous fluctuations.

If the paper is not a full legal tender, or if it is issued in too great quantity (more than the growth of business can absorb), or if the government is tottering and unable to en-

---

[1] See Chapter II. for further reasoning on this point.
[2] See Chapters II., III. and IV.

force the legal tender quality, the currency may depreciate in value, as in the case of the French Assignats, the Continental currency, the Confederate scrip, the Colonial money of Massachusetts, etc. The North depreciated most of its money during the War of the Rebellion by denying it a full legal tender quality, and issuing too much of it—it was legal tender *except* for the payment of duties on imports and interest on public debt. There were, however,

### SIXTY MILLIONS OF DEMAND NOTES

that were *receivable for public dues* and they remained substantially at par with gold thru all the vicissitudes of the war until they were retired.

The Acts of July 17 and August 5, 1861, authorized the issue of fifty millions of demand notes in denominations of $5 and upwards, bearing no interest and receivable for public dues. The Act of Feb. 12, 1862, authorized a further issue of 10 millions. These 60 millions of notes were afterwards (March 17, 1862) made legal tender.[3]

The first demand notes were issued in August, 1861, being paid out for salaries at Washington. Before the suspension of specie payments, December 28, 1861, $33,460,000 of the demand notes were in circulation, and the whole amount authorized was issued prior to April 1, 1862. These demand notes, not being at the start a legal tender, were received with hesitation by merchants and shop-keepers. Railroad companies refused them and leading bankers in New York would not take them except on special deposit.[4]

When the notes were made a legal tender of course these difficulties vanished.

---

(³) Walker, "Money," p. 373, Bolles "Financial Hist. U. S. 1861-1885," p. 75, Gen. Weaver's "Call to Action," p. 214, John Jay Knox on United States Notes, p. 89 et seq.; Statutes of the U. S.

(⁴) An interesting anecdote is told on page 225 of Schucker's life of Secretary Chase. "About the time of the suspension of cash payments, a wealthy New Yorker came into the possession of a large sum approximating to one million of dollars in 'demand notes.' He offered them for deposit in a leading bank of New York, the officers of which refused to receive them, however, in the ordinary course of business, or in any other way than as a special deposit. Having no alternative, the gentleman reluctantly consented. The demand notes being receivable for customs the same as coin, kept pace pari passu with the advance in the price of coin, and when the depositor in the bank withdrew his deposit 'demand notes' were worth nearly or quite one hundred and fifty per cent. premium measured in legal tender."

The notes were of the size of greenbacks and were of the following form:

**Washington,** **1861**

*ACT OF JULY 17, 1861*

*ON DEMAND THE*

**UNITED STATES**

*PROMISE TO PAY THE BEARER*

**TEN DOLLARS**

*RECEIVABLE IN PAYMENT OF ALL PUBLIC DUES*

Now note the situation; war; gold and silver scarce; specie payments suspended; greenbacks issued for war expenses, a legal tender except for duties on imports and interest on the public debt;[5] and 60 millions of demand notes, legal tender to the same extent as the greenbacks plus the quality of being receivable for public dues. Coin had three utilities the greenback did not possess—coin could be exported, it could pay interest on the public debt, and it could pay duties on imports. The demand notes would pay duties but could not pay interest on the public debt, and were not available for exportation. What was the result? I take the answer from page 97 of the History of the United States Notes by John Jay Knox, the highest authority on the subject.[6]

| DATE. | | PRICE OF DEMAND NOTES IN GREENBACKS. | PRICE OF GOLD IN GREENBACKS. |
|---|---|---|---|
| 1862 | May 10 | 100¼ | 103⅜ |
| | June 7 | 101 | 104⅛ |
| | July 5 | 105¼ | 109⅞ |
| | August 2 | 105¼ | 115¼ |
| | September 6 | 108 | 119¼ |
| | October 4 | 122⅝ | 123 |
| | November 1 | 126¼ | 131¼ |
| | December 6 | 125 | 132 |
| 1863 | January 3 | 129 | 134½ |
| | February 7 | 155 | 157⅞ |
| | March 7 | 153 | 155½ |

(5) The act of February 25, 1862, authorized the issue of 150 millions of U. S. notes, "receivable in payment of all taxes, internal duties, excises, debts and demands of every kind due the United States except duties on imports, and of all claims and demands against the U. S. EXCEPT for interest on bonds and notes, which shall be paid in coin. Fifty millions of said notes shall be in lieu of the demand treasury notes authorized by the act of July

The above data show that the premium upon the demand notes kept within a very few points of the premium on gold. February 7, 1863, the difference between the demand notes and greenbacks was 55 points and the difference between the demand notes and gold was but $2\frac{1}{8}$ points.

The slight difference between the "demands" and gold was due to the exportable quality of the latter, and the fact that the notes would not pay interest on the bonds. This inability of the notes, together with their power to pay duties, caused their early withdrawal by the government. Mr. Knox says (p. 90): "Efforts were made to retire them as rapidly as possible, for as they were receivable for duties they embarrassed the government in providing for the gold interest upon the public debt. On July 1, 1863, more than 56 millions had been retired, and a much larger amount of legal tenders (with the exception clause) had been placed in circulation."

Thus we see what may be effected by the presence or absence of the legal tender quality.

### SILVER CERTIFICATES.

The Act of February 28, 1878, provided that any holder of the coin (standard silver dollars) authorized by the Act might deposit the same with the Treasurer or any Assistant Treasurer of the United States in sums not less than ten dollars and receive therefor certificates of not less than ten dollars each. The coin deposited for or representing the certificates shall be retained in the Treasury for the payment of the same on demand. Said certificates shall be receivable for customs, taxes, and all public dues. The Act of August 4, 1886, authorized the issue of silver certificates in denominations of $1, $2, and $5. In Circular No. 123, issued by the

---

17, 1861; which said demand notes shall be taken up as rapidly as practicable and the notes herein provided for substituted for them." July 11, 1862, another 150 millions were authorized and March 3, 1863, still another issue of equal amount.

(*) John Jay Knox graduated from Hamilton College in 1849, was a banker and bank officer till 1862, when he received a treasury appointment from Secretary Chase; in 1867 he became Deputy Comptroller of the Currency; in 1872 he was appointed Comptroller and held the office till 1884, when he resigned and became President of the National Bank of the Republic in New York. His History of the U. S. Notes was published in 1884 by Chas. Scribner's Sons.

United States Treasury Department, July 1, 1896, and signed by John G. Carlisle, Secretary of the Treasury, we find on page 11 the following statement:

"Silver certificates have practically taken the place in circulation of the standard silver dollars which they represent. The amount outside the Treasury July 1, 1896, was $331,259,509, while the amount of standard silver dollars outside the Treasury was only $52,175,998. *Neither silver certificates nor silver dollars are redeemed in gold.*"[7]

Yet these silver dollars and certificates pass at par with gold. Why? Simply because they are legal tender for debts, duties and taxes, and are not issued in excess. No one takes

---

[7] There is a popular impression that silver certificates are redeemed in gold. This has arisen from confusing the Treasury Notes authorized by the act of July 14, 1890, known as the "Sherman Act," by which the Secretary of the Treasury was directed to buy 4½ million ounces of silver per month at the market price and pay for the same with Treasury notes redeemable on demand IN COIN (gold or silver in the discretion of the Secretary) and legal tender for all debts, public and private except where otherwise provided in the contract. The purchase clause of the act was repealed November 1, 1893, up to which date $155,931,002 Treasury notes had been issued under the Sherman law. "The amount of Treasury notes redeemed in gold up to the close of the fiscal year, 1896, was $80,073,325, and the amount redeemed in standard silver dollars was $26,247,722." (Carlisle Circular U. S. Treasury No. 123 p. 12.) On March 1, 1897, the Treasury reported $85,546,621 of these Treasury notes in circulation. They are redeemable in gold or silver at the Secretary's discretion, but the $363,700,501 of silver certificates issued under the laws of February 28, 1878, and August 4, 1886, are not redeemable in gold; the law does not authorize their redemption in anything but silver and they are not redeemed in anything but silver. On page 328 of "Coinage laws of the United States" published by authority of the Senate, Secretary Carlisle writes as follows in answer to a request from the Senate for information as to "whether silver dollars or silver coin certificates have been redeemed by the treasury department or exchanged for gold or paper that is by law or practice of the government redeemable in gold:"

Treasury Department, October 17, 1893.

To the President of the Senate:
 The law providing for the redemption or exchange of silver certificates, which requires that such certificates shall be redeemed or exchanged in kind or for standard silver dollars, has, so far as this department has information, been strictly complied with by the treasurer of the United States and the various sub-treasury offices, and no gold has been given in return for such certificates or standard silver dollars. J. G. CARLISLE.

The Secretary proceeds to state that in New York and San Francisco the sub-treasurers have sometimes paid out paper that was by law or practice redeemable in gold, in payment for silver dollars or certificates deposited with those offices. Such payments of gold paper were made not as matter of right nor even at request of the depositor of the silver, but as a mere matter of convenience to the payor, the silver funds specified in the law for the redemption not being at hand at the given time and place. These cases the Secretary says were infrequent and the amounts involved insignificant. The opposite sort of exchange has been much more frequent and considerable, viz., the payment of silver certificates and silver dollars ($167,858,132 from 1880 to 1893) in exchange for deposits of gold coin, at the request or with the willing assent of the depositor.

September 10, 1894, Secretary Carlisle wrote:
 "The department does not redeem either silver dollars or silver certificates with gold." April 29, 1895, he wrote:
 "The policy stated on page 328 of the 'Coinage Laws of the United States' has been pursued by the Treasury Department ever since the passage of the Bland Act." And July 1, 1896, he said: "Neither silver certificates nor silver dollars are redeemed in gold."

a silver dollar certificate for a dollar's worth of goods or service because it is redeemable in gold, for it is not so redeemable, nor because it is redeemable in silver, for the silver behind it is only worth a little more than fifty cents. No, he takes it at its face because he knows that it will pay a dollar's worth of debt and taxes; and that everybody else in the United States will honor it for a dollar's worth of service or commodities, which makes it as good as a gold dollar, and better, for it is not so easily lost.

In March, 1897, there were in circulation $363,709,501 of silver certificates, $55,378,762 standard dollars and $60,709,595 subsidiary silver coin—a total of $479,797,858 "redeemable" only in silver worth a trifle more than fifty cents on the dollar, all of it passing at par with gold because everybody knows it is a good legal tender and will pay their debts and taxes as well as gold. When a merchant or banker or anybody else receives a payment in bills he doesn't stop to see whether they are gold bills or silver bills; he only looks to see if they are genuine. He knows that if they are not counterfeit the government will take them for taxes and duties, the courts will enforce them in satisfaction of debt, and the people will take them for goods and services at their face value, and that is all he wants to know about them.

### THE CRISIS OF 1857.

The notes of the suspended banks of New York and New England remained almost or quite at par after the suspension of specie payments in 1857.[8]

### COUNTY SCRIP.

Our counties frequently pay the expenses of constructing public works with county scrip, receivable for county taxes, and even this paper money, with its very limited legal tender qualities, passes at par, if not too largely issued.

### LEATHER MONEY.

One of the earliest mediums of exchange consisted of the skins of animals, and from this intrinsic money was developed

[8] Professor Dunbar of Harvard in the Quarterly Journal of Economics Vol. 6, p. 333.

a system of representative money consisting of small pieces of leather usually marked with an official seal. Such a currency was long in use in Russia, in China, in Carthage and probably in Rome before the time of Numa.[9] With the growth of trade the transfer of skins and furs would naturally be found an inconveniently bulky method of exchange. Small pieces might be clipped off, and handed over as tokens of possession. By fitting into the place from which they were cut, they would prove ownership. After the people became accustomed to the circulation of these bits of leather as money they would continue to circulate without regard to what may have become of the skins from which they were cut,[10] and a representative money was evolved from the use of skins and furs under the operation of the same laws that in later days developed paper money and money of account as substitutes for gold and silver, in order to avoid the trouble and risk of handling the precious metals, the difficulty of obtaining them in sufficient quantity, and the expense and burden of keeping them safely.[11]

### INDIAN MONEY.

When the Mayflower touched New England the pilgrims found the Indians using wampum, or black and white beads made of clam shells and periwinkle shells, as a medium of exchange. The pilgrims adopted this Indian money and it became the chief currency of the early settlers.[12]

Another sort of money used by the Western Indians teaches a lesson our people have shown less power to learn. I heard it described when a boy by an Indian orator who had been educated in our Eastern colleges and who lectured in a most interesting manner on the customs of his people. He said that when a man did a day's work for the government the chief cut a notch in a stick and gave it to the worker, and that notched stick would buy a day's work from any other Indian, or pay for a day's work's worth of the provisions and stores

---
[9] Jevons Money and the Mechanism of Ex., pp. 20, 196-7. M. Bernardakis' Journal des Economistes, Vol. xxxiii. pp. 353-370.
[10] Ibid.
[11] Jevons' Money & Mechanism of Ex. pp. 200-1.
[12] Prof. Sumner's History of Amer. Currency.

belonging to the tribe, as the product of property they jointly owned, or purchased with the proceeds from sales of their land, etc., or produced or procured by their joint efforts.

Here was a money without a metallic base, not convertible into coin, redeemable only in goods and services, and yet it kept its value and did justice in exchanges, because (1) it was legal tender by custom; (2) the volume of genuine notches was limited by the method of issue and redemption; and (3) as the speaker stated with peculiar emphasis, "No Indian was ever known to counterfeit or inflate the currency."

### NORTH CAROLINA.

Hon. John C. Calhoun said in the United States Senate in 1838:

"North Carolina, just after the Revolution, issued a large amount of paper, which was made receivable in dues to her; it was also made a legal tender, but which, of course, was not made obligatory after the adoption of the Federal Constitution. A large amount—say between four and five hundred thousand dollars—remained in circulation after that period, and continued to circulate for more than twenty years at par with gold and silver during the whole time, with no other advantage than being received in the revenues of the State, which were much less than one hundred thousand dollars per annum.[13]

### CONNECTICUT.

In early years Connecticut, like Massachusetts and Rhode Island, had overissued bills of credit, and had suffered from their depreciation. She was one of the States prohibited by Parliament in 1751 from issuing legal tender paper, and for twenty years she kept her commerce on a specie base. Between October 1771 and October 1774, however, she issued £39,000 in bills for the expenses of government, seasonable and sufficient taxes being provided for their redemption. These "irredeemable" bills were not even a legal tender except for taxes, and yet "as they did not exceed the sums

---

[13] "Money of Nations," p. 65, and Arena, February, 1894, p. 366.

required by the trade of the Colony, they did not depreciate."[14]

#### NEW YORK, NEW JERSEY AND PENNSYLVANIA

during their Colonial days possessed an independent paper money that did not depreciate until the English Parliament destroyed its legal tender quality.[15] The fullest data are obtainable in relation to the paper of Pennsylvania, which will therefore be taken as an example of the financial policy of the middle colonies before the Revolution.

#### PENNSYLVANIA PAPER MONEY.

For half a century, beginning in 1723, the colony of Pennsylvania had an independent or "irredeemable" paper money, which did not depreciate but kept its value, and was an important factor in the unparalleled prosperity of the colony during the period named. The money was issued and the whole financial system managed directly by the Government. Some of the money was loaned at low interest on the security of lands and houses, a part of the principal being repaid each year with the interest. The rest of the money was issued in payment of salaries and other public expenses. The bills were not redeemable in gold or silver, but were made full legal tender, and not being issued in excess of the needs of business, they did not depreciate.[16]

---

([14]) Dr. Bronson's Connecticut Currency, p. 84.
([15]) The prices of some exported articles varied considerably after the middle of the 18th century in consequence of changes in the foreign market, but with this exception, prices remained substantially level in the middle colonies during the half century of independent legal tender paper. Prices and exchanges were practically at the same level in New York and New Jersey as in Pennsylvania, while in Massachusetts, Rhode Island and other colonies they rose in 1749 to more than six fold the Pennsylvania rates.
Franklin's Works (Sparks) Vol. II., p. 351.
Paper Currency of the Colonies by Henry Phillips, Jr., 1865.
U. S. Notes by John Jay Knox, p. 5.
Walker on Money, pp. 321, 322, 314.
Hist. Amer. Currency by Prof. Sumner, p. 36.

([16]) For details see below, and the following authorities:
Franklin's Works, edited by Jared Sparks, Vol. II., pp. 254 to 276.
"Administration of the Colonies," by Governor Pownall of Massachusetts, (London, 1765, fifth ed., 1768).
"A Discourse Concerning Paper Money," Phil., 1743 by John Webbe.
Adam Smith's Wealth of Nations, 1776, p. 262.
"Paper Currency of the Colonies," by Henry Phillips, Jr., Roxbury, Mass., 1865.
Annals of the Amer. Academy of Polit. and Social Science, July, 1896, article by C. W. Macfarlane.
Pres. F. A. Walker's book on "Money," p. 322, et seq.
Hon. John Davis, M. C., in Arena, February, 1894.
Laws of Pa.; Colonial Records; Journals of Assembly.
Hazard's Register of Pa.
Gordon's History of Pa.
Anderson's History of Commerce.
Douglass' Summary.
Gouge's History of Paper Money, Phil., 1833.

In 1764 Benjamin Franklin, "full of years and wisdom," wrote of the independent money of the middle colonies:

"It has continued now nearly forty years without variations upon new emissions, tho in Pennsylvania the paper money has increased from £15,000 to £600,000 or near it. Nor has any alteration been occasioned by the paper money in the price of the necessaries of life when compared with silver."[17]

Pennsylvania was exempted from the Act of Parliament passed in 1751 to restrain the Northern Colonies from issuing legal tender paper,[18] but in 1764 an Act was passed in England "to prevent paper bills of credit hereafter to be issued in any of his Majesty's Colonies in America from being declared to be legal tender in payment of money, and to prevent the legal tender of such bills as are now subsisting from being prolonged beyond the periods for calling in and sinking the same."[19]

A second Act seemingly[20] more stringent and imperative than the first was passed in 1773. The result of these laws was a progressive contraction of the legal tender currency, and a final extinction of the full legal tender quality the bills had so long enjoyed. The consequences were commercial loss, inconvenience and industrial distress of such severity that according to high authority[21] this parliamentary destruction of financial freedom in America was really a powerful factor in causing the compound discontent and resentment that produced the revolution.

Governor Pownall of Massachusetts said in 1768:

"I will venture to say that there never was a wiser or better measure—never one calculated to serve the interests of an increasing country; that there never was a measure more

---

([17]) Franklin's Works (Sparks), Vol. II., p. 351. Testimony that is corroborated by careful study of the price lists of the period, 1723 to 1773, see below. The £600,000 named by Franklin, was more than the outstanding circulation of Penn. notes—either he did not allow for withdrawals or included bills of other colonies circulating in Pa.
([18]) Phillips, p. 23 note.
([19]) Phillips, p. 25. Other authorities give the date of the act as 1763 (Gouge, p. 23, Walker, p. 324). The truth appears to be that the act was proposed in 1763; reasons were given by the Board of Trade for it, and by Franklin and the Colonial Assemblies against it in 1764, and it was passed in the latter year (Macfarlane, p. 63, Phillips, p. 70 et seq., and action of N. J. Assembly in 1764 while the bill was pending).
([20]) Cobbett's Parliamentary History does not give this act, but it is referred to by several authorities. Gouge p. 24. See also Davis, Cooper, Twells, etc. Appendix A.
([21]) See Appendix A.

steadily pursued or more faithfully executed for *forty years together than the loan office in Pennsylvania*, founded and administered by the assembly of that province."[22]

### THE CONTINENTAL MONEY.

The total circulation of the thirteen colonies just before the Revolution was estimated at 12,000,000 of dollars, between 4 and 5 millions of it being specie.[23] In June, 1775, the Continental Congress voted to issue 3 millions of paper; in November 3 millions more; February, 1776, 4 millions; May and July, 10 millions. The States also issued paper to cover war expenses—about 2 millions in 1775 and $3\frac{1}{2}$ millions in 1776.

Before the middle of 1776, 9 millions of Continental paper had been issued, and before the close of the year the emissions amounted to 20 millions. What was the result? Professor Sumner, of Yale, says: "Continental paper for 9 millions was issued before depreciation began.[24]

Including the State issues nearly 12 millions of paper had been put out without depreciation. On the approach of danger a considerable part of the coin had vanished, so that the total circulation was now about 21 millions—an addition of 75 per cent. to the circulating medium in about a year's time, changing the per capita from $4.28 to $7.05 without depreciation. *The transformation thus effected was equivalent to an addition of $1,200,000,000 to our currency now, changing the circulation from $21 to $37 per head.*

There is high authority for the conclusion that no appreciable fall in the value of the Continental money took place until after 20 millions of it had been issued. The historian, Dr. David Ramsay, after reciting the issues from June, 1775, to August, 1776, says:

"These several emissions amounting in the aggregate to 20 millions of dollars circulated for several months without any

---

[22] For those who wish to go more deeply into the history of this interesting matter, a fuller account is given in Appendix A., p. 161.
[23] Phillips' "Paper Cur. of the Colonies," p. 155.
[24] "History American Currency," p. 44, see also Gouge "History of Paper Money," p. 26, citing the concurrent testimony of Jefferson and Paine to the effect that the issues exceeded 9 millions before depreciation began.

depreciation, and commanded the resources of the country for public service equally with the same sum of gold or silver. The United States for a considerable time derived as much benefit from this paper creation of their own, tho without any funds for its support or redemption, as would have resulted to them from the free gift of as many Mexican dollars. But there was a point in time and quantity beyond which this Congressional alchemy ceased to operate. That time was about 18 months from the date of their first issue, and that quantity about $20,000,000."[25]

Upon this statement of the great historian, including the State issues, 25 millions of paper were issued before depreciation occurred. The circulation of the States was nearly trebled, and yet, so intense were the times, the Continental paper passed current at its face value thruout the greater part of the country till near the end of 1776. *Such a change to-day would mean the addition of $2,880,000,000 to our $1,600,000,000 of circulation!*

The Continental Congress had no power to tax. It did its best, however, to get the States to tax themselves for the withdrawal of the Continental paper, so that its volume might not become excessive. The States neglected to do this. Early in the proceedings, before depreciation began, Franklin urged that Congress should borrow back its notes rather than unduly increase the mass outstanding. But his wise counsel was disregarded, and by the close of 1776 depreciation began, and continued with subsequent issues until 1781, when the Continental paper stood at 500 to 1. The total issues are stated by the American Almanac for 1830 at 357 millions, and by the Merchants' Magazine at 387 millions; but these estimates include re-issues, and the true figure is about 242 millions.[26] During the same period, 1775 to 1781, the States issued about 209 millions, so that the total circulation of genuine notes in 1781 was $460,000,000—*38-fold the circulation of 1775, or a change from $4.28 to $150 per head in seven years.*

---

[25] History of the United States. See "Finance" in the Index, as the paging varies in different editions. See also Walker on "Money," p. 327.

[26] Prof. Sumner's "Financier and Finances of the American Revolution," 1891, Vol. 1, p. 98, and Walker on Money, p. 329, gives nearly the same figure.

The rise of exchange is shown by the following table taken from Gouge, p. 26:

| DATE. | | EXCHANGE AT PHILADELPHIA. |
|---|---|---|
| 1777 | January | 1¼ per cent. |
| | March | 2 " |
| | July | 3 " |
| 1778 | January | 4 " |
| | August | 5 " |
| | November | 6 " |
| 1779 | January | 7, 8, 9 " |
| | February | 10 " |
| | April | 12 to 22 " |
| | August | 20 " |
| 1780 | January | 40, 45 " |
| | March | 60 " |
| | August | 65, 75 " |
| | November | 80, 100 " |
| 1781 | January | 100 " |
| | February | 100, 120 " |
| | March | 120, 135 " |
| | April | 135, 200 " |
| | May | 200, 500 " |

There was not the slightest hesitation among the people about taking the bills at any time—they circulated as lively as ever at 500 to 1. On May 31, 1781, they ceased to circulate, but were afterward bought on speculation at from 400 for 1 to 1000 for 1.

The rapid depreciation of paper from 1776 to 1781 caused a great deal of misery. Dr. Ramsey says:

"Many opulent persons of ancient families were ruined by selling paternal estates for a depreciating paper currency, which in a few weeks would not replace half of the real property in exchange for which it was obtained."

Mortgages, debts, rents, incomes, were swept away; properties changed hands; people could live only by producing, for money withered in their hands; industry and diffusion of property were favored; debtors were freed and creditors ruined—results in large part beneficial, but reached by an unjust path. If the States had taxed themselves, or Congress had taken Franklin's advice, the currency might have been kept within reasonable bounds, and diffusion of property, unburdening of debtors, etc., might have been attained by means more wise and just. It is needful to remark that in order to sustain the currency, something more would have been necessary besides the limitation of the volume of notes issued by Congress and the States by taxation or borrowing; viz.: great care in the execution of the bills would have been requisite in order to prevent imitation, or else a frequent recalling of the circulation to weed out counterfeits, or both; for the reader must not imagine that the depreciation of the Continental money was due entirely to over-issue. Besides the effect of over-issuing genuine bills, the volume of money was enormously increased and its circulation debased by the systematic injection of counterfeit notes. Bolles says:[27]

"Counterfeiting was not confined to individuals. The British Government also embarked in the business. General Howe abetted and patronized those who were engaged in making and pushing these spurious issues into circulation. In the same papers which published British official documents and proclamations might be found advertisements like the following:

'Persons going into the other colonies may be supplied with any number of counterfeited Congress notes for the price of the paper per ream. They are so nearly and exactly executed that there is no risk in getting them off, it being almost impossible to discover that they are not genuine. This has been proved by bills of a very large amount, which have been successfully circulated.' * * * Persons accompanying an English flag of truce are known to have largely made use of the opportunity for disseminating the fraudulent notes; emissaries from New York endeavored to obtain paper from the mills similar to that used by Congress for its emissions. Many in Great Britain and elsewhere believed that if Continental paper money could be destroyed the Americans would be obliged to submit, from lack of funds to maintain their cause. This is why the British Government promoted so extensively the business of counterfeiting. But General Clinton wrote truthfully in January, 1780:

---

[27] Financial History of the United States, 1774 to 1789, pp. 151 to 153.

"Every day teaches me the futility of calculations founded on its failure. No experiments suggested by your lordship, no assistance that could be drawn from the power of gold or the arts of counterfeiting, have been left unattempted. But still the currency, like the widow's cruse of oil, has not failed the Congress. My hopes on this head, I must acknowledge, were much higher twelve months since than to-day. With the appearance of an enormous quantity, still it is all the debt which the people have to struggle with, and in this view, and when compared with that of other nations, it shrinks into a very inconsiderable sum. I shall, nevertheless, my lord, continue assiduous in the application of those means intrusted to my care; if they cannot work its destruction, yet they can embarrass the government and make the carrying on of the war more precarious, burdensome, and less energetic."

Phillips says: "A shipload of counterfeit Continental money coming from Great Britain was captured by an American privateer."[28]

The Continental money did not die a natural death. It was mortally wounded on the field of battle, while bravely fighting for its country, from which metallic money had fled at the first sign of danger. It won the fight before it breathed its last, and conquered Great Britain with all its gold and limitless resources.

## ENGLAND.

In 1797 the Bank of England, the monetary heart of Great Britain, suspended specie payments, and legal tender inconvertible paper was the principal medium of exchange till 1821, when specie payments were resumed. For the first ten years and more the "iredeemable" paper money did not depreciate; afterwards in consequence of excessive issues prices rose considerably. In 1815 the battle of Waterloo closed the war with Napoleon and the period of expansion came to an end. In 1816 England demonetized silver and began to contract the currency preparatory to the resumption of specie payments. Prices fell heavily and continued to fall until

---

([28]) Cont. Paper Money, p. 71.

the middle of the century, when the floods of gold began to pour in from the newly discovered mines of California and Australia.

The period of expanding currency 1797-1815, tho an epoch of exhausting war, was a period of remarkable prosperity. Merchants, manufacturers, farmers, laborers, all classes in the community, prospered in a high degree, and wealth was created in a hitherto unheard of ratio.

Early in the war with France (which commenced in 1793) metallic money began to disappear, producing financial stringency and commercial disaster till specie payments were suspended and irredeemable paper came to the rescue. The paper money of England enabled her to put vast armies in the field, to subsidize Europe, to conquer Napoleon, and to develop her own resources to an astonishing extent. Wm. Pitt said of the suspension of specie payments that its effect "was like finding a mountain of gold."

The second period, 1816-1849, the epoch of contraction and appreciating gold, was one of panic and industrial distress. The fall of prices paralyzed business. Profits and wages shrank. Vast numbers of workers were thrown out of employment. Riots broke out in many manufacturing towns, and agricultural laborers burned corn stacks and hay ricks, for which some of them were hanged. The ruined farmers petitioned the government for loans at low interest, based on land and agricultural products, but they were told the trouble was with the tariff—when that was fixed all would be well. But years of tariff and no tariff were alike disastrous. Prices fell 30, 40, 50, 60 per cent., and harvests were abundant, yet the laboring classes were unable to get bread, and famine desolated Ireland. Hundreds of banks were ruined, as were tens of thousands of enterprising merchants and manufacturers; and the land holders of England, Ireland and Scotland were reduced in numbers from 175,000 to 50,000, a change precisely contrary to that produced by the expanding paper of France in the years of the Revolution.

The English period of expansion, 1797-1815, corresponds in our own history to the period from 1860 to 1866, when the suspension of specie payments and the expanding volume of "irredeemable" national notes produced the same effects that characterized the paper epoch in England. The English period of contraction, demonetization of silver and rising gold, 1816 to 1849, corresponds to our period from 1866 to the present time (1897) and the effects have been the same as in Great Britain.

The course of events in England and America in the eras under consideration may be broadly presented thus:

| CAUSES. | RESULTS. |
| --- | --- |
| Danger. | Financial stringency and Industrial distress. |
| Disappearance of coin. | |
| Suspension of specie payments and issue of inconvertible paper. | Expanding money. Revival of business and marvelous prosperity. |
| Contraction, demonetization of silver and resumption of specie payments. | Scarcity of money. Rising gold and money and obligations based on gold. Panic and industrial depression. |

In view of the immediate revival of business on the suspension of specie payments and issue of irredeemable notes in 1797, and the unparalleled prosperity which England enjoyed at home and abroad during eighteen years of expanding paper, in spite of the heavy drain of the war, it may seem strange that England's statesmen should not have learned the laws of money sufficiently well to avoid the contraction and the golden fetters of 1816 and following years. Perhaps they would if it had not been for inherited theories and the interests of bond holders.[29]

England might have retained forever the glory of 1815, had she continued the policy of supplying her people with an abundant but not excessive currency, raised the needed rev-

---

(²⁹) See the fuller account in Appendix B.

enue by graded income and property taxes, and continued the public employment and direction of all the "surplus" labor[30] in the country, not in army and navy as during the war, but in the construction of roads and public improvements. — —

The same remarks apply to our history for thirty years past, the evils of which in very great part would have been avoided if Congress had made *all* the war *notes a full legal tender to and from* the government, placing duties on imports and interest on bonds on a level with all other payments, making the people's money as good as the banker's, and paying the bond holders in the same money that was good enough for soldiers, farmers, mechanics, merchants and manufacturers, and then had been content to take the funds of the wealthy as well as the lives of the poor for the service of their country, establishing a graded income tax that would have *made excessive issues* of greenbacks *unnecessary*—and, after the war, had increased the volume of the currency (as France did after the German war in '71) and entered upon public improvements, in order to absorb with ease the labor freed by the cessation of hostilities, and provide a currency equal to the new demands of a re-united North and South.[31]

### FRANCE AND GERMANY.

From 1870 to 1878 France kept her inconvertible paper close to par,[32] and finally reduced the premium on gold to zero, not by contracting her currency or resuming specie payments, but simply by expanding the volume of her irredeemable paper in judicious manner.[33]

The war with Germany left France in a very serious condition. She had been ravaged over nearly half her territory, she had had to maintain not only her own army, but in a

---

([30]) The unemployed are not really "surplus," tho often spoken of as such. There is plenty to be done. The unemployed are simply out of place and out of adjustment in our complex system.

([31]) The history of England during the periods above referred to is so important that we give in Appendix B a fuller account for those who wish to study the subject more deeply.

([32]) Prof. Dunbar in the Quarterly Jour. of Economics, April, 1892, p. 333.

([33]) See writings of Henry Carey Baird and Baron Wubnitz, mentioned below, also "Money of Nations," by Warwick Martin, 1880, p. 21.

large degree that of her enemy also. In addition to the presence of a victorious invader, her industries had to stand the shock of a domestic revolution. By the peace she lost two of her finest provinces containing a million and a half of her most ingenious and industrious citizens, and was required to pay 5 billion francs (one billion dollars) war indemnity with 5 per cent. interest on the debt each year.

Germany had suffered little, had only the partial support of her own army to pay for, her soil had not been devastated by battle, she was full of the enthusiasm of victory and conquest, and exultant over the billions of gold she was to receive from France.

What was the outcome? The French bankers made advances to merchants and manufacturers amounting to $36,000,000 during the first fortnight after the defeat of the French armies in August, 1870, and the consternation had seized the people at the triumph of the German arms, not one failure of consequence took place, and the loans were promptly repaid.[34] In September, 1870, specie payments were suspended and the notes of the Bank of France were made a legal tender. After the first payment of coin to Germany in 1871, gold went to a premium of 1½ per cent., but the volume of paper was expanded cautiously and the premium fell and finally disappeared. In June, 1870, before the war, the circulation of the bank was $275,000,000; by the end of 1870 it had become $460,000,000; by the end of January, 1872, it had been expanded to $490,000,000 and the premium had fallen to 1 per cent.; by the end of October, 1873, it had been further expanded to $614,000,000, when the premium on gold and silver disappeared. Coin now began to come into the country and the bank began to contract its paper volume. By June 25, 1874, the withdrawals amounted to $107,000,000. The contraction was found to be too great, bringing

---

([34]) A similar course had been followed by the bank in the Revolution of 1848, when the inconvertible notes of the bank were made legal tender and immense advances were made to public resources, and to private parties on receipts for merchandise stored in warehouses opened for the purpose by decree of the National Assembly. These merchandise receipts alone were discounted to the value of $12,000,000, and the increase of the currency revived business and saved the nation from panic and collapse (H. C. Baird, "Money and Bank Credit," 1891).

financial distress and industrial depression, especially at Paris. An expansion was immediately begun again and kept up till December 31, 1874, when the paper volume had been increased $62,000,000 and the specie $81,700,000 and prosperity was fully restored. During the early part of the first expansion the debt to Germany was completely paid, not, as Germany expected in French gold, but in German bank notes and bills of exchange on Berlin, Amsterdam, Frankfurt and other German cities and on London. Nearly seven-eighths of the war indemnity was paid in this way, about one-eighth of the seven being in exchange on London, and the other six-eights in German notes and bills. The Germans, elated with success, full of victory and plunder, bought with a lavish hand. The French flooded Germany with advertisements, sold their wines and silks and other luxuries and made the Germans pay a large part of the indemnity themselves. The war fine was really paid in merchandise for which France drew her bills of exchange on the German people who paid *their cash* into the German treasury. Germany had demonetized gold in 1857 and remained on a silver basis until 1871, when, relying on the expected billions of gold from France, she decreed the establishment of the single gold standard. In fact, however, she only got $54,600,610 in gold and $48,000,000 in silver from France, and the outcome of the whole affair was a contraction of circulation and panic in Germany, forty-one banking houses being compelled to suspend, while France was prosperous beyond the dreams of any one who saw her in the hour of defeat.[35]

Even as late as 1880 the bank had still a large volume of "irredeemable" paper. It made no promise to pay its notes in coin, and yet they were at par with gold, because they were by law receivable for everything gold was receivable for, and they were not issued in excess.[36]

---

[35] These and many other facts relating to this period of French history have been given to me by Henry Carey Baird, the noted Philadelphia publisher and economic writer who studied the subject on the ground, and has written numerous accounts of the splendid achievements of French banking in the seventies: "Money and Bank Credit," "The Lesson of German and French Finance," "The Franco-German War Fine of 1871," etc. The detailed official statement of the Bank of France as to the manner in which the indemnity was paid is of the greatest interest.
[36] "Money of Nations," by Warwick Martin, 180, p. 21. See also Warren's American Labor, pp. 22-4.

President Walker, writing in 1876, says:

"The occurrence of the war with Germany in 1870 caused a suspension by the bank, which has lasted to the present time; but during all this period the condition of her circulation has constituted a triumph of sound finance. Altho irredeemable, her paper has never been allowed, at any moment, to become greatly in excess. The premium in gold has never gone above 1.5 per cent., and during the greater portion of the period has been five-tenths of one per cent., or even less. 'The failure of the French armies,' wrote the late Mr. Bagehot, in November, 1874, 'has not been more striking than the success of French banking.' "[37]

Baron Wabuitz, a distinguished German author, says:[38]

"France had, by the war of 1870, incurred a burden of debt which (in proportion) far exceeded that of the United States. It had been compelled to permit the issue of unsecured notes, which up to that time amounted to about $240,000,000, was increased at the very commencement of the war by about $160,000,000, and in December, 1870, received a second increase of about $60,000,000. All these bank notes were given the quality of legal tender. * * * Yet after the conclusion of peace the financial administration had the courage to still further increase the issue of notes in 1871. * * * Instead of fixing a date for the resumption of specie payments, France merely made an arrangement with the bank management, according to which, as soon as the part of the national debt assumed by the bank should be paid back to it, the forcible character of the legal tender notes should cease. * * * The results of this French financial policy have been as follows: (1) The immediate reappearance of coin in circulation. * * * (2) The par exchange of bank notes when their legal tender character was removed. (3) Increasing prosperity of the country, which is so little affected by the great commercial and financial crisis visiting the whole world, that even the collapse of the recent gigantic swindling establishments of Philipart made scarcely an impression upon the public credit."

---

[37] "Money," p. 366.
[38] "The old Standard," pp. 25-7.

"The contrast between the events in France and the operations which the United States permitted under similar antecedent conditions, is, as will be confessed, a glaring one."

France has experienced the bad effects of a currency planlessly issued, as well as the benefits of paper properly managed. The John Law episode, 1717-1721, was a scheme by which 12 billions of francs were loaned to the King to pay off his debts. The plan was to make the colonial possessions of France one grand mortgage to secure the currency. The notes circulated at par at first, but as the volume became excessive they sank in value. Even under the best conditions mortgage notes could not be converted into land with sufficient readiness to drain off the excess of voluminous issues in the interest of an impecunious and ignorant young King, and when the land relied on for redemption of the notes was across the ocean, in the wilds of the Mississippi valley, it is easy to see that people would rather keep the money than pay it to the government for such lands, and so there was nothing to call in the excess, and the over-issues depreciated the currency.[39]

The French *Assignats* put out by the Revolutionary Government, 1790-1796, were also issued against land, and were supposed to be secured thereby. The holders of the notes had a right to purchase with them the lands confiscated from the church and emigrant nobles, but *the price of the land was not fixed, no proportion was established between land and paper*, the holder of the assignats had simply the right to buy land at its market value, and as the assignats depreciated with excessive volume the land rose in price, and the security was shown to be merely a name.[40] Even if a definite value in assignats had been put upon specific portions of land, the convertibility would have been too cumbrous to constitute an efficient limitation on the volume of a currency issued with the reckless prodigality that characterized the Revolution. The land security of Pennsylvania was altogether different;

---
[39] Jervons on "Money and the Mechanism of Exchange," International Scientific Series, p. 228.
Walker on "Money," p. 304.
Hon. John Davis in Arena, June, 1894, p. 99.
[40] Jevons, p. 228.

the money was issued on loan to those who *already* owned realty, and it had to be paid back with interest or the land would be taken by the Government. In this way *the relation of the notes to land constituted an effective limitation upon their volume* and so prevented their depreciation; but in France the relation of the notes to land had nothing to do with the volume issued by the Government, and little influence in drawing off the excess that was issued.[41] The issue began in 1790, and by the beginning of 1796 over 9 billions of dollars had been issued,[42] $7,200,000,000 of which were in actual circulation[43]—a steep ascent in the space of six years from about $20 of money per head to a circulation of $300 per head! Imagine a change in six years from our circulation of $1,600,000,000 to a circulation of $22,000,000,000! The largest circulation claimed for the United States at the close of the Rebellion was $2,000,000,000. The assignats were rudely executed and easily counterfeited. In addition to the overissue of genuine notes, the country was flooded with counterfeits from England, Belgium and Switzerland. Europe was at war with France and made a business of trying to break down its money by counterfeiting. The English Government sought to put down the French Revolution as she had tried to put down the American Revolution—by forgery. Wm. Pitt, Prime Minister of England, organized and superintended the business. Seventeen factories were in full operation in London with a force of 400 men, devoted to the production of false assignats. In May, 1795, it was found that 12 to 15 billions of francs of forged assignats were in circulation.[44] No wonder the assignats sank to a small fraction (1-200) of their nominal value. Issued by an unstable government, issued in overwhelming excess, executed poorly and systematically counterfeited with tremendous effect by foreign governments

---

([41]) Besides the fact that no fixed relation existed between the land and the notes, there was the further important fact that the title to the land was regarded as doubtful. If the revolutionary government failed and the nobles returned to power, the confiscated lands might be reconfiscated, and those who obtained estates by way of redemption of their assignats might find the security worth less than the paper on which the assignats were printed.

([42]) Garnier's "Traite de Finances," p. 408.
([43]) Walker on "Money," p. 344.
([44]) "Assignats and Mandats," by Stephen D. Dillaye, 1877, pp. 32-33. Doubleday's Financial Hist. of England.
John Davis, Arena, June, '94, pp. 91-2.
Walker's "Money," p. 345.

beyond the reach of the French criminal laws, they lacked every element of virtuous paper. If the notes had been carefully executed in the highest style of art, and called in now and then to weed out counterfeits, and after seven or eight hundred million dollars were issued the further needs of the government had been met by taxation or loan, there is every reason to believe that the notes would have kept their value, and prices would have remained substantially level. In other words, if the same policy had been pursued in 1790 that was afterward followed in 1870, it is probable that the results of 1790 would have been similar to those of 1870.

In 1796 the Revolutionary Government began to issue *territorial mandates* exchangeable for land in substantially the same way as the assignats. Eight hundred millions were to be used in cancelling assignats at 30 to 1, the rest to serve the government. They rose to 80 per cent. of their nominal value after the first limited emission, but additional issues sent them down to 1-1000 of their face. They were really nothing more than assignats under another name; they had some value for a time because the withdrawal of the assignats at the rate of 30 to 1 materially diminished the volume of the circulation. The paper of the revolution went down with the revolution. The last insurrection was put down by Napoleon in 1795. In July, 1796, a decree was issued authorizing every man to do business in the money and on the terms he chose, mandates to be taken at their market value. With Napoleon's power, coin and a comparatively stable government returned to France. Napoleon's wars kept France supplied with specie during his ascendency; he took the gold and silver from all the countries he conquered.

The evils of the rapid depreciation of the curency in the French Revolution were doubtless very great; industrial calculations could not be made with any certainty for any considerable period in the future, and creditors were cheated to an enormous extent. Two things, however, must never be forgotten. First, that these evils are not inherent in inconvertible paper, as the French experience of 1870 has shown, but belong to the bad management of the Revolutionary Government; and second, that in spite of all its evils, the revolutionary paper accomplished wonders; coin was invisible for danger was in sight; paper was necessary, and the assignats, ill-managed as they were, nevertheless enabled France to conquer the enemies of liberty on every hand; nation after nation with metallic money yielded to the French and their poor paper, debtors thruout the land were liberated, unjustly to a large extent no doubt, but nevertheless liberated, a result in itself a benefit; the first moderate upward trend of prices gave an enormous impulse to industry; the national domains were purchased almost for nothing by the holders of government paper, many large estates were divided into little holdings and became daily more productive from the number and energy of the new cultivators; the diffusion of property that resulted was of inestimable benefit.[45] It was a great thing to get rid of some of the old burdens, oppressions and aristocracies, and tho it might have been done in a better and juster way, we must give the rag credit for wiping the slate, even while we recognize that it was not as clean a rag as it should have been.

### THE ALLIED POWERS.

During the Napoleonic Wars part of the gold and silver of Austria, Prussia, and Russia went into hiding or emigrated of its own notion, and the rest was carried to France by the conqueror, and "coin became improcurable within their territories." An inconvertible paper money was issued by the Powers, and guaranteed jointly by Great Britain and all the other allies, and this "irredeemable" paper alone rendered possible the vast military operations of the allies which resulted in the defeat of Napoleon. Paper money overthrew him, altho his stolen millions of metallic money constituted one of his best props.[46]

### RUSSIA.

Paper money (to the amount of 40,000,000 roubles or $32,000,000) was first issued in Russia under Catharine II in

---

[45] "History of Europe," by Sir Archibald Alison, Vol. IV., p. 371.
[46] Such is the verdict of one of the best and most authoritative European writers on finance, "The New Golden Age," by R. H. Patterson, London, 1882, Vol. ii. pp. 24-5.

1768, on the ground that the copper money, then forming the legal tender was inconvenient.[47]

"The manifesto accompanying the issue of this paper," says Mr. Tooke,[48] "left it in doubt whether the payment to bearer was to be in copper or silver; and acording to Storch, opinions were still divided when he wrote in 1815. The agio in favor of silver varied only from 1 to 3 per cent. in that interval, from 1768 to 1787, while there was an agio of 1.5 per cent. *in favor of paper against copper.*"

"In 1787 60,000,000 roubles were added, and during a series of wars with Sweden, Turkey, Poland, Persia and France the Russian government, instead of taxing the wealthy, issued new volumes of paper till the amount outstanding in 1810 was computed at 577,000,000 roubles, or $461,600,000, a paper advance in twenty-three years from $1.50 per head to $11 per head. This rapid increase of volume was accompanied by a considerable depreciation. The paper rouble (par value 80 cents) was worth in silver:[49]

72 cents in 1787.
48 cents in 1796.
36 cents in 1800.
24 cents in 1810.
18 cents in 1817.

### AUSTRIA.

For twenty years Austria-Hungary has had a legal tender paper which does not profess to be based on gold or silver or have any relation therewith. The price of gold has fluctuated chiefly from political causes,[50] but in reference to commodities in general, this baseless, promiseless, irredeemable paper has at no time fallen in value; on the contrary it has appreciated, prices have fallen somewhat,[51] the notes not being issued fast enough to keep the movement of the currency volume even with the growth of business.

---

[47] Jevons, 202, Walker, 366.
[48] See Tooke's Hist., Prices, ii., 67, 209-16, also i., 103-1
[49] Mulhall's Dict. of Statistics, title "Money."
[50] Walker on "Money," p. 368.
[51] Mulhall, tit. "Prices," subhead "Austria."
   Tit. "Money" for exchange rates

I said the paper was promiseless; I mean that the issuing government does not promise to *pay* anything for the paper; it merely promises to *receive* the paper for debts due it, and makes it legal tender with slight exceptions in cases where coin payment is expressly provided for. This Austrian currency is so well described by Consul-General Post that I quote a few paragraphs from his report:

"Prior to 1866 the currency of the Empire cconsisted of National bank notes—promises to pay silver florins which were the standard. In 1866, however, the government (Austria Hungary) commenced to issue legal tender state notes which do not pretend to be promises to pay anything, anywhere, at any time. They read on their face, after stating the denomination, one, five, or fifty gulden as the case may be, as follows : 'This state note will be received and paid out by all imperial and royal depositories and offices for all payments which are not required by law to be in coin.' "

"It will be seen that these notes are a promise to receive, not 'to pay,' and that they do not claim to be redeemable, and have no more reference to silver florins than to gold florins. As the National Bank was compelled to accept these irredeemable state notes, the Government exempted the National Bank by law from redeeming its notes, so long as state notes are issued, so that legally and practically the business of the empire is conducted with a paper currency absolutely irredeemable, and having no reference to either silver or gold, its value being derived from its legal tender character. The average amount of National Bank notes in circulation in 1876 was 291,000,000, and of state notes 342,000,000 florins."

"The legal tender promises to receive issued by the state not only furnish the larger part of the circulation, but fix the character of the entire currency. *That currency which some American philosophers and statesmen are reported to be dreaming of and longing for, has been established by law, and is in actual use in this country—a paper currency with a value stamped thereon, and which costs nothing but the printing. It is not silver, it is not gold, nor is it a promise to pay silver or gold, nor is it a promise to receive as equivalent to silver or gold.* It is a paper florin, a legal tender for all debts, except debts which are by express law or by express agreement payable in coin."[52]

### BRAZIL.

Brazil kept an independent paper currency at par with gold for many years, and even sent it to a premium. After the Paraguayan war Dom Pedro refused to paralyze the country's energies by contracting the circulating medium. In-

---

[52] Hon. Philip S. Post, U. S. Consul General to Austria-Hungary, Consular Reports, July 13, 1878.

stead of doing that he decided to stimulate them by vigorous expansion (as France did after the Franco-German war), and the consequence was that within seven years after the war the paper money which, during the war, had depreciated nearly one-half, measured in gold, rose again to par, and even commanded a premium of 1⅜ d. in gold.[53]

The appreciation was not accomplished by diminishing the volume of the currency. On the contrary the first step was an expansion, to the enormous extent of 50 per cent. in one year, which was followed by an advance of 11¾ per cent. toward par. It took the United States fifteen years to bring its paper to par with gold via the contraction road, while Brazil reached the same goal in less than half that time, by way of the expansion turnpike. Moreover, our people suffered inexpressible hardships during the journey, while hers were never more prosperous and happy.[54]

The Herschell Commission says:

"The case of Brazil is, perhaps, the most remarkable of all, as showing that a paper currency, *without* a metallic base may, if the credit of the country is good, be maintained at a high and fairly steady exchange, altho it is absolutely inconvertible, and has been increased by act of government out of all proportion to the growth of population and its foreign trade. The Brazilian standard coin is the milreis, the par value of which is 27 d. A certain number were coined, but long since left the country, and the currency is, and has, since 1864, been inconvertible. The inconvertible paper was more than doubled between 1865 and 1888, but *the exchange was about* the same at the two periods and very little below the par of 27 d. It has gone down to 14 d., in 1868, the date of the war with Paraguay, but has risen again, and was in 1875 as high as 28¾ d. In 1869, when the quantity of paper was increased from £12,648,000 to £18,320,000, the mean sale of exchange showed an advance of 11¾ per cent."

Since the Commission wrote, the currency of Brazil has met with serious depreciation thru enormous overissues, but so long as the conditions of steady value—a stable government and due limitation of the money volume—were maintained, the inconvertible paper kept its value.*

---

([53]) Report of the Herschell Indian Currency Commission composed of some of the ablest statesmen of England, every member signing the Report.
([54]) "The Key Note" by Albert Griffin, pp. 98-9.
*Paper circulation in Brazil rose from 192,800,000 milreis (196,300,000 gold) in 1889 to 785,941,000 milreis (209,296,090 gold) in 1898. The government

## THE BANK OF VENICE.

In the year 1171 a Venetian fleet was sent to avenge an outrage perpetrated by the Grecian Emperor Manuel upon Venetian merchants in his empire. To meet the charges of this war against the Emperor of the East and sustain the burden of hostilities with the Emperor of the West, in which the Republic was also involved, the Duke Vitale, Michael II., had recourse to a forced loan from the most opulent citizens of Venice, each being required to contribute according to his ability. By determination of the Great Council, a Chamber of Loans was established, and the subscribers were guaranteed 4 per cent. interest. The contributors were constituted a special board for their own protection and the management of the loan; the book in which the loans were inscribed was authenticated by the Government, and made evidence of the whole amount of the debt, and the proportion belonging to each subscriber.[55]

It was an easy step to commence the transfer of the loans upon the books as a means of paying debts or obtaining money, and the advantages of the book credits seem to have led to a very rapid circulation of the loan.[56]

---

then began to contract the paper volume so that in August, 1899, it was reduced to 735,759,000 milreis (equal to 219,736,530 milreis in gold or £25,717,000). In 1889 paper was at a premium of 1.8¢ above gold. The next year thru a large increase of volume, it began to depreciate, and by 1898 the depreciation rose to 73.4¢ and 74.5¢ (the maximum) in March, 1899, three months after the withdrawals of paper began. In August, 1899, when the withdrawals had been going on for eight months, the depreciation was reduced to 70.1¢. In March, '99, the volume of paper in circulation was 773,802,000 milreis, worth 197,087,470 in gold, or almost exactly the same as 200,000,000 milreis were worth in 1889. (For further details, see L'Economiste Européen, vol. 16, p. 613, Nov., 1899; vol. 17, pp. 324, 389—by Feb. 1st, 1900, the volume of paper had been further reduced to 725,719,854 milreis.)

[55] McPherson's Annals of Commerce (London, 1805), Vol. I., p. 341. Colwell's "Ways and Means of Payment," pp. 288-9. Stephen Colwell was a learned and wealthy Philadelphian who collected a large library rich in Italian literature. He made a very careful study of the Bank of Venice and wrote the best history of that institution that has been put into English. It was published by J. B. Lippincott & Co., in 1859. In October, 1878, the Bankers' Magazine of New York commended Mr. Colwell's work in high terms, printed his chapter on the Venetian Bank, saying that it was considered the best account in the English Language. The American Cyclopedia, Art. "Bank." cites Colwell as "an eminent economic writer." In fact he is universally regarded as an able and trustworthy writer, which is important in view of fact that his writings furnish the only available source of complete information on this subject for those unable to read Italian.

[56] Colwell, p. 289.

Thus originated the Bank of Venice, which for more than six centuries (until overthrown by Napoleon in 1797)[57] dominated the finances of Europe.

The facility of transfer coupled with the superior security of funds guaranteed by the State, and the regular payment of interest, soon opened men's eyes to the advantages of the Venetian Bank over common banks, and the demand for Bank credits rapidly grew. In an ordinary bank the depositor might lose his money by robbery, or defalcation, or maladministration of the officers; but funds in the Bank of Venice were secure from these dangers. Payment in coin was slow, inconvenient and unsafe. There was a great admixture of coins in Venice, which her widely spread commerce brought from all over the world. These coins not only belonged to different systems and nationalities, but were new and old, counterfeit and genuine, light weight and full weight, and it required special skill to tell the value of the coins. Under such circumstances the ready transfer of book credits by which thousands of ducats could be paid in a moment in a medium secure from counterfeiting and light weight, of entirely certain value and perfect divisibility, became a matter of the highest importance. If all the merchants of a city had the same banker who kept an account with each one of them, this banker could make all the reciprocal payments without moving a cent of their money.

The capital of the bank did not consist of gold or silver, but simply of a debt due by the Republic to its citizens. The government took the money and gave in return an inscription on the books of the bank. The Government used the cash in war or foreign expenditures, or turned it again into the channels of domestic commerce. Depositors in this bank could not withdraw their deposits. "It was perfectly under-

---

[57] 1171 to 1797 is the period given by Colwell; by Pres. E. Benjamin Andrews, in his Institutes of Economics, p. 131; by Hon. John Davis, Arena, December, 1893, p. 35; by Wharton Barker, in his Bimetallism, p. 10; see also Hazlitt's History of Venice, Sidney Dean's "History of Banking and Banks from the Bank of Venice founded A. D. 1171, etc"; Edw. H. G. Clark in the North American Review, September, 1885, p. 205; and see the Cyclopedia Britannica, the American Encyclopedia, the International Cyclopedia, La Grande Encyclopedie, art. "Banque," p. 251, etc. Prof. Dunbar, in Quar. J. of Econ., April, 1892, says the bank was opened in 1619 instead of 1171, and closed by Napoleon in 1806; but the overwhelming weight of authority is against him.

stood that no coins passed, neither any right to any, on the transfer in the bank."[58] If the amount of bank credits exceeded the demand for them in business transactions, the Government paid off a part of the debt so as to remove the superfluous funds. When the bank funds were in large demand, the bank was open to receive further loans to the government. This policy of adjusting the volume of credits so that they should not exceed the needs of business, not only kept the inconvertible credit currency of the bank at par with specie, but, in connection with the peculiar advantages of the credits, kept them for the most part far above the level of gold and silver.[59]

The Government itself made payments by drawing on the bank, and received bank credits into the public treasury on payment of sums due the State. A law was passed that all bills of exchange above 300 ducats might be paid in money of the bank, which could not be refused unless the right to refuse had been stipulated for.[60] In 1423 it was decreed that *all* bills of exchange payable in Venice *should be* paid in the bank unless otherwise stipulated.[61]

It was further enacted that all payments in gross for merchandise and all payments whatever for oil and quicksilver should be in bank. These measures brought the mass of payments of that great commercial city to the State Bank, created a great additional demand for bank funds, and brought large sums into the public coffers.

The Government no longer paid interest, but the bank funds were exempt from execution for debt and from encumbrance by mortgage, and were not merely legal tender, but the required medium of payment for bills of exchange and purchases at wholesale. No promise was made to repay the coin with which new credits were bought. The Government took the coin and used it in foreign wars, etc., and the depositor

---

[58] Colwell, p. 306.
[59] Colwell, pp. 6 and 7, 306, 309, 311. Temporarily, during the stress of war on two or three occasions, the government's policy of adjusting the bank funds to the needs of business was not perfectly carried out. (See below note 8.)
[60] Daru Hist. Venice, Vol 3, p. 73.
[61] Colwell, p. 292.

had only his transferable credit,[62] which was, however, worth more to him than the coin, else he would not have bought it. The superior advantages of bank funds and the limitation of their volume[63] resulted in sending them to a premium above coin, which rose at times as high as 40 or 50 per cent. When it had risen with various fluctuations to an average of 20 per cent., a new law was passed fixing the agio or premium at that amount, hoping to do away with the fluctuations in the relation between coin and credit; but the law was unsuccessful; the real agio at times fell below 20 per cent. by reason of the sale of bank credits at a discount of 10 or 15 per cent., and at other times rose above 20 per cent. by reason of demand for bank funds, inducing merchants to offer a *sur*-agio of 20 or 30 per cent. in addition to the 20 per cent. allowed by law.[64]

[62] In the course of time a "Cash Office" was opened as a branch of the Ancient Bank, and in this cash office coin could be deposited and withdrawn at pleasure; but money deposited in the main bank went into the public treasury and could not be withdrawn. Merchants kept in the cash office money they might find convenient to use directly in trade, and even those who had bills to pay in a short time, making it necessary to carry their money into the ancient branch of the bank, might wish to keep the coin in their power until the payments matured. (Colwell, p. 299.) Experience showed that the establishment of the cash office did not cause any sersible diminution in the business of the main bank. (Savary, Dict. de Com., art. "Banque," p. 276.)

[63] Colwell says, p. 311: "The public debt was wisely kept at that amount which not only preserved its value, but furnished the full quantity of currency required for trade, with the means of increasing or diminishing the amount according to the demand." And p. 309: "The money brought in to pay bills was taken by the government as fast as it was received, until the amount of the deposits, or debt of the state, was adequate by rapid circulation to the current payments of commerce." After this point was reached in the judgment of the authorities, merchants desiring bank credits would have to buy them of other merchants in possession of the desired credits. And, if the government needed further coin for foreign purposes, it issued bonds or borrowed from the cash office. At times, however, either through temporary departure from this policy and an over production of bank credits, or through a falling off of commerce reducing the demand for bank funds, their value fell somewhat below the usual 20% premium level; at other times it rose above that level.

[64] Professor Dunbar, in the Quarterly Journal of Economics, April, 1892, sets forth the opinion that the agio or premium of 20% established by law was not due to any superiority of the bank credits, but resulted from the arbitrary selection of an imaginary ducat 20% more valuable than the real ducat as a unit of account. Upon this point it may be said: (1) That such a complication of commercial transactions would seem incredible as a mere arbitrary regulation. (2) That abundant reasons existed for the preference of bank funds to coin, reasons quite sufficient to produce the recorded phenomena without any arbitrary measure. A payment by transfer of credit was quick and safe and inexpensive, sure to give full value and free from the trouble of counting and valuing a multitude of diverse coins, many of them mutilated and not a few of them depreciated coins of alien origin. (Colwell, p. 306, see also to the point that the agio in ancient banks arose from these natural causes, Jevons' Money and Mechanism of Exchange, p. 200, and Adam Smith's Wealth of Nations, Bk. IV., Chap. III.) (3) That Prof. Dunbar's theory does not explain the sur-agio of 20 or 30 per cent. (4) That Prof. Dunbar does not adduce a single fact in support of his assertion, all the citations made by him agreeing far better with the idea that the difference between the bank ducat and the coin ducat was the result of the superior utility and safety of the former. And (5) That historians clearly state that the agio was first developed by the merchants and afterwards

fixed by law. Colwell says (p. 305): "The bank's funds rose to 30% premium over the current coins and continued to fluctuate near this high rate until the government limited the premium to 20%." And (p. 308): "The government so far from producing the agio, attempted to limit it to 20%, an attempt which was rendered wholly abortive by the introduction of a sur-agio." The premium was not caused by the government nor by the bank, but by the acts of the merchants themselves competing for bank credits with which to pay their debts. The amount of bank funds was limited as we have seen, and this circumstance together with their superiority to coin in large commercial transactions, sent them to a premium.

In the same article Prof. Dunbar contends that the Bank of Venice paid coin on demand except during suspensions beginning in 1691 and 1717, and some earlier suspensions of uncertain date. This contention appears to arise from a confusion of the main bank with the cash office. Colwell clearly states that money once deposited in the main bank could not be withdrawn, and that the cash office was established on purpose to provide for those who wished to deposit their money subject to call. (Ways and Means of Payment, pp. 299 and 307; see also Dict. de Com. par Savary, art. "Banque," p. 276.)

After stating the inconvertibility of the bank credits as a matter of historic record, Colwell adds the opinion that, "If the credits had been convertible at will into the precious metals, the agio could never have originated" (p. 307). On Prof. Dunbar's theory that the main bank was a bank where money could be deposited and drawn out at will, it is clear that no agio could have arisen, since the laws requiring payment in bank would have been satisfied by payment in specie as well as by payment in account, and if credits had been advanced in price, specie would have become at once the medium of payment as the cheaper medium; the debtor owing 1,000 ducats and having an account worth 1,200 metal ducats would have gone with the creditor to the bank, taken out his metal, paid his debt with 1,000 coins and had 200 ducats left.

The historic fact that not only an agio, but also a sur-agio existed in Venice, proves the error of Professor Dunbar's hypothesis as to convertibility. The debtor had to pay in the main bank; the only way to do this was by transfer of credit on the books of that bank; it could not be done with cash, for there was no cash in that bank (except cash received on loan to the government and in transitu to the public treasury—no cash demandable on the credits). As the credits were limited in quantity by the policy of the government, the competition for them among debtors sent them to a premium. That is the story history tells, and it is perfectly clear and consistent and apparently the only story that will fit the facts. The debtor could not demand cash for his credits; the government had taken the cash originally given for the credit, and neither government nor bank promised to redeem the credit with cash; the credit was simply a debt due from the government which reserved the right to cancel the debt with cash if it chose, but did not engage to do so within any specified time; if the debtor had a deposit in the cash office and a bill of exchange coming due, he could not draw out his cash and pay the bill with that; the only way to liquidate the bill was by a transfer of credit on the books of the main bank. If the depositor in the main bank could have withdrawn his deposit, the primary purpose of the government in starting the bank, and one of its chief objects in maintaining the institution, would have been defeated; for the government could not have used the deposits in foreign wars without depressing business at home, and incurring the danger of bankruptcy. In the stress of war and disaster, at the very time the government had most need of the money, there would have been a run on the bank compelling disbursement or closing of the bank. This is what did occur to the cash office, but not to the main bank, showing once more that its credits were not convertible.

In the Quarterly Journal of Economics, January '93, p. 210, Professor Dunbar admits that he made several mistakes in the previous article above referred to. He acknowledges that his assertion that the history of the bank since 1619 had not been written was an error; and that the long suspensions of the cash office were from 1630 to 1666 (36 years) and from 1713 to 1739 (26 years), instead of beginning in 1691 and 1717 as he had formally stated.

In view of these things it is not difficult to imagine that the Professor may have confused the main bank and the branch, and applied the statements to the former which related only to the latter. But the most important consideration is that even if we accept all that Professor Dunbar says about the Venetian Bank, our main conclusions in respect to it are not in the least affected. The Professor says that cash payments were suspended for 62 years and more, and during these years, at any rate, the bank credits were admittedly inconvertible, whatever view he may take of their character at other times. Yet he admits that the bank credits remained good during the suspensions, with temporary exceptions, when the exigencies of war caused the government to depart from its policy of keeping the bank credits within moderate limits, or the influence of hostilities seriously diminished the volume of business in Venice.

The Professor explains the continued value of the bank credits in spite of suspensions covering whole generations by saying: "It is plain that a cur-

Here we have a currency consisting simply of bank credits having the power by authority of law and usage to pay debts.[65] Men were willing to take bank credits in payment of debts due *to* them because they knew they could use those credits to pay debts due *from* them. They were *more* willing, in case of large payments, to take the credits than coin, because of their superior safety and convenience. And when the law increased the advantages of credits over coin by requiring the payment in bank of all bills of exchange and wholesale purchases, merchants were ready to give a considerable premium for these bank credits which were most convenient in large transactions at home, and were almost essential to extensive commerce abroad. In consequence of their superior advantages as a medium of exchange, these "irredeemable" bank funds, these "fiat" book credits without an ounce of gold or silver behind them, went to a premium above gold and silver in all the great markets of the world, and with slight exceptions for more than 400 years the precious metals were at a discount as compared with the funds of the Venetian Bank.[66]

Venice had not only the main bank with its "irredeemable" credits in which large payments had to be made, and the cash office for special purposes, but there were also interest bearing Government bonds, and these bonds with all their in-

---

rency which, for important purposes, is a legal tender, would not lose its ease of circulation by becoming inconvertible, and might even be kept at par with specie, if its supply were strictly limited to the demand for the special purposes referred to, as, for example, in this case, the settlements for exchange. In short, the good credit sometimes enjoyed by the bank after suspending payment, which excited the wonder of foreign observers, is the same phenomenon which has been observed in other cases where inconvertibility has not been made the excuse for over issue." Citing the notes of the Bank of England during the first ten years after the suspension of 1797, the notes of the suspended banks of New York and New England after the suspension of 1857, and the inconvertible notes of the Bank of France from 1870 to 1878.

The chief differences between Prof. Dunbar and other writers on the Bank of Venice lie in the matter of dates, the cause of the agio, and the relation of the cash office to the main bank. On the vital point of the value and circulating power of the inconvertible legal tender bank credits he is at one with all the rest.

([65]) Paper money has well been defined as "a portable system of bookkeeping."

([66]) Colwell, pp. 306-310. He further says that the demand for funds that would pay bills of exchange was greater than for gold or silver for export or retail trade or any other use. The great mass of purchases were made in the first instance by bills of exchange, and the chief operation of payment consisted in liquidating those bills. "To comprehend the extraordinary fact of a credit on the books of the bank with no money in its vaults, and not bound to make that credit good in later times even by the payment of interest, or to redeem it in any way, having been for hundreds of years at a high premium over gold and silver, we need only remember that these credits were the funds in which debts were chiefly paid." ((Pp. 306 and 307.)

terest (profit) and their promise of coin redemption, were quoted at 60 per cent. of their face value, while the bank credits, with no interest and no promise of coin redemption, were at a premium above gold. The quality of paying debts was worth more than the interest and future redemption in coin put together.[67]

*For six hundred years Venice had no money panic. In this country as many as ten disastrous panics have occurred within a single life—a rate that would have given Venice over a hundred panics during the life of her credit bank.*

The people of Venice appear to have been entirely satisfied with their bank. Colwell says, p. 294: "Not an objection to the bank is extant; neither book, nor speech, nor pamphlet have we found in which any merchant or dweller in Venice ever put forth any condemnation of its theory or practice." On the contrary, the Venetians had every reason to be proud of their banking system. The law that required all bills of exchange and wholesale purchases to be settled in the bank might seem unjust as intended to give a forced currency to the bank credits; but it was found to work so well in practice that it brought an immense accession of business to the city and the bank. In fact the bank became a great clearing house, or place of adjustment for merchants of many countries. Merchants everywhere found it convenient to have funds in Venice. It was for centuries the greatest entrepot of commerce in Europe. And the credit bank was, as Colwell says (p. 289): "For many ages, the admiration of Europe, the chief instrument of Venetian finance, and the chief facility of a commerce not surpassed by that of any European nation."

*The Bank of Venice lasted longer than any other money system known to history, and it clearly proved that an "irredeemable" legal tender, receivable in the revenues and*

---

[67] Hon. John Davis, in "Money in Politics," Arena for August, '94, p. 328: Similar facts occur elsewhere in history. During the Napoleonic Wars the non-interest bearing irredeemable legal tender British paper was worth twice as much as the 3% gold bearing bonds of England. (Ibid., citing Alison's History of Europe.) The same thing was seen during the Rebellion, when our specie bonds were frequently 20% or more below par in coin, while that part of our irredeemable paper which was receivable in the government revenues remained substantially at par with gold.

*enforced in the payment of debts, may have far greater convenience, safety and stability than coin or any money redeemabe in coin.*[68]

In his summary, Colwell says (pp. 7, 8): "The history of these celebrated banks (of Venice and Genoa) furnishes lessons which would richly repay the most careful attention."

"They demonstrated the efficacy of circulating deposits as a means of payment, and that the deposits were just as effective when they consisted of a debt due from the government, as if they were gold or silver; and they showed that it was possible to keep the amount of this public debt, as held by the depositors on the books, within a range of amount, which not only prevented depreciation, but kept the deposits always from fifteen to thirty per cent. above gold and silver."

### NUMERARY MONEYS OF ANTIQUITY.

Ancient nations understood that receivability and limitation of volume were the essential attributes of money; that intrinsic value was not necessary; and that money could and ought to be regulated.

The Middle Ages went back to barter and commodity money. Modern nations have not yet outgrown the commodity money, and "intrinsic" theories of barbarous times, but are beginning to understand something of the philosophy of the symbolic money which characterized the civilizations of antiquity, and will probably characterize the civilizations of the future. Some account of ancient thought and usage may be helpful here.

Aristotle says in his *Politica:* "Money (nomisma) by itself is but a mere device which has value only by law (nomos) and not by nature." And in his *Ethica:* "By virtue of volun-

---

[68] The fullest, clearest and most authoritative account of the Venetian Bank in the English language is that contained in Colwell's "Ways and Means of Payment," Philadelphia, 1859. Next to this may be mentioned the series of articles by Hon. John Davis, M. C., in the Arena for December, '93, April, '94, and August, '94. Considering its condensation, the statement of Edw. H. G. Clark, in the North American Review, September, 1885, is admirable. In addition to these and other accounts already named, the curious reader may consult Postlethwaite's Dictionary, London, 1755; Hayes' Negotiators' Magazine, London, 1739; Traite Generale du Commerce, par S. Ricord, 1732; Marperger on Banks, pp. 180 to 189, Leipsic, 1717; Econ. Politique, par Henri Storch, Vol. IV., p. 95; Broggia Trattale delle Monete, Vol. II., p. 270; in Vol. V. of Custodi's collection of the Economisti Italiani, Il Banco Giro di Venezia, by Prof. Amadeo Soresina, Venice, 1889.

tary convention, money has become the medium of exchange. We call it 'nomisma' because its efficiency is due, not to nature, but to law (nomos), and because it is in our power to regulate it."

Alexander Del Mar, one of the greatest of modern writers on monetary subjects, gives a fine account of the numerary[69] moneys of ancient times. In his "Science of Money," p. 31, he says in substance: Among highly civilized nations of antiquity, before paper was invented, symbols for such money consisted of porcelain tablets, as in China; thin iron discs, as in Sparta; artistic copper discs, as in Rome; discs of secret composition, as in Carthage; or tablets of stamped clay or leather, as in several other States. Where these moneys permanently retained their original value it was by means of limiting the number of symbols employed, by protecting them from counterfeiting (which is another point in the limitation of their volume), and by abolishing all other kinds of monies. The bits of material which represented the numbers, whether porcelain, sheet-iron or leather, counted for nothing. The devices or legends upon them promised nothing. Their value was derived from the legal-tender quality and their numbers; from the legal obligation to receive them for debts, fines, taxes, commodities and services of all sorts, and from the legal interdiction of all other kinds of money. Such numerical monies followed pre-existing commodity monies.

The facts collated by Del Mar exhibit with tremendous emphasis the power and importance of limitation of the monetary volume. The statements of Del Mar are so well represented by the selected quotations in President Will's financial lectures that I will use his abstracts of Del Mar's "History of Money in Ancient Countries," instead of attempting the hopeless task of improving upon his selections.

The numerary monies we are discussing were, as a rule, absolutely destitute of "intrinsic" value, possessing practically no commodity value; almost absolutely worthless for any other purpose than money; and yet, when the proper condi-

---

[69] A numerary money is one in which the number and value of the pieces is specifically limited by law.

tions of receivability and limitation of volume were observed, they did the work of money, and did it admirably well. The value of these monies was determined, not by their intrinsic quality, not by the labor cost or any other cost of producing them, but by the limitation of the number of pieces and by the legally established and enforced condition that this money should be good for all public and private debts and dues. Here are the abstracts:

1. China. The Chinese more than once caught sight of the true principles of money, and at times put them into operation. The theory of money is very correctly outlined in a memorial to one of the emperors of the present century. (Chinese Repository ii, 279.) It was known, however, in China ages before. At present it is forgotten.

The cash of the empire was always issued as numerary moneys. Several circumstances at times affected its character. (a) The vicissitudes of the government, leading it to break down the limits set to emissions. (b) Inefficiency in guarding counterfeits. (c) Emission of private bank notes. These circumstances lowered the value of copper cash to its commodity value (p. 41).

2. Egypt. The gold mines in Egypt failed for twenty centuries, i. e., until 525 B. C. Egypt must have been without gold * * * yet it could not have been without money; otherwise it could not have maintained its civilization; paste-board, parchment, leather, papyrus, nummulites and scarabei may have been used as money. * * * This money must have been numerary; otherwise it could not have passed, since its commodity value was so slight.

Over-valued iron money was used in Kordofan, the pieces varying in weight from 121 to 428 grains each, yet all were of similar value; this fact proves that monetary value is determined by numbers and not by weight.

Glass numerary money was used under the reign of the Fatimite Caliphs, A. D. 909-1171. It was used continuously or at intervals for upward of six hundred years. It could not have passed at its "intrinsic value." * * * The author believes these numerary moneys were all badly over-issued and so fell to their commodity value or thereabout (p. 150).

3. Persia. 1294 Kai Khatu, noting the lack of precious metals and the mischief occasioned thereby, tried to substitute over-valued copper coins for gold and silver coins. The scheme utterly failed. (a) No specific limit was set to the emission. (b) The coins were easily counterfeited. (c) The concurrent circulation of gold and silver coins was permitted. (d) The government was weak and despotic. The people were enslaved and ignorant; no confidence was felt in the value of the new coins, which were refused almost as soon as issued. The prince's own nephew set the example of

refusing these coins, which after this rapidly fell into disrepute (p. 152).

4. Greece. The supplies of coining metals were always irregular. Gold and copper had to be imported, while the silver mines were controlled by Athens; hence the other Greek states were compelled to employ numerical moneys. This was resorted to so commonly and at so many different times as to familiarize the Greek mind generally with the idea that money was an institution of law; and hence the name of law, prescription, limit, numbers or nomos was the generic name always conferred upon it (p. 162). (See Aristotle's Definitions of Money in Gide's Political Econ., p. 216, and Senator Jones' silver speech in United States Senate Oct. 18 and following dates, 1893, p. 29).

5. Sparta. The famous iron money of Sparta, upon which Plutarch has poured such ridicule, is believed by Del Mar to be a purely numerary money adopted by Lycurgus either because of "scarcity of metals, or of the desire to emancipate the country from the trammels of a metallic basis of valuation." The intrinsic (i. e., commodity) value of this iron was destroyed in advance by dipping the coins while redhot into vinegar. Inflation of the currency was discouraged by absolutely prohibiting the production and importation of gold and silver. There is every reason to believe that Sparta used this system of numerary iron money for three and one-half centuries; that is, until she lost the hegemony to Athens. B. C. 479. After this her fall was rapid (pp. 164, 165; also Boeckh, Pol. Econ. of Athenians, p. 763).

6. Clazomenae. A numerary money of iron discs was used. The number is not stated. To each was given an arbitrary value probably equal to that of the same weight of gold. Iron having been put into circulation, and having supplied the place of silver (gold?), the amount of ready money in the state was not diminished. Iron money performed the same service in the state which silver (gold?) had previously done, and the silver which remained could be employed for purposes of foreign commerce. To that extent iron money was identical in its uses with the paper money of modern times.

Clazomenae, however, was not able to maintain the system (pp. 165, 166; also Boeckh, p. 763, and Aristotle, Economics, II., pp. 2, 16).

7. Byzantium, a colony, rose rapidly to affluence and power. During the period B. C. 431-404 the favorable condition of its civilization and credit enabled it to employ numerical money. Discs of sheet-iron, having an impression on one side, were employed. Such a disc was known as a "sidareous." As the resources and credit of the government declined, its money was supplemented by corporative issues. A bank was chartered and given a monopoly; it issued highly overvalued gold and silver coins. The bank afterward ran down, and its issues depreciated to their commodity value (pp. 166, 167).

8. Athens. About B. C. 405 a numerary money of copper discs, highly over-valued, was adopted (p. 168). After the Peloponnesian war the rehabilitated republic issued a numerary money of copper discs, highly over-valued; this was receivable for all payments, public dues included, and was nominally redeemable at an indefinite time in silver; a promise of whose performance we have no record. (Boeckh, pp. 399, 766.) With the Social War, Athens and her numerary system fell together (pp. 171, 172).

9. Syracuse. About B. C. 387 Dyonisius issued over-valued coins of tin and of silver. He attempted to force their circulation, but failed. The coins fell to their commodity value. (Perhaps the people feared the tyrant would not receive the coins at face in payment of taxes.)

10. Carthage. Issued a numerary money of some unknown substance, probably tin, wrapped in leather or parchment. This probably went out of use within the half century after the gold and silver mines of Spain were opened, about B. C. 408. * * * The introduction of gold and silver into Carthage, and its "fatal effects," are noticed by Heeren, IV., 144. (Del Mar, pp. 174-176.)

11. Rome. The monetary history of Rome is of profound interest. Various systems were tried. Del Mar proves exhaustively that the early "Roman system was a numerary one, and that the numismatic relics that have so long been regarded by the learned world as copper coins were essentially irredeemable notes stamped, for lack of paper, on copper and devised and designed to pass in the exchanges for a much greater value than that of the metal of which they were composed." He shows "that from year of Gaulish invasion, B. C. 385, until about the year B. C. 269, the monetary system of Rome consisted of copper nummi, formerly known as Ases; that the whole number of these nummi was limited by the senate; that they were a full legal tender; and that they were rendered secure from counterfeiting by the artistic beauty and mechanical excellence of the pieces, and the vigilance of the law officers:" That between B. C. 269 and B. C. 250 the patrician class, by permission of the senate, introduced the over-valued silver denarius. That, B. C. 207 the numerical system gave way before the free coinage of silver, and its adoption as full legal tender commodity money; and that, B. C. 46, Julius Caesar introduced the gold standard, doubtless that he might thereby create a home market for the gold he had secured in Spain and Gaul (p. 186, et. seq.).

Exploiting, by slave labor, the gold mines of Spain and Gaul, then seizing the sovereign power at Rome, and forcing upon the people the single gold standard, he cleared away an enormous personal debt (25,000,000 sesterces or $1,250,000) and grew enormously rich in a few years.

We shall see that the effect of Caesar's policy on the prosperity of Rome was not so good as upon his own.

## THE FALL OF ROME.

One of the main causes of the downfall of the Roman Empire was the appreciation of the precious metals used as money.

During her days of conquest, "Rome seized the accumulated treasures of Carthage, Spain, Gaul, Greece, Persia, Asia Minor and Egypt, throwing into circulation as money, among her people, what had been hoarded as royal treasure, or devoted in vast masses to sacerdotal uses, thus raising the prices of all commodities thruout the Empire, but especially in Italy and the countries nearest the capital."[70] Prices rose almost 400 per cent. between the Punic Wars and the time of Augustus,[71] and industry flourished; but soon after Rome became an Empire a contrary movement began. The influx of precious metals ended when conquest ceased. The product of the mines was not sufficient to maintain the volume of money. A chief source of labor supply for the mines, viz., the slaves captured in war, was no longer available. The men to whom the mines were "farmed" out took only the richest ores and rapidly exhausted the deposits. They also terribly maltreated the criminals and slaves whose labor worked the mines. The value of money increased and prices began to fall. Gold and silver were hoarded. Coin was exported for luxuries. The wealthy had ornaments and trinkets made of gold. The fall of prices ruined the debtor classes, depressed industry and threw the wealth of the world into few hands. Paper money was unknown, and even if it had been understood might not have been used, for the Goverment was in the control of the moneyed classes who profited by the appreciation of gold. At last the "barbarians appeared on the borders of the Empire, offering a refuge to those who had the courage, born of despair, to attempt an escape from the power of Rome," and many convicts and slaves deserted the mines. Then the barbarians came into the Empire and the first lands invaded were those on the produce of whose mines the world was most dependent for its supply of gold and silver,

---

([70]) Genl. Walker's "Money," pp. 124-5.
([71]) E. B. Andrews' "An Honest Dollar," p. 16.

and the "production of the precious metals received a shock from which it was not to recover for more than a thousand years."[72] From 480 to 680 A. D. there does not appear to have been any mining at all,[73] and it was not until the discovery of America that the mining of precious ores revived.

Jacob, who is the leading authority on the subject, estimates that in the year 14 A. D., in the time of Augustus, the stock of money in the Empire was £358,000,000. By the year 482 it had sunk to £87,000,000, and the product of the mines had ceased entirely. By the year 806, in the time of Charlemagne, he estimates that the stock of gold and silver in Europe was only about £33,674,000, or less than one-tenth of what it was in the reign of Augustus, and it remained nearly the same until the beginning of the Sixteenth century, when American metal began to make its appearance in Europe.

President Andrews, of Brown University, says that "Between Trajan (A. D. 98) and Charles the Great (A. D. 768-814) prices had fallen in nearly the ratio of 5 to 1, and the purchasing power of money had increased 400 per cent. The main cause of this tremendous change was the decrease in the volume of money metal used in trade.[74]

As if the cessation of the supplies obtained by conquest and the falling off of the product of the mines were not enough, the value of money was still further increased arbitrarily by an edict (221 A. D.) depriving silver of its money quality and making gold the only legal tender money.

The burdens of the producing classes increased with the scarcity of money and the fall of prices. Their debts and taxes remained the same while their labor and property diminished in value. Their property being at last exhausted without paying their debts, they became the slaves of the creditor class. All incentive to energy was destroyed, agriculture decayed, industry was paralyzed, the classes that once formed the strength of Rome, from which the invincible legions were drawn in former times, were now reduced to miser-

---

[72] Walker, "Money," p. 128.
[73] Jacob, "Inquiry into the History of the Precious Metals," p. 131.
[74] An Honest Dollar, p. 18.

able dependents ready to welcome any change as a relief, while the ruling classes were enervated by idleness and luxury born of unearned wealth.[75] "I for one," says President Andrews, "am convinced that the slow contraction of money was among the most potent causes of the dissolution of Rome.[76]

Sir Archibald Alison says: "The two greatest events which have occurred in the history of mankind have been directly brought about by contraction and expansion of the circulating medium. The fall of the Roman Empire so long ascribed in ignorance to slavery, heathenism and moral corruption was in reality brought about by a decline in the silver and gold mines of Spain and Greece."[77]

The failure of the money supply to keep pace with business caused an appreciation of money which meant progressive ruin for all but the very wealthy and powerful, so that at last it is said, a group of 1800 men owned practically the whole known world, and the rest of mankind were dependents, obliged to get permission even to till the soil or labor to earn the means wherewith they might continue to live. The disturbance of just distribution of wealth and power resulting from the appreciation of money was a fundamental cause of the industrial, political and moral debasement which destroyed the strength of Rome and made her fall a prey to barbarian invaders.[78]

### THE DARK AGES.

For centuries after the fall of the Roman Empire the money volume in Europe continued to shrink. This, however, while a very natural accompaniment, was not the cause

---

[75] Wharton Barker, "Bimetallism," pp. 8-11.
[76] "An Honest Dollar," p. 16.
[77] Hist. Europe, 1815-1852, Sec. 33. The other "greatest event" was the revival of energy and enlightenment following the discovery of America and the increase of money volume thereby produced—of that hereafter.
[78] See further on this absorbing topic, Andrews' "An Honest Dollar;" Barker's "Bimetallism;" Walker's "Money;" Alison's "Hist. of Europe;" Jacob's "History of Precious Metals."
For further discussion of the relation of appreciating money to the fall of Rome, see Del Mar's "Hist. Precious Metals," p. 19, Senator Jones' speech in Senate, October, 1893, p. 117 et seq., and p. 43 of "Facts About Silver," issued by the American Bimetallic League. The dark ages in the Levant, with the decay of Tyre and Sidon, resulted in part at least from appreciating money. Pres. Wills' Lectures on Finance, and Del Mar's Hist. Precious Metals, pp. 9, 10. The dark ages in Japan appear to have been due to the same cause. Del Mar's "Hist. of Money in Ancient Countries," p. 53.

of the darkness in this case. The appreciation of money in Rome was a main cause of its fall whereby the darkness of the North enfolded the whole of Europe, but the subsequent shrinkage of money was not the cause of continued darkness. Indeed the destruction of property and the reversion to primitive conditions so far diminished production that prices rose considerably in the Fifth and following centuries. For a long period the lack of social organization and the insecurity of possession would probably have neutralized the stimulus of even a very rapid increase of gold and silver.

In the Ninth and Tenth centuries mining began again, social organization and security improved and commerce grew. Credit money came into use. The Bank of Venice (1171) and the Bank of Genoa (1407) satisfied the needs of commerce in their localities. But taking Europe as a whole, tho the volume of money increased somewhat from the Ninth to the Sixteenth centuries, population and business increased so much faster in the later centuries of the period that by 1510 the value of money was almost, if not quite as great as in the last period of the Empire.

### THE DISCOVERY OF AMERICA.

In 1492 Columbus made his grand voyage, and in the following century the treasures of the new world flowed into Europe. Its money supply was increased about 500 per cent., and prices rose nearly as much, or from a price level of 100 to 470, according to the highest authority.[79] We have already referred to the passage in which Sir Archibald Alison deals with the failure of Roman civilization and the awakening that followed the discovery of America as the two greatest events in history—the failure caused by a contraction, the awakening by an expansion of the money volume. He continues: "Columbus led the way in the career of renovation. When he spread his sails across the Atlantic he bore mankind and its fortunes in his bark. The annual supply of the pre-

---

[79] Jacob, Hist Precious Metals. Other estimates by Prof. Leslie, Hume, Alison, etc., place the rise at 200 to 300 per cent. See American Economic Assoc. "Economic Studies," Vol. I., No. 1, p. 30, and Genl. Walker's "Money," pp. 81, 135.

cious metals for the use of the globe was tripled; before a century had expired the prices of every species of produce were quadrupled. The weight of debt and taxes insensibly wore off under the influence of that prodigious increase; in the renovation of industry the relations of society were changed; feudalism was cast off; the rights of man established. Among the many concurring causes which conspired to bring about this mighty consummation, the most important, tho hitherto the least observed, was the discovery of Mexico and Peru."[80] The rise of prices stimulated industry and commerce, reduced the pressure of debts and all fixed charges, rents, pensions, mortgages, etc., swept away the resources of the idle rich, made it increasingly difficult to live without labor, enlarged the profits of merchants and manufacturers, and enabled the producing classes to throw off the yoke of the creditor classes.[81] Widespread distress resulted to certain classes. "The creditor class was very generally impoverished, if not hopelessly ruined. Debts were, in many cases, almost confiscated by the rapid depreciation of the money in which they were to be paid."[82] Pauperism visited the homes of many who had lived without labor, and misery was the portion of dependents. The benefits, however, that came to current labor far outweighed the evils to those who lived on the fruits of past labor. The lightening of debts, rents, taxes, and all the obligations of the past, the diffusion of wealth, the levelling of classes, the discouragement of idleness and parasitism, and the stimulation of industry thru the increased rewards to the active and skillful members of society more than balanced the evils of depreciating gold, and united with intellectual and moral causes to make the Sixteenth and Seventeenth centuries luminous with progress and grand with the mighty energies of a new born hope. Even in its most glorious epoch, however, metallic money bought its benefits with devastation and distress, and sought for progress at the cost of grievous injustice. It is not a wise money system that pauperizes one class to bene-

---

[80] Hist. of Europe, 1815-1852, Sec. 33.
[81] Genl. Walker's "Money," pp. 85-89 and 135-6.
David Hume's "Essay on Money,"
Alison's "Hist. of Europe."
[82] Walker's "Money," p. 136.

fit another, and ruins multitudes of honest, law-abiding citizens thru the sudden confiscation of resources on which it had previously led them to rely.

#### A METAL BASE IS A BUILDER OF DEBT AND AN ALLY OF GAMBLERS.

The recent issue of 262 millions of bonds in time of peace illustrates one of the serious evils of our metallic system. The necessity the Government is under of redeeming greenbacks in gold upon demand enables scheming men to draw large amounts of gold from the Treasury and then to say to the Government, "Your reserve is getting low; you must have gold or you will be in danger of failure to keep your promise in respect to specie payments; issue bonds and get the gold back again." So the schemers get bonds for their gold, sell the bonds at a premium, take the greenbacks they get for the bonds and draw the gold out of the Treasury again, till the Government is frightened into a new issue of bonds, and so on in an endless chain, with a premium profit for Wall Street on every issue of bonds and nothing but accumulating debt for the nation. It is not wise or just for the nation to go into debt, in time of peace, especially when it can easily raise all the money it needs by taxation. It is wrong to burden the people with needless interest payments for 20 or 30 years on loans not required for public expenditure, but negotiated for the benefit of the bondholding classes who desire the bonds, as the safest modern means of compelling labor to pay tribute. The Government might start with thirty millions of gold in the Treasury, and thru the repetition of the above described process, issue a billion of bonds, and at the end have only thirty millions of gold in the Treasury and not a thing to show for the billion of debt but some money which it could and should have obtained by taxation without saddling the nation with the burden of an interest bearing debt, and the keeping of a promise (gold redemption) that is of little advantage to any one except the schemers who have found out how to gear it to a bond-printing press and make it turn the people's millions into their coffers as fast as they dare to turn on the current.

It is a heavy count in the indictment against our metallic system that it places our industries, our debts and even our Government at the mercy of unscrupulous gamblers, who are able to heap hundreds of millions of useless debt upon the nation, govern to a large extent the general movement of prices, exert great influence over the business interests of the country, capture millions of unearned profit, and bring the Government to its knees before them, offering tribute for their protection—all by controlling the floating supply of gold.

The bond record stands as follows:

December, 1891, fifty millions of bonds issued to get gold for the Treasury, and in two months the gold thus obtained was gone from the Treasury again.

March, 1894, fifty millions of bonds, and in three months the gold was gone.

February, 1895, sixty-two and a half millions of bonds, and by 1896 the gold had vanished again.

January, 1896, a new issue of bonds brought in $116,000,000 of gold, nearly the whole of which departed within six months.

July, 1896, a new issue seemed necessary, but Bryan was nominated; the rising of the people was too serious to be trifled with; it would not do to goad the people further at the very gates of a National election, and the bankers decided that the bond business must rest till after election, to accomplish which they supplied the Treasury with twenty-odd millions of gold.

In respect to where the gold went so fast after its capture by the Treasury we have some evidence in one of President Cleveland's messages.

"The results of previous bond issues," he says, "have been exceedingly unsatisfactory, and the large withdrawal of gold succeeding their sale in open market gave rise to the reasonable suspicion that a large part of the gold paid into the Treasury in such sales was promptly drawn out again by the presentation of notes, Treasury notes, and found its way into the hands of those who had only temporarily parted with it in the purchase of bonds."

On the $62,500,000 loan the Morgan-Belmont syndicate offered but 104½, altho United States bonds were selling in Wall Street at the time for 120. The Government was unwilling to accept the bid, but according to Mr. Morgan he was able to persuade the Government by going on to Washington in person and assuring the authorities that they could not get gold except thru him and his associates, and there would be a panic if his figures were refused.

So Morgan, Belmont, Rothschild & Co.
Got the bonds for ........................$65,112,943.
And sold them to jobbers for ...............  69,928,587.
Who sold them to the public for ............  73,531,700.
Profits of speculation on this one deal ........   8,418,757.

More than eight millions of dollars in the pockets of gold gamblers that should have gone into the Treasury of the United States.

The remarks of William J. Bryan on this subject in one of his campaign speeches last year are so fine that I quote them at some length:

"The first $50,000,000 of bonds were advertised for, and the advertisement stated that only gold would be received for the bonds. Suppose a man had gone to the Secretary of the Treasury with $1,000,000 in greenbacks and Treasury notes and said to the Secretary: 'I want to buy $1,000,000 of bonds.' The Secretary would have said: 'We can't sell you these bonds for greenbacks and Treasury notes. These bonds are issued to get gold and, therefore, we can only sell them for gold.' This man would say : 'Well, if you won't sell them for greenbacks and Treasury notes, I will just deposit the greenbacks and Treasury notes and have you redeem them in gold.' The Secretary would have said: 'Well, that's what we are here for, and would have given him the $1,000,000 in gold. Then the man would say: 'Do I understand that you have some bonds for sale?' 'Yes.' 'Well, here is your $1,000,000 in gold, give me the bonds!' "

"Don't you think that can be done? It can be done. Do you think it would be done? It has been done. When they issued the first $50,000,000 of bonds they drew out $18,-000,000 in gold to pay for those bonds, and to the extent of $18,000,000 the Government had no more than when it commenced, altho it had agreed to pay interest on $18,000,000 of bonds."

"Then they issued $50,000,000 more and drew out a larger percentage of the gold than the first time. Then they made the Rothschild contract. There was a contract by which the Government sold to a private syndicate bonds at 104½ which were at that time worth 120 in the market."

"That contract contained a stipulation by which the Rothschild and Morgan syndicate agreed for a certain length of time to do their best to protect the Treasury of the United States. They hired two men to back the Treasury. If this Government is going to admit that it depends for its financial existence upon two banking firms, one foreign and one domestic, then it puts itself where those people can charge this Government whatever they please."

"Yet they issued $100,000,000 more. It was suggested that they were going to be issued at private sale, and J. Pierpont Morgan, who had been in the bond deal where they made such a profit on the bonds that he refused to tell about it, when brought before a committee of investigation, after stating that he did it largely because of his interest in the country, refused to tell how profitable it was to be interested in the country just at that time, J. Pierpont Morgan organized another syndicate, and it was advertised that he was going to submit a bid for various parties at about 105, and when a circumstance arose that made it necessary for the President to advertise for public bids, did the Morgan syndicate put in a public bid for the same amount it would have at private sale? No, that syndicate waited until just before the time to open the bids, and then their bid was put in more than $5,000,000 above the bid that they expected to put in if they had secured the bonds at private sale."

"Now that is business sagacity. Of course, no financier would condemn a man who tried to get the bonds at 105 and then had to bid 110 and a fraction and got them. If that is business sagacity, then I believe it is the business of this Government to protect the people against such sagacious financiering instead of turning the finances over to them."

"You may call it patriotism on their part if you will, but I want that kind of a patriot to serve some other country and not mine. If some petty individual who did not have a high financial standing were to try to beat the Government out of $100 they would put him in the penitentiary and make an example out of him. But if a man tries to beat the Government out of $5,000,000 he becomes a patriot, and deserves to be the chief guest where Treasury officials are banqueted. I do not believe the man who manages the financiering should be the bosom friend of the conspirators who never lose an opportunity to bleed the people."

But when the metallic system puts it in the power of a few speculators to wreck the credit of the Government, by exercising their lawful right to purchase and hold out all the gold they can obtain, is it strange that Government officials anxious to sustain the public credit and filled from boyhood with the belief that the maintenance of metallic redemption is essential to honest finance—is it strange that such officials under such circumstances seek to placate the scheming owners of gold and bargain for their help? It is simply the reductio ad absurdum of metallic redemption.

Writing in 1895, Major Winn, a powerful and careful thinker, used the following significant language: "The most striking display of monetary power is shown by the action of the foreign syndicate in stopping the gold drain of a million or more a week from the Treasury. It seems, with the gain in gold and some expansion by the banks, to have restored confidence and revived business, and to show that, under a gold system, *a few men hold National prosperity on tap to be sold to the highest bidder.* In this view the six or eight millions profit paid by Mr. Cleveland seems reasonable. Terror is reported at Washington and a stock decline in Wall Street from fear that these bankers will not protect the United States till October. A great nation grovels at the feet of a foreign syndicate."

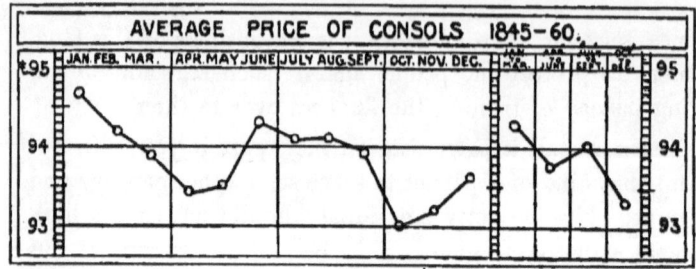

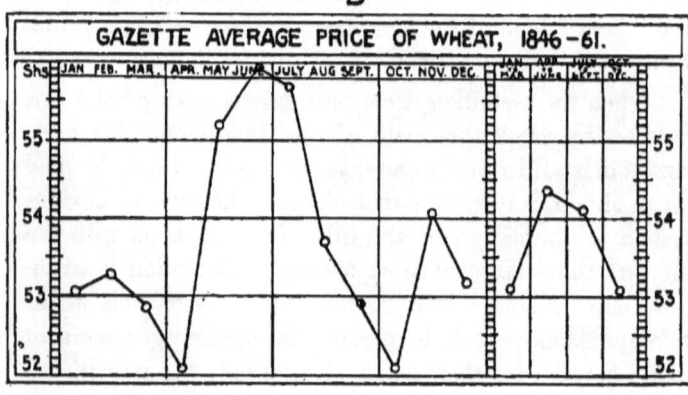

per cent. in one year from January 1, 1893, to January 1, 1894, and nearly 19 per cent. in two years from January, 1893, to January, 1895.[85]

The farmers sell mostly when money is dear and products cheap, and buy mostly when money is cheap and products dear. The movement of the crops, the settlement of the year's business, the preparation for the Christmas holidays, etc., make special demands upon the circulating medium. Instead of expanding to meet the need, money becomes more difficult to get in proportion as it is needed, and the stringency ruins many honest merchants and debtors of various sorts each autumn, while riches come by the stroke of a pen to the men who devote themselves to studying the movements of money instead of wasting their energies in producing and distributing goods and merchandise, and who are not too scrupulous to use their knowledge to capture for themselves the wealth of the producers.

The larger variations of value are disastrous in the extreme, especially the appreciation of money. Rising prices may cause a serious injustice to creditors of every class, from bondholders and mortgagees to savings bank depositors. Labor too may suffer if goods advance in price more rapidly than wages and salaries, which is almost sure to be the case. The stimulation of industry creates a new demand for labor; the unemployed find work, employment is less interrupted; and wages rise, but not till after the rise of goods which gave new energy to production and caused the new demand for labor, so that injustice in the shape of diminished reward for a given amount of labor of hand or brain is sure to result.

---

([85]) See the tables published quarterly by "The American." The fall of prices from 1873 to July 1, 1897, using the figures of Sauerbeck and the American, was 49.9 or practically 50%; in other words gold doubled in value. Using the Aldrich tables and the American, the fall would be about 41% and the rise of gold between 80 and 90 per cent. The Sauerbeck data are considered by economists to be the more reliable.

Even the quarterly price levels vary in a marked degree. The following figures are taken from Sauerbeck in the Journal of the Royal Statistical Society, Vol. 59, p. 189 (1896).

1894, 1st quarter price level,.... 65
1894, 2nd quarter price level,... 63.3
1894, 3rd quarter price level,... 62.8
1894, 4th quarter price level,... 60.9
1895, 2nd quarter price level,... 62.2
1895, 3rd quarter price level,... 63.3
1895, 4th quarter price level,... 62.8
1895, 1st quarter price level,.... 60.3

Some writers affirm that rising prices lead to panic, while others believe a rising market to be a blessing so great as to more than offset the injustice to creditors and the scaling down of the wage rate. Each of these views contains a truth, but neither is unqualifiedly true. It is clear that rising prices do not *necessarily* lead to panic—they may lead to remarkable prosperity as during the long age of rising prices that followed the discovery of America, and in England during the Napoleonic wars, and in America during the Civil War. There are, however, two ways in which, *under the present system*, rising prices *may* lead to industrial disaster: (1) The decreasing proportion of product that goes to the wage receiving class under rising prices, and the increasing share of the entrepreneur is apt to augment the production of common goods and necessaries of life beyond the power of the community to buy and consume them. The rich can buy but need only a very limited quantity, the poor need much but can buy little, and their power of purchase is diminishing relatively to the volume of goods produced; so that there is apt to arise what is called "over-production," which would generally be more accurately described as under-consumption, or false distribution of the power of purchase; tho it is possible, of course, that a particular class of goods may be produced beyond the amount the community could consume even if every member of it had a full share of purchasing power. On the other hand, if the increasing profits of the entrepreneur are used for the production and consumption of luxuries, or goods and services wanted by the rich and well to do, the new distribution of labor may keep the system in balance and prevent the glutting of the market. (2) A rise of prices, especially if rapid, may lead to careless expansion of credit and speculation of a rash and dangerous sort on the part of overconfident and reckless investors, and *under our present system*, the collapse of these undertakings may involve the entire community. Industry would be safest if protected from any rapid rise of prices as well as from falling prices. But the continuous and emphatic inflation is unwise, throwing investors and business men off their guard and leading to collapse and failure of many imprudent individuals, yet it by no means follows that even a rapidly ascending market need produce a panic, if the financial system were sufficiently elastic to check an extreme rise and soften the reaction—reduce the grade of the *upward slope* and bring it to a *level* by a gradual gentle change, instead of leaving industry to climb the steep to the top and tumble over a precipice of falling prices. Individual failures there would be under any system, but they would not become the widespread failure and depression that constitute a panic, except for the effect of falling prices, which are by no means a necessary consequence of a period of rising prices, but result from the failure of the legal tender money volume to expand so as to offset the temporary shrinkage of credit.

The fall of prices acompanying panics is shown in the following table. The figures are taken from the data of Sauerbeck, Wharton Barker and the Aldrich Committtee for six of our first class crises:

| PRICE LEVELS JUST BEFORE THE PANIC OF | | SUBSEQUENT PRICE LEVELS. | |
| --- | --- | --- | --- |
| 1825 | 117 | 1827 | 97 |
| 1837 | 102 | 1837 | 94 |
| 1847 | 95 | 1848 | 78 |
| 1857 | 105 | 1858 | 91 |
| 1872 | 138 | 1875 | 127 |
| 1893, April, | 99¾ | 1895 Jan. | 79¾ |

The fall of prices is partly the cause of panic, partly the effect of it—the first fall leading to a further fall in the absence of elastic currency. The above figures do not fully express the facts. For example, the 105 expresses the average price for the whole year 1857 including several months of panic prices; it is likely that 108 or 110 would more truly represent the real level before the crisis.

The worst injustice and dangers of rising prices are far exceeded by the evils of falling prices or appreciating money. A falling market is a calamity almost as much to be deplored as civil war. It ruins merchants, manufacturers and farmers, throws men out of employment, and leads in a double way to failure, depression and panic. A very slight fall between the time a merchant or manufacturer buys his goods or materials and the time he sells, may turn his expected profit into a loss. He borrows money to tide him over, hoping next year to recover; but prices fall further the following year, and instead of relief he finds the loan an ever-increasing weight about his neck. Year after year he struggles to regain what he has lost, but prices continue to fall and his difficulties to increase, until at last he fails. His creditors, some of them wrestling like himself with falling prices, are further embarrassed by his bankruptcy, and their names are soon upon the list of wrecks. Failures and the natural impairment of industry due to the discouragements of a falling market throw many out of work. Having no employment they cannot buy as they used to, and a shrinking demand is added to the dangers and perplexities of commerce, causing a further fall of prices and new ruin; and so the inter-acting causes continue their sad work till stoppage and destruction reach such vast dimensions that we call them panic.

Falling prices are unjust to debtors; their debts remain the same, but their means of payment shrink. The note calls for as many dollars as ever, but the number of bushels of wheat or bales of cotton that must be sold to get those dollars is double what it was when the money was borrowed and the note was written.

Here is a table that tells the story of the farmers' falls—the Niagara of agriculture: it is taken from "The Key Note," by Albert Griffin, p. 197:

VALUE OF AN ACRE'S PRODUCT.

|  | 1866-70 | 1871-5 | 1876-80 | 1881-85 | 1886-90 | 1893 |
|---|---|---|---|---|---|---|
| Corn | 12.84 | 11.30 | 9.62 | 10.25 | 8.81 | 8.35 |
| Wheat | 13.16 | 11.90 | 12.00 | 10.20 | 9.07 | 6.00 |
| Oats | 10.2 | 9.81 | 8.58 | 9.17 | 7.50 | 5.75 |
| Hay | 13.28 | 14.38 | 11.57 | 11.15 | 10.19 | 10.00 |
| Cotton | 28.01 | 28.55 | 17.65 | 15.63 | 13.84 | 10.65 |
| Total | 78.21 | 75.94 | 59.42 | 56.40 | 49.44 | 40.75 |
| Average | 15.64 | 15.19 | 11.88 | 11.28 | 9.89 | 8.15 |

Such is the history of our thirty years' war upon the products of the soil. As the value of an acre's yield diminishes, the value of the acre itself decreases also. Many a man who put his savings into farm land years ago, giving a mortgage for the balance of the purchase price, finds to-day that the mortgage has swallowed up the farm. Suppose he had saved five thousand dollars, borrowed five thousand more, and bought a ten thousand dollar farm in Kansas, giving a mortgage for the money he had borrowed. To-day the farm is not worth the face of the mortgage; falling prices have devoured his five thousand dollars and left only the debt. At the start the farmer and the mortgagee had equal interests in the farm; now the mortgagee's interest covers the whole farm, and the farmer has nothing. This is a fair example of one of the disastrous processes that have been going on all over the country, and especially in the West and South, and no one can wonder that our people should become desperately hostile to a monetary system that causes or permits such evils.

*The entire product of our farms in 1895 was worth less by 6 per cent. than in 1873, altho the increase in the number of hands was about 50 per cent., in the number of acres also about one-half, and the product in tons and bushels had grown about 100 per cent.*

One of the most striking illustrations of the extent and effects of falling prices in the last thirty years is the fact that, after having paid over four billions and a half in interest and principal on the National debt, the people have still to pay more in terms of commodities to settle the remainder of the debt than would have sufficed to cancel the entire debt at its maximum figure just after the rebellion. Upon an average of 25 leading commodities, including land and labor, the debt is bigger now than in 1866, in spite of the hundreds of millions that have been paid on the principal since that date. President Andrews says: "Our National debt on September 1, 1865, was about 2¾ billions. It could then have been paid off with 18 million bales of cotton? When it had been reduced to a billion and a quarter, 30 million bales would have been required to pay it." ("An Honest Dollar," p. 13.) Careful estimates by the eminent historian, John Clark Ridpath, will be found in the Arena for January, 1896, p. 271. The results briefly stated are as follows:

## AVERAGE PRICES.

|  | MARCH, 1866. | CLOSE OF 1895. |
|---|---|---|
| Wheat, per bushel | $1.90 | $0.58 |
| Flour, per barrel | 10.75 | 3.50 |
| Cotton, per lb. | .48 | .085 |
| Mess pork, per barrel | 28.37 | 8.20 |
| Sugar, per lb. | .11125 | .05 |
| Wool, per lb. | .53 | .215 |
| Beef, per cwt. | 15.25 | 9.50 |
| Bar iron, per lb. | .0675 | .0267 |
| Superior farm lands, Ohio and Mississippi valley, per acre | 75.00 | 35.00 |

The National debt, March, 1866, was ........ $2,827,868,959
The National Debt at the close of 1895 was .. 1,126,379,106

It will cost more to pay the little debt now than the big one then:

| | |
|---|---|
| More of wheat by about | 43% |
| More of flour by about | 38% |
| More of cotton by about | 140% |
| More of pork by about | 50% |
| More of wool by about | 8% |
| More of bar iron by about | 10% |

It will cost a little less in sugar (2½ per cent.), beef (30 per cent.) and land (6 per cent.) to pay off the remnant of the debt; but to pay a *billion* now will take about *double* the sugar, beef, and land that was required to pay a billion of the debt in 1866, and upon the average of the nine great staples above mentioned it requires a great deal more of them to pay a billion now than it did to pay three billions at the close of the war.

On the average of all commodities a dollar now (1897) will buy nearly 100 per cent. more than in 1873, and over 100 per cent. more than in 1866. These changes have benefited labor in some respects—a day's wages, as a rule, will buy more than in 1873 or 1866; but the disastrous effects of falling prices upon productive activity and the distribution of wealth have more than counterbalanced the advantages of the change. The appreciation of money is of little avail to the workman out of employment, or the merchant whose business has shrivelled into insignificance, or the farmer whose mortgage appreciates as fast as the dollar. The increased power of the dollar is of no use to the man who can't get the dollar; a positive detriment to him when it is that very increase of power that crippled his business or threw him out of work, and a terrible disaster to the man whose debt grows bigger with the growth of the dollar, while the crops or other property with which he expects to pay the debt depreciate and disappear.

The United States Monetary Commission, Vol. I., p. 50, says that "falling prices, misery and destitution are inseparable companions," and our great economist, Francis A. Walker, says: "Mr. Balfour was fully justified in saying that a slow appreciation of the standard of value is probably the most deadening and benumbing influence which can trouble the springs of enterprise in a nation.[86]

The tables prepared by R. A. Southworth, Secretary of the National Farmers' Alliance, show in another way how fierce has been the fall of prices and how strong has been the tendency to pour the product of the country into the laps of the official and directing classes. I have taken Cleveland, 1896, instead of Harrison, 1892.

Lincoln's salary, 1866, $25,000, equal to 10,310 bushels of wheat.
Cleveland's salary, 1896, $50,000, equal to 86,000 bushels of wheat.

| PAID TO | 1866. | 1894. |
|---|---|---|
| Congressman .. | $3,000=1,240 bu. wheat. | $5,000=15,000 bu. wheat. |
| Governor ....... | $3,000=1,240 bu. wheat. | $5,000=5,000 bu. wheat. |
| Legislator .... | $4 a day=1 2-3 bu. wheat. | $7 a day = 21 bu. wheat. |
| Lawyer ........ | $5 a day = 2 bu. wheat. | $10 a day=30 bu. wheat. |

Mr. Southworth has taken the average prices given by the American Almanac, but even if the very conservative averages of Prof. Ridpath are taken for the calculation, the results still show that while the farmer has continually greater difficulty in obtaining the means of livelihood, the "upper classes," as they are called, obtain 6 to 8 times as much wealth in return for their services as they did in Lincoln's time.

---

[86] American Economic Association, Economic Studies, Vol. I., No. 1, April, 1896, p. 44.

The contrast is not by any means confined to wheat. Some of Mr. Southworth's other figures are as follows:

|  | LINCOLN'S YEARLY SALARY 1864 TO 1868 WOULD BUY AT AVERAGE NEW YORK PRICES. | HARRISON'S SALARY 1892 WOULD BUY. |
|---|---|---|
| Corn | 18,248 bushels. | 100,000 bushels. |
| Cotton | 132,275 lbs. | 625,000 lbs. |
| Wool | 48,356 lbs. | 166,666 lbs. |
| Rice | 110 tons. | 960 tons. |
| Butter | 68,870 lbs. | 250,000 lbs. |
| Sugar, raw | 193,708 lbs. | 1,111,111 lbs. |
| Mess pork | 959 barrels. | 5,263 barrels. |
| Mess beef | 1,042 barrels. | 6,060 barrels. |

Mr. Southworth remarks that in the early period, from 1864 to 1868, when the people were comparatively free from private debt, $100 for payment of interest or principal could be obtained with 40 bushels of wheat; while now, when the people are weighted with debt, it takes 2 or 3 hundred bushels to get the same number of dollars that used to be bought with 40 bushels. These tremendous injustices are caused or permitted by our system of metallic money.

It is said that falling prices are caused by cheapened production, and this is partly true. Part of the fall in the last thirty years has been due to the appreciation of gold, and another part has been due to cheapened production and intensified competition under a money that failed to counteract the downward tendency of prices. The system is as much to blame in one case as in the other. It makes no difference whether gold moves away from commodities or commodities move away from gold; whether gold has appreciated or commodities depreciated, or both; the result has been a falling market with all the disastrous consequences which a proper system would prevent. There is abundant evidence in the table given above that gold and silver *have* vibrated through enormous arcs, becoming less valuable with each new mining discovery and growing more valuable as the sources of supply failed to keep pace with the growth of business requirements. The movement of production will not account for the facts.

The centuries following the discovery of America witnessed a vast industrial advance and cheapening of production, yet prices did not fall; they rose because the movement of money was more than sufficient to counteract the cheapening effects of organization and invention. Again, from 1850 to 1866 art and invention and business grew marvellously; the railroad, the steamboat, the telegraph and thousands of labor-saving devices worked their wonders on America, yet prices rose. It is not disputed that the movement of gold produced the great fall of prices in the later years of the Roman Empire, and there can be no rational question, I think, that it has shifted its position to higher values since the demonetization of silver in 1873.

But this is entirely immaterial to the question of monetary responsibility for falling prices. Falling prices are disastrous, whether they result from the movement of business and invention while the gold stands still, or from the movement of gold while business stands still, or from the combined effect of the two movements in opposite directions. If a merchant buys at 50 and the price falls to 40, he is ruined just the same whether the fall is due to cheapened production or to a relative scarcity of gold. And if such cases are numerous, as they will be, where the average price level of commodities is sinking, widespread embarrassment will ensue. In a competitive society, falling prices and disaster are inseparable companions regardless of the cause of the falling prices. It is the business of a monetary system to adjust itself to changing conditions, so as to maintain a uniform level of prices in reference to the great staple commodities on which our industries are based, in order that injustice to both debtors and creditors may be avoided, and security given to the whole industrial system so far as possible.

History shows that this has been done and can be done by means of a regulated paper money, and it is equally emphatic that it has never been done and probably never can be done with a system based on gold or silver or both. The vicissitudes of mining, the movements of production, the contingencies of foreign markets and the conspiracies of speculators make a uniform level of metal prices a practical impossibility. Even if the Government should become the owner of the mines of gold and silver and carefully regulate their coinage and issue (the only way in which it appears to be possible to make any approach to a fair and rational metallic system) even then it would be difficult if not impossible to counteract the effect of changing prices in other countries using the same metals. Our stock of gold and silver would be subject to exhaustive emmigration, and at the best the system would not outlast the life of the mines.

### A METAL BASE IS A CAUSE OF INDUSTRIAL CRISES.

The variations of money due to natural or artificial causes constitute a prolific source of panic, originating or permitting and intensifying every industrial crisis.

Wendell Phillips said: "The great lie called 'specie basis' has destroyed the commercial prosperity of the United States once every six years since the nation started."[87]

Looking over the history of England and America we find that panics of the first magnitude occurred in England in 1763, 1783, 1793, 1797, 1816, 1825, 1837-8, 1847, 1857, 1866, 1875 and 1890-3, and in the United States in 1819, 1825, 1837, 1839, 1847, 1857, 1873 and 1893 (with a plentiful supply of lesser disasters in intermediate years), and every one of them was either directly caused by the movement of money, or grew to ruinous dimensions because the money volume failed to expand at the proper time to relieve the financial pressure, metallic money being far more apt to shrink away and hide itself in time of danger than to come to the rescue of commerce when credit money is shaken.

A few great failures from rash speculation, a contraction

---

[87] See North Amer. Rev., Sept., 1885, p. 205. Phillips called specie basis a lie, because coin is not really the basis of our money, but only a regulator, or rather a misregulator of it. The true basis of money, that which makes it pass as money is not the specie reserve but the legal tender quality of the currency. The vital fact is not specie redemption but utility redemption. Men do not take greenbacks because they are convertible into gold, but because they are convertible into food and clothes, shelter and service, and will pay debts and taxes. As a matter of fact they are not convertible into gold except to a very limited degree. Complete redemption is impossible. The holder of bills and silver token monies could not get gold for them since there is not half enough gold in the United States to make the redemption. Even partial redemption is apt to fail. "The gold dollar is never behind the dollar-bill except when no one wants it."

of the currency, an adverse balance of trade, a foreign panic, large sales of American securities held abroad, purchase of gold by foreign governments or banks, any drain of gold to foreign countries, a corner on gold in New York, or a rapid withdrawal of loans by concerted action of powerful bankers and capitalists, destroys confidence, produces financial stringency, and brings the mercantile classes face to face with ruin. We have seen that France, at such a time, averted panic by expanding the volume of her independent paper money. And that is the simple common sense cure for a crisis, or rather the common sense means of preventing a crisis, for it will not come if the remedy is promptly used. When one part of the money force is disabled, the other part should be increased sufficiently to do the work of the injured part. When credit money or non-legal-tender money fails, and prices begin to fall, legal tender money should expand to take its place. People fear to do business with checks and private notes in panic times for the individuals behind the paper may prove unable to make it good, and the power of individual paper to pay debts and make exchanges diminishes in proportion to the loss of confidence. The failure of credit and the necessities of merchants and manufacturers who must meet maturing liabilities, causes them to offer their goods at lower rates to raise the needed money. The fall of prices discourages industry and deepens the difficulty. Men are afraid to do business on a falling market. But men are not afraid to do business with cash on a steady market or a rising market. Full legal-tender money backed by Federal law and not issued beyond the needs of trade retains the confidence of men in spite of panic, because the nation is behind it to make it good in service and see that it pays its face in debt, wherefore it does not lose its power of settlement and transfer in periods of disturbance as individual paper does; and if in threatening seasons legal-tender currency were issued in sufficient volume to take the place of the vanished credit, and counteract the tendency to falling prices, no panic would ever materialize. For over six hundred years Venice had no commercial panic. Her independent National money, under a wise public management, was always adjusted so well to the needs of trade that a crisis was impossible. We have had eight *tremendous* panics in less than eighty years.

The adjustment we have spoken of would be easily possible with Postal Savings Banks and Independent National Currency under public control. But with the metallic system the legal-tender money shrinks when credit shrinks, instead of expanding to fill its place. No sooner does panic show its head than people begin to run upon the banks, compelling the latter to draw in their loans and not infrequently to close their doors, thus intensifying the pressure instead of relieving it. People would not withdraw their money en masse from Postal Banks in times of disturbance, because the money would be safer in the Government Banks than anywhere else, at such times as well as at any other times; and even if they should run upon these banks with all their might, and draw out every dollar of their deposits, not a bank would close its doors.

There would be failures still, so long as the competitive system may last, for men will speculate and some of their ventures will not succeed, but panic there need not be if reasonable care were taken to prevent the pestilence of failure from spreading over the whole community and involving the sound and valid members of the industrial system as well as the reckless speculators. Some men undertake too much, especially when times are prosperous and prices going up. When it becomes evident that their enterprises will not succeed, they have to sell out or be sold out to pay their debts. This gives a fall to prices, embarrasses many who had business relations with the bankrupts, and leads capitalists to distrust the future. Loans are called in, money is hard to get, merchants hard pressed to pay their debts raise money by offering their goods at lowered prices. Many a man whose assets are far greater than his debts, is nevertheless ruined because he cannot collect what is due him in time to meet his own obligations. The falling market paralyzes industry. The merchant feeling the pressure and fearing worse to come, is determined not to be caught with a large stock on his hands, so he orders little or nothing from his manufacturer and discharges all the employees he can possibly spare. The manufacturer with shrunken orders diminishes his force and runs on half or three-quarters time, or may be closes his mill entirely. Labor out of employment cannot buy, the market shrinks still more, additional discharges and new shrinkages follow, and so hard times go on intensifying themselves in a grievous circle, like the bitter words of angry brothers. The quarrel could be avoided by a gentle word at the first rebuff, and the panic would never exist if the first shock were met by easy loans from the Government to the embarrassed merchants and business men of solid worth, in order to tide them over the trouble, as Pitt did long ago in England, and as our own Government did in 1881.[88]

A panic may come with the turn of the tide from rising to falling prices, or with the accumulated effects of a long term of falling prices. The bursting of a bubble of speculation, a change in the foreign market,[89] a falling off in the production of the mines, a corner in gold, a deliberate plan to draw in large loans, the demonetization of one of the money metals—any of these may produce a falling market and industrial panic. But of all the causes of panic none deserves more note than the contraction of the currency.

---

(**) See pp. 72-3. Some slight relief was also afforded in 1873 by an expansion of $5,000,000 issued from the Treasury, but the issue was too small to put the industries of the country on their feet. (Prof. Sumner's Hist. of Currency, pp. 218-9.) The British "Bullion Committee" of 1810, the doctrines of whose report Prof. Sumner says (p. 248) are no longer disputable, being matters of experience and demonstration, recorded among the said doctrines an emphatic statement that in presence of a panic it is the duty of the Bank of England to discount freely for all solvent parties. In 1825 the Bank, at the request of the Government, lent money even on goods. In 1857 its loans on private securities went up 55 millions in a few months. In the crisis of 1866 it had only 20 millions cash but loaned 65 millions in the first few days of the panic, the Government assisting. In 1890 the Bank again came to the aid of embarrassed commerce (Hon. Henry Winn, American Magazine of Civics, Dec. 1895, p. 586.) It is well to use the Treasury presses to fight the hoarders and panic makers, but it would be better to stop the fluctuations of price that lead to panic than to await the explosion—better prevent the conflagration than merely to fight it when it comes. Our banks are more apt to assist the flames than to allay them, and the Government seldom comes to the rescue. In the panic of 1893 the National banks, instead of relieving the money famine, actually contracted their loans 140 millions in the worst of the crisis, and in the whole of the critical period from May 4 to Oct. 3 they contracted their loans 819 millions, altho their cash resources had increased meantime by 26 millions. (Winn, pp. 576,587.)

(**) The falling of prices in England brought upon us a falling market and the panic of 1825, which, tho not so severe in the United States as in England, was nevertheless a well developed panic here. (Sumner's Hist. Currency, p. 85.) In 1836 the failure of some British banks precipitated the crisis of 1837 on both sides of the water. (Sumner, p. 133.) The panic of 1893 was partly due to disturbances in the London money market. (See Quarterly Journal of Economics Jan. 1894: "Panic in United States in 1893," by A. C. Stevens.) But there were other facts in the case with us. (See below.)

Some years ago an eminent economist went over the history of industrial crises and found that a contraction of the currency was an antecedent factor in every panic that had occurred up to his time (Asa Walker's Political Economy)—not always the initial cause, not always the principal cause, but always present as at least a part cause of the crisis. During the rebellion the currency expanded, prices rose and prosperity was great. Contraction began with the National Banking Act of 1863, which provided for retiring greenbacks and issuing National bank notes—$90,000 in bank notes for every $100,000 of currency cremated—a contraction of 10 per cent. on the whole volume of currency used in supplying a basis for the National banks, tho population and business were growing all the time. But this was only the prelude. The curtain rose on the real contraction act April 12, 1866, when it was enacted that the Secretary of the Treasury should be authorized to sell 5.20 bonds and with the proceeds retire United States currency. In 1865 the circulation is estimated to have been between 1¾ and 2 billions, while the funded debt was $1,109,568,191. From September, 1865, to September, 1867, the Secretary of the Treasury reported the reduction in the curency as $797,725,000. By June 30, 1869, the money in circulation had fallen below ¾ of a billion and the National bonded debt had grown to be $2,166,568-920.[90] Prices fell from 216 in 1865 to 153 in 1869 and 137 in 1873. The folowing table shows the results:

TABLE XII.

| YEAR. | NO. OF FAILURES. | LIABILITIES. |
|---|---|---|
| 1865 | 530 | $17,625,000 |
| 1866 | 1,505 | 53,782,000 |
| 1867 | 2,386 | 86,218,000 |
| 1868 | 2,608 | 63,774,000 |
| 1869 | 2,799 | 75,054,000 |
| 1870 | 3,551 | 88,242,000 |
| 1871 | 2,915 | 85,250,000 |
| 1872 | 4,069 | 121,058,000 |
| 1873 | 5,183 | 228,499,000 |

([90]) See Comptroller's Report 1880, p. 35. Sec. Treas. Rep. Mess. & Docs. 1867-8. pp. 27-29. Rep. of J. T. Power, May 10, 1878. United States Treasury Circular No. 123, July 1, 1896. Care must be taken in dealing with the statements of the circular and those of recent United States abstracts, since the currency figures given for some of the earlier years differ materially from the figures given for the same years in earlier United States Abstracts and statements of the Treasury Department made at the time.

The embarrassment of business was so severe that by 1873 the accumulated effects produced a terrible panic from which the country has not even yet entirely recovered. It is said that in 1865 labor was well employed, but by 1873 about 500,000 men were idle; a year or so later an army of tramps began to travel, and three years later there were more than a million of them on our highways, and another million of idle workmen in our homes.

Some of our foremost financiers, including John Sherman, vividly predicted the ruin that would follow the contraction of the currency incident to the scheme for resuming specie payments. The United States Monetary Commission of 1876 thoroly investigated the panic of 1873, and concluded that it was caused by the contraction of the currency and consequent fall of prices. The Commission says:

"However great the natural resources of the country, however genial its climate, fertile its soil, ingenious and enterprising its inhabitants, or free its institutions, if the volume of money is shrinking and prices are falling, its merchants will be overwhelmed with bankruptcy, its industries will be paralyzed and destitution and distress will prevail."

General Ewing, in a strong speech in Congress eighteen years ago, estimated that the depreciation of values due to contraction amounted to one-third of the whole, and that the resumption law constituted a practical confiscation of $3,500,000,000 of property.

The loss to the laboring classes was $3,000,000 a day, or more than $900,000,000 a year.

In recent years, altho the currency has not contracted absolutely, but on the contrary has increased in volume, yet it has not increased sufficiently to keep pace with business and changing conditions of production, so that prices have continued to fall, and the industrial thermometer, tho showing slight yearly movements up and down, has on the whole persisted in a downward course.

During the early years of the Napoleonic Wars (1793-1797) England was in a most alarming condition. Her money had fled (as our money did at the breaking out of the rebellion, as metallic money always does in time of calamity), a financial stringency crippled her business, a panic swept over her commerce and ended in a run on the bank and mutiny in the fleet. The Government was induced to give relief by loans to the business classes, and was at last, in 1797, compelled to suspend specie payments, and rely entirely on a paper currency. Immediately the business of the nation revived, and for eighteen years England enjoyed unparalleled prosperity in spite of the heavy drain of the war. And she might have retained her industrial glory forever had she retained the policy of supplying the people with an abundant currency and raising revenue by a heavy income tax and continued the public employment and direction of all the surplus labor in the country, not in army and navy as during the war, but in the construction of roads, parks, buildings and all manner of public improvements. But in 1816 she demonetized silver for amounts beyond $10, provided for the resumption of specie payments by a bill passed in 1819, and in preparation therefor began to fund the paper currency into public bonds. Prices immediately began to fall. Profits and wages declined. Riot and ruin followed. The farmers petitioned for loans from the Government at low interest, but without avail. Crops were good and prices low, yet the working people could not buy bread. The net results of the contraction and accompanying fall of prices were wreckage, poverty, decades of misery, enormous growth of the fortunes of the wealthy, and ruin of all others.

Speaking of the post-contraction period in England, 1819 to 1845, the historian Alison says: "There never was a period in which a greater amount of financial embarrassment has been experienced by the Government or more widespread and acute suffering endured by the people. Wages were in many trades low, employment difficult, suffering general, and yet the period was one of great increase in material resources. It may safely be affirmed that the anxiety and distress which were felt during this brilliant period of natural growth have never been surpassed. The distress among the mercantile classes for years after the dreadful crisis of 1825, of the agricultural interests during the low prices of 1832-35, and of the whole community from 1837 to 1842, was extreme. The extraordinary fact has now been revealed by statistical researches that in an age of unbounded wealth and general and long continued peace, a seventh part of the whole inhabitants of the British Isles are in a state of destitution, while 70,000 persons have among them an income of 200 million pounds or $14,000 each per year. Frightful strikes occurred. Crime made unexampled progress, serious detected offenses having multiplied seven-fold while population increased but 70 per cent.; with rapid growth of wealth and great effort at instruction, crime has augmented ten times as fast as the numbers of the people. The co-existence of so much suffering in one part of the people with so much prosperity in another is unparalleled. Capital exists to profusion, labor adequate to any expansion of industry is at hand, yet millions are pining for employment." Mr. Alison examines the various theories advanced to account for the above situation (so like the story of our own country since the beginning of contraction here), and finally concludes, as we have already seen when speaking of England, that "the contraction of the currency which was made to accompany the resumption of cash payments has been the chief cause of all these effects."

Contraction and falling prices oppress the poor, ruin the middle classes, and increase the power and affluence of many of the wealthy.[91] Those who control large amounts of money are able to take advantage of the distress of others to accumulate vast property for themselves; the power of the dollar and its possessors is increased; the congestion of wealth in the hands of a few materially favored; and the industrial interests of the nation in every way disastrously affected. Contraction and its sister, failure of due expansion, are among the most powerful, insidious, and to the masses of the people, unrecognizable causes of evil that exist in this world of mischief.

---

[91] Writing of the United States in 1820, when panic prices had brought wheat to 20 cents a bushel and flour to $1 a barrel, Prof. Sumner says: "Money was plentiful in the hands of those who had no debts to pay, where of course it must settle whenever the social machinery comes to a stand still. (Hist. Currency, p. 82.)

Even the wealthy as a rule misunderstand the effect of falling prices. They see the more obvious effect of increasing the value of their loans, and fixed returns, but they do not appreciate the remote effects. If they realized the fact that the discouragement of industry and the diminution of the total product more than balances the increased proportion of product that goes to the creditor, they would know that falling prices are really a detriment to the moneyed classes as well as to the rest of the community. The lender gets a larger share of the product than under steady or rising prices, but the total product is so much diminished that his share is less in actual amount than it would be if prices were steady. If this were understood and the insecurity of investment incident to falling prices were given due weight, there would be none to favor or be content with a falling market, except the gamblers and wreckers, who profit by the misfortunes of others rather than by the development of commerce and the growth of industry.

It must be remembered that aside from natural causes and the movement of gold to foreign parts, serious contraction of the currency may occur not merely thru legislative action, but thru individual action; not merely by withdrawal of greenbacks or demonetization of a money metal, but thru the recall of loans and the hoarding of money that generally follow any disturbance of credit or appearance of danger; and worst of all perhaps, thru deliberate conspiracy to wreck the market by cornering gold or calling in loans, or contracting the circulation in order that the conspirators may secure desired legislation or possess themselves of railroads, factories, mines, lands and other properties at prices that represent but a fraction of their cost.

In 1881 there occurred a sudden and simultaneous action on the part of a number of National Banks in withdrawing about 18 millions of gold and U. S. currency from circulation to deposit with the Government in order to redeem their bank notes. Interest on call loans went up to $1\frac{1}{2}$ per cent. a day, 371 per cent. a year. New York was on the verge of panic and probably would have gone over the edge if it had not been for an order from the Secretary of the Treasury for the redemption of $25,000,000 of bonds on presentation. This concerted disturbance was created apparently for the purpose of killing a bill then pending in Congress that was obnoxious to the National Banks. It was killed. The following autumn Secretary of Treasury Windom recommended Congress to prohibit National Banks from withdrawing their circulation without notice, and President Arthur concurred in the recommendation; but no such restriction has been enacted.[92]

There is evidence tending to show that the panic of 1893 was not entirely a natural phenomenon. The moneyed interests desired the unconditional repeal of the silver purchase law. It was openly said that "The quickest if not the only way to repeal the silver purchase law is to precipitate a panic upon the country, as nothing short of that will convince the silver men of their error and arouse public opinion to a point which will compel the next Congress to repeal the Sherman law whether it wants to or not."[93] The panic came and the silver law was repealed.

In 1896 it was commonly understood and accepted on all sides that if Bryan were elected there would be a panic. If the moneyed classes cannot have the President they want, and the kind of money they want, then there will be an earthquake.

Once get a system of Postal Savings Banks and a National currency into full operation and no class in the country could cause a panic; but under the present system a very few men can wreck the industries of the nation.

Is a monetary system with such a history, and saturated with such disasters and iniquities, worthy the acceptance or retention of a civilized people?

Even the banks, tho strongly attached to the metallic sys-

---

([92]) See Appleton's Annual for 1881, pp. 129, 779; and "The Money Question," by G. H. Shibley, pp. 410, 676. If there were a law requiring the Government in case of stringency to loan money on United States bonds or other good securities at a reasonable interest, it would go far to prevent a corner, collapse or temporary contraction from developing into a panic. In Germany, money is loaned by the Government in this way, but only to banks. The system has been adopted in Austria-Hungary and Japan.

([93]) See "Banker's Magazine," New York, May, 1893, p. 806.

tem, abandon it in panic time. Prof. Sumner says: "The banks suspend, escape the results of a folly in which they had full share, and then loan their notes at exorbitant rates to the merchants who are still out in the financial storm. This has been the process here in every crisis and probably will be as long as the people stand it without complaint."[94]

### COIN IS A COWARD.

Metallic money is very timid. It goes into hiding upon the approach of danger. When the country needs it most it retires into seclusion or journeys to foreign shores. In battle it deserts the flag, while independent paper goes to the front unmindful of the roar of cannon, ready to do its duty bravely in the face of the enemy.[95]

### ENGLAND'S BATTLE MONEY

was not gold, but paper, when she fought the great Napoleon. And paper carried the Allies thru to a finish at Waterloo and conquered the greatest soldier of modern times. Coin vanished at the bugle call, and paper came to the front for service. Napoleon fought with gold because he was able to keep his coffers full by taking the treasures of nations he subdued. Nothing but martial law could make it do its duty, and even then it failed against the English paper.

### THE PATRIOT PAPER OF THE CONTINENTAL CONGRESS

burdened as it was by overissue, and brought to ill repute by

---

[94] Hist. Currency, p. 137. When the specie basis brings a crash, the banks suspend specie payments and let paper money do the work of recuperation.

[95] When the French Revolution broke out metallic money disappeared and the assignats, tho terribly watered by overissues and grievously corrupted with heavy injection of British counterfeits, carried the Republic thru the storm to years of comparative safety when coin was ready to come out of doors and go to work again. The depreciation of paper caused very great hardships, ruining creditors and those who lived without labor or settled income, but it helped to diffuse the wealth of the nation and distribute among a multitude of active producers a large amount of property that had formerly been held by a few individuals.

In China more than a hundred years before the Christian era, the Emperor raised funds for war in a way that showed a keen appreciation of the value of the legal-tender-limited-volume principle. An independent currency made of the skins of white deer was used as money. The Emperor collected into a park all the white deer to be found and prohibited his subjects from possessing any animals of this monetary variety. Having obtained a monopoly of the material, the Government issued pieces of white deer skin leather as money at a high rate. (Jevons Money & M. of Exc., p. 107.)

spurious rivals tresspassing incognito in its domains, nevertheless enabled the Colonies to carry the battle thru and free themselves from the English yoke. Coin vanished with the musketry of Lexington, and the commerce and military operations of the Revolutionary period had to be carried on with paper. The British commanders recognized the fact that the Continental paper constituted the sinews of war, and did their best to destroy it; but tho it was mortally wounded on the field of battle, it lived long enough to win the victory for America.

### THE GREENBACKS OF THE SIXTIES

saved the Union. Gold and silver disappeared quite early in the conflict. In 1861 the banks of Boston, Philadelphia and New York agreed to loan the Government $150,000,000 in specie, but were unable to carry out the agreement, and the last $50,000,000 of the loan was paid by the banks to the Government in *demand notes* of the United States which the banks had at first refused to recive as money.[96]

Instead of borrowing coin from the banks, we think, as we have already intimated, that the Government ought to have abandoned the recreant metals, issued full legal tender greenbacks, opened Postal Savings Banks, so that the circle of issue and deposit would have brought the funds round again to public use and not into the vaults of Wall Street, and when the volume of the currency showed signs of more rapid growth than might be deemed wise, the Government should have

---

([96]) Speeches of Thaddeus Stevens in the House, Feb. 5th and 20th, 1862. (Cong. Record, Part I, 1861-2, pp. 679, 200.) It has been said that "if the banks had been permitted to exercise their own methods, they could have continued their advances in sums of 50 millions for an indefinite period." (Geo. S. Coe, Pres. Amer. Ex. Bk. N. Y., in Bankers Magazine, Jan., 1876, p. 540.) Before the first payment the associated banks in New York had $49,733,900 in coin, and after $80,000,000 of the loan had been paid they had $42,318,010 of coin, a reduction of only $7,415,880; that is, if the banks could have made loans to the Government in moderate installments with an interval between each two installments sufficient to let the coin get into circulation and come round to the banks again in payment and deposit, why the banks could have kept right on loaning specie to the Government. What a beautiful plan! The banks had loaned nearly twice as much specie as they possessed and had the Government's bonds for about eleven times as much coin as they had lost, and if they had only been allowed to keep on without interference from greenbacks, they might have been able to pile up billions of Government bonds in their vaults. The greenbacks stopped the scheme for a few years, but a very good substitute was carried into effect when bonds were issued to call in the greenbacks and burn them up preparatory to the resumption of specie payments.

called upon opulent citizens to give their money to their country as freely as it called upon the poor to give their lives for the Union.

At the close of the war when the greenbacks had the field, the Government should not have contracted the currency 50 or 60 per cent. in order to return to specie payments against the advice and warnings of many of the ablest statesmen in the country. It should rather have made the whole body of greenbacks a full legal tender without regard to coin, and expanded instead of contracting the volume of money, as did France at the close of the Prusssian war, so as to meet the larger demands upon it incident to a reunited North and South, the entire commerce of both sections being thereafter dependent on the currency that had previously had to do service for one section only; and last but not least, the nation should have had a care that its million defenders found employment when they came from the ranks, and provided employment on the public works for those whose labor was not absorbed by private industry. If these plain principles of justice and common sense had been heeded, if statesmanship instead of capital had ruled our councils, the prosperity of the period of the war would have been redoubled in time of peace. As it was, the burden of battle was no sooner lifted from our industries than the burden of falling prices was fastened upon them; the industries that had prospered and grown strong under the load of civil war, languished and grew feeble under the load of appreciating gold.

In closing these remarks upon the unreliability of metallic money under fire or in any stress of danger, I cannot do better than quote the words of Senator Ingalls in his noble speech in the United States Senate, February 15, 1878:

"No people in a great emergency ever found a faithful ally in gold. It is the most cowardly and treacherous of all metals. It makes no treaty it does not break. It has no friend it does not sooner or later betray. Armies and navies are not maintained by gold. In times of panic and calamity, shipwreck and disaster, it becomes the agent and minister of ruin. No nation ever fought a great war by the aid of gold. On the contrary, in the crisis of the greatest peril it becomes an enemy more potent than the foe in the field; but when the battle is won and peace has been secured, gold reappears and claims the fruits of victory. In our own Civil War it is doubtful if the gold of New York and London did not work us greater injury than the powder and lead and iron of the South. It was the most invincible enemy of the public credit. Gold paid no soldier or sailor. It refused the National obligations. It was worth most when our fortunes were the lowest. Every defeat gave it increased value. It was in open alliance with our enemies the world over, and all its energies were evoked for our destruction. But as usual, when danger had been averted and the victory secured, gold swaggers to the front and asserts its supremacy."

### CONCLUSIONS.

Upon the facts revealed by monetary history we come to the following conclusions:

(1) Metallic money is not to be relied upon in war. It caresses the conqueror, but deserts the oppressed. It cares nothing for justice, liberty or country. The money of patriotism is independent paper.

(2) Metallic money, by its fluctuations, is a cause of industrial disturbance and panic, and by retiring instead of expanding in time of stringency, it adds to and intensifies the disturbances produced by other causes.

(3) The history of metallic money is characterized by long periods of falling prices more disastrous than war or pestilence.

(4) A nation with a metallic system is peculiarly open to industrial and political disturbance arising from monetary changes in other countries, whereas an inconvertible paper currency remains serenely unaffected by the vicissitudes of foreign moneys.

(5) Metallic money is the friend of gamblers and speculators, affording them innumerable opportunities for plunder in its periodic, annual, monthly and sometimes daily variations, offering them thru combinations among themselves the

inestimable privilege of controlling prices, and placing at their mercy even the Government, the public credit and the National debt.

(6) The volume and value of metallic money in circulation is governed by chance and private manipulation; the contingencies of mining, the movements of international trade, the changes of opinion and political action across the sea, the narrowing or expanding policies of combinations of capitalists in New York, London and other money centres.

(7) Steady prices are unknown to our metallic system. Prices are always rising or falling, and continual injustice is being accomplished thereby. Creditors cheated by rising prices, debtors cheated by falling prices, the normal relations and efforts of industry disturbed in both cases. And altho the stimulating effects of a moderate rise of prices may sometimes justify the accompanying injustice, especially after a period of falling prices, when a rise is necessary to bring industry back to its normal level, yet when once the normal level is attained and idle labor is absorbed at reasonable wages, there is reason to think that steady prices should become the rule. Whatever may be thought of slowly expanding prices when not required to overcome the effects of depression, it is clear that no possible justification exists for falling prices, which mean only ruin and despair to the producing classes and unjust advantage and aggrandizement to the owners of money. A wise financial system would subject the movement of money to scientific control in the public interest, aim to avoid all needless injustice betwen class and class, all panic and depression, or undue stimulation of industry. In other words, it would keep prices steady except, perhaps, where a serious emergency or calamity called for the aid of a rise, which if ever deemed justifiable as a deliberate measure after considering all less objectionable means of industrial stimulation and adjustment, should at least be very carefully administered and discontinued as soon as possible.

(8) History shows that independent paper if well managed yields steady prices, freedom from industrial disturbance, immunity from gambling with the money volume, security from

the vicissitudes of mining and the change of foreign markets and policies, and entire protection against the disastrous dominion of chance and private manipulation. Even when not well managed, paper money produces no panics, does not desert its country and prove false to its creator in time of danger, and mainly places such injustice as it brings upon the shoulders of the rich, the idle rich, and not upon the laboring poor, and the active managers of industry. On the contrary, steady prices appear to be impossible under metallic money. Fluctuation is inherent in it and no nation can control it. And it is very apt to build the fortunes of the idle rich, pouring into their laps unnumbered millions of unearned increment at the expense of the active and owing classes.

Independent paper properly managed does not fluctuate.

When not properly managed its fluctuations favor the debtor and producing classes, diminish the relative power of the idle rich, bring the classes nearer together and help to diffuse the wealth of the world.

Metallic money has fluctuation in its heart—it is inherent in it.

And its changes in our generation oppress the poor and favor the rich, burden the active debtor and bestow a gift on the idle lender, discourage production and encourage gambling, widen the breach between the classes, and give to the few the wealth created by the many.

Which is just money?
Which is rational **money?**
Which is the people's money?

# CHAPTER II.

### THE BEST MONEY.

Turning from the history of the subject to its philosophy, we have to consider:

First.—The purposes or functions of money.

Second.—The attributes, essential or convenient, which more or less perfectly fit a material or commodity for service as money.

Third.—What sort of money combines these attributes in the highest degree of perfection, and is, therefore, best fitted to fulfil the functions of money.

### PURPOSES OF MONEY.

The functions of money in civilized society appear to be five, since money acts as:

1. A medium of exchange.
2. A measure of value.
3. A means of storing or transmitting value or power of purchase.
4. A standard of deferred payments.
5. A regulator of production and distribution.

Barter is too complex, cumbrous, and difficult to answer for the exchanges of a highly developed community. Some article is, therefore, selected, first by custom and afterward by law, to act as a medium in terms of which all exchanges may be made. This device lubricates the action of exchanges, avoids the transfer of bulky articles, permits the indefinite division of wealth and value, and renders easy a volume and variety of commerce that would otherwise be impossible.

### MEASURING VALUES.

A necessary consequence of its action as a medium of exchange is the power of money in the measurement of value.[1]

---

[1] Jevons "Money" &c., pp. 5, 13; Mill. Polit. Econ. III, ch. 7, sec. 1 and ch. 15; Rogers Pol. Econ. p. 22; Marshall Prin. Econ. sec. 5; Prof. Bowen Pol. Econ. 203; Walker, "Money," pp. 4-9, 64, 280-9. The latter doubts the

Value is a ratio. If cotton is selling at 10 cents a pound, corn at 50 cents a bushel, and wheat at $1, the value of a bushel of wheat in terms of corn is two bushels at that time and place, and the value of a bushel of corn in terms of cotton is 5 lbs., etc. Little or no idea of the real exchange value of a commodity can be obtained by comparing it with one or two other things.[2] The value of a commodity is its general pur-

---

validity of ascribing to money the function of measuring values, claiming that it acts as a common denominator of values, but not as a measure of them. It is true that our money does not measure values by final test of a constant something inherent in itself as in the case of a quart measure or a pound weight. We measure with it as we would with a quart that swelled and shrank and had to be compared with a standard back of it in order to know the meaning of its results. It would not be wise to use such a method of measurement unless it were easier to compare a commodity with the real standard by comparing it with the variable measure (money) and then comparing this with the standard behind it, than it would be to compare the commodity with the real standard directly without the intervention of money. Money serves as an intermediator between the commodity to be valued and other commodities in general. Its power of representing those commodities (its relation at the given time and place to the real standard) being known thru prices) it becomes a means of measuring the said commodity against commodities in general, with less trouble than would be required by the complex processes and statements incident to the direct measurement of a commodity against others by way of barter.

"In a state of barter the price-current list would be a most complicated document, for each commodity would have to be quoted in terms of every other commodity, or else complicated rule-of-three-sums would become necessary. Between one hundred articles there must exist no less than 4950 possible ratios of exchange, and all these ratios must be carefully adjusted so as to be consistent with each other, else the acute trader will be able to profit by buying from some and selling to others." (Jevons "Money" &c., p. 5.)

All such trouble is avoided if some one thing is chosen and its ratio of exchange with each other commodity is quoted.

The real nature of the process being understood, the statement that money is used to measure values seems to be a convenient and unobjectionable form of stating one of the functions of the circulating medium.

Speaking of money as a measure and recalling the fact that the value of money varies with its volume, Dr. C. F. Taylor calls attention to the fact that: "This does not apply to yardsticks and bushels. The length of a yardstick does not depend in any way upon the number of yardsticks in existence; and the size of a bushel measure does not in any way depend on the number of such measures in a country." (Medical World, Aug., 1807, pp. 347-8. Unless the facts are fully understood, analogies between the money measure and other measures are likely to be misleading until a system of finance is adopted that shall keep the dollar in harmony with the real standard of exchangeable values.

(²) The fact that a bushel of wheat commands two bushels of corn affords very little information as to the value of either. The ratios of both to other commodities may be high or low or medium, i. e. both wheat and corn may be dear or cheap or of medium price compared to other commodities.

So with the relation of any commodity to money; the price of a commodity or service tells us practically nothing of its value till we know the prices of other commodities and in the fullest sense we do not know its value till we ascertain the prices of all other commodities and services, and so understand its relative position to the entire body of purchaseable things, its power of command over the whole range of products. If I were told that at a certain period wheat sold for $10 a bushel I would not know its value; but if I were also told that during the said period a hat cost $30, a pair of boots $40, a pound of beef $2, &c., I should begin to get a glimmering of the value of the wheat. When I read that in the latter days of Rome one two-hundredth of an ounce of gold (about 10 cts. worth now) would buy a bushel of wheat, I get no idea of its real value; the general exchange power of gold may have been (was) so great that (notwithstanding the said low price) a man could get more in exchange for a bushel of wheat in Rome than in the United States to-day or at the close of the Revolution, when it took a pocket full of money to buy a loaf of bread.

chasing power, and its relation with other commodities as a whole must be understood in order to get a knowledge of its purchasing power or command over commodities in general. This, money enables us to do with the greatest ease and simplicity. Having the price of a bushel of corn and the prices of other commodities, we can ascertain its ratio to any one commodity or any combination of commodities, and so measure its purchasing power or exchange value in terms of one commodity or all. Money serves to express and compare the ratios that constitute value, measuring one commodity against another or one against all others or any combination of others. The selling price of wheat being ascertained to be $1 a bushel, the farmer measures by that fact the value of the 1,000 bushels he possesses, and puts it down as $1,000, which means as to real values that 1,000 bushels of wheat are equivalent to the quantities of other commodities which can be bought for $1,000—a quantity dependent on the prices of those other commodities.

### STORING THE POWER OF PURCHASE.

A further result of the use of money in exchanges is that it may become a means of storing value or power of purchase.[3] If I do a piece of work for $50 or sell goods to that amount, receiving five ten dollar bills, and do not care to buy anything with the money now, preferring to keep my power of purchase for some future need, or take it to a distant place, I can accomplish my purpose by simply keeping the money. In such case the bills in my pocket become a store of purchasing power or exchange value always ready to my purpose. If I wish to transmit say $50 of value or power to a distant friend, I can do so by sending the bills.

### STANDARD OF PAYMENT.

Money performs another function of great importance in connection with borrowing and lending, and the settlement of debts of various origin. When A borrows from B and is to pay B at some future date, the money used becomes a stan-

---

[3] Jevons "Money, &c.," p. 15. Compare Walker, "Money," p. 12.

dard of deferred payment[4]—a means of measuring back to the lender at a future time an equivalent for what he lent. The same is true if A buys goods of B at a specified price and pays for them at a later date. Any debt, whatever its origin, that is to be paid after an interval, brings into play the same principle.

### A REGULATOR OF PRODUCTION AND DISTRIBUTION.

None of the powers of money arising from its use as a medium of exchange are of more importance than its power to regulate enterprise, and modify the distribution of wealth. The movement of the money volume in reference to the business to be done with money, or its failure to move, causing or permitting a rise or fall of prices, will change the relative proportions of product that go to laborer, landlord, capitalist and entrepreneur, stimulate or depress industrial motive,[5] increase or diminish the weight of every debt, and exert upon the industrial system an influence so profound that panic or prosperity may wait upon its whim.

Wages, rent, interest and profits represent the classes among which the yearly product is divided: Wages to the workers, rent to the landlords, interest to the capitalists, profits to the entrepreneur or manager and director of industry who borrows capital, employs labor, and takes the responsibility of enterprise for the sake of profit. The money value of wages, rent and interest has a considerable stability or inertia due partly to the effect of time contracts, and partly to the fact that a change in the purchasing power of money is not readily seen, and appreciated. The result is that every change in general prices seriously alters the distribution of product. A rise in prices increase the share of the entrepreneur and decreases the shares of laborer, landlord and capitalist. Wages, rent and interest do not go up at once upon the rise of goods, but follow after an interval if at all. To bring out the case, sup-

---

[4] Walker, "Money," p. 10. Jevons, "Money, &c," p. 14.

[5] See the discussion by Prof. J. Allen Smith, Annals of Amer. Acad. of Polit. & Social Science, Vol. VII, No. 2, pp. 3-6. And Gen'l. Francis A. Walker's "Money in its Relation to Trade and Industry." Most economists, when speaking of the functions of money, say little or nothing of its power as a regulator of industry and distributor of wealth, but Professor Smith and Pres. Walker give proper emphasis to this most vital function.

pose that prices are doubled. The entrepreneur has for a time the same interest, rent and wages to pay as before, but receives twice as many dollars for his goods; his profits are consequently very much increased; he is eager to push his business, borrows more capital, employs more labor, embarks in new enterprises, and business is very lively; too much so sometimes for safety to men of insufficient caution. The worker on a fixed salary renders services which bring his employer twice as many dollars as before the rise, but he only gets the same wage, until it slowly dawns upon him that the prices of what he has to buy are higher than they used to be and that business is good with his employer; then he asks for more pay. The employer gives him a small increase, often a mere fraction of the rise in goods, and the worker is satisfied as a rule because he is used to thinking of the dollar as something absolute, and since he is getting more dollars, he must be better off. He sees the rise of wages and does not clearly comprehend the general rise of prices and its precise quantitative bearing upon his interests.

A fall in prices has exactly the contrary effect. The entrepreneur cannot scale down the debt he owes, or the rent or salaries he has agreed to pay; his liabilities remain the same, while his income shrinks and his profits are cut down or may be turned into a loss. He is discouraged, has no motive to undertake the risks of business in face of a falling market, and as he constitutes the active force in industry, the man who takes the initiative in production, the result is that industry languishes. It makes no difference what may be the cause of falling prices, the result will be the same. If prices fall because of invention and improvements in production, the effect is the same as when they fall because of increasing scarcity of gold. If the entrepreneur, merchant or manufacturer has to sell for less than enough to pay the fixed charges resting upon him—the rent, interest and wages he has agreed to pay, and the price of materials and goods he bought on time—he is ruined just the same, whatever the cause of the fall in the market.[6]

---

[6] Inventions and improvements in production while they are of the highest advantage to society when their benefits are justly distributed, may

Falling prices injure labor also, unless employed on time contract or at a fixed salary. It is true that falling prices increase the purchasing power of the wages received by ordinary labor, but it does not follow that labor is better off. The total amount of wages must be considered as well as the rate.[7]

A falling market reduces production, throws labor out of employment, compels factories to close or run on short time, and the amount of wages received per worker in the course of a year is often so much less as to more than balance the effect of the added purchasing power in the few dollars that are obtained. Better have 500 normal dollars than 100 dollars of double the normal value.

It appears then that money thru its action upon prices has a vital regulative influence on the whole industrial system. This power of money to control and direct industrial forces

---

for a time cause serious disturbance and large injustice to laborers and active business men thru the imperfect distribution of the burdens attending the destruction of capital and the displacemnt of labor that accompany their introduction. Workers are thrown out of employment, and reduction in the value of existing capital occasioned by the invention or improvement falls entirely upon the entrepreneur. Industrial capital is owned by two classes, interest receivers and profit receivers. The latter have the management. The property of the interest receiving class exists in the form of a mortgage or fixed money claim upon the capital and product of economic society. Their principal and interest constitute a first claim on the capital and earnings of industry. Dividends and profits come afterward. The entrepreneur must, therefore, sustain the loss of capital occasioned by improvements. His debt to the interest receiver is as large as ever, and the machinery he bought with the borrowed money is worth less than before by the whole effect of the improvement. It is one of the great injustices of the present system that the active capitalist, the initiator and manager of industry has to bear the whole burden of depreciation caused by improvements, while the passive capitalist escapes. If either class of capitalists is to receive a special benefit at the expense of the other, equity would demand that favor should fall on the active and not on the passive capitalist. Those who take no active part in industry should not fare better than the captains of production. Progress should not punish the progressive in preference to the non-progressive. (See the admirable discussion by Prof. J. Allen Smith, Annals A. A. P. & S. S., Mar. '96, of which this note is a condensation.)

([7]) The facts in relation to the movement of wages as prices change are of the utmost interest and importance. We must carefully distinguish between wage rates and aggregate wages. According to the Aldrich Report, money wages rose in the ratio of 100 to 148 per cent., from 1860 to 1865, while general prices rose in the ratio of 100 to 232. From 1873 to 1879, money wage rates fell in the ratio of 166 to 134, while general prices declined in the ratio of 129 to 95. The accuracy of these figures is not, however, satisfactory. They are suggestive, but not absolutely reliable. Dr. Chas. B. Spahr, economic editor of The Outlook, has written an article on "The Gold Standard and the Wage Earner," which is to appear in the National Review, London, and which contains the results of some very valuable researches on this subject. The author finds that average wages have considerable inertia, but that aggregate wages move very quickly. From 1873 to 1879 the reduction in average daily wages had been 14 per cent., the reduction in the number employed 17 per cent., prices had fallen 17 per cent. and aggregate wages had fallen 29 per cent. From 1879 to 1883 prices rose above 10 per cent., the average daily wage rose about 13 per cent., while aggregate wages rose 58 per cent. From 1893 to 1895, by the Mass. Labor Reports, aggregate products fell 17 per cent. and aggregate wages 16 per cent., while average wages fell about 7 per cent. By the Pennsylvania Labor Reports, aggregate products and wages fell off about 33 per cent., while average wages and prices declined only about 13 per cent.

and determine the distribution of wealth is of the utmost moment economically, politically and socially, and must be most carefully considered in constructing a scientific system of finance.

### ATTRIBUTES OF MONEY.

Coming now to consider the attributes necessary or desirable in the performance of the above functions, we find that the following qualities will be either essential or advantageous to whatever may be chosen to act as money.

1. General receivability or acceptabilty—willingness of people to receive in exchange for commodities and services and in payment of debt, etc.
2. Limitation of volume.
3. Steadiness of value.
4. Portability.
5. Ease of keeping.
6. Ease of concealment.
7. Difficulty of counterfeiting.
8. Durability.
9. Divisibility.
10. Elasticity.
11. Uniformity.
12. Cheapness.

Concerning most of these qualities a word will be sufficient. Durability and elasticity are needful for steadiness of value, and may be referred to that head. Large susceptibility to division is convenient but not always essential—the cattle used as money in many countries did not possess it. In a state of advanced commerce however a considerable divisibility becomes quite necessary. The same thing may be said as to uniformity—one cow was not always the equivalent of another unit of bovine currency. There was one uniformity about it tho. The taxpayers of Massachusetts, when cows were legal tender, quite uniformly paid their taxes in the smallest and leanest kine. Portability is good but not essential; living money had little of it; grain has been found very bulky, and gold and silver very heavy when large payments have to be made. Ease and safety in keeping are good, but not necessary—cattle cannot be put in your inside pocket, and you could not keep that sort of money very well in a Boston flat. Difficulty of counterfeiting is an excellent thing in money, but not essential. The Continental money and the French assignats were very faulty in this respect, but nevertheless they did undoubted duty as money. Cows are perhaps superior in this respect to either gold or silver coin or paper money. Cheapness is good, other things equal; i. e., if a money that costs very little labor can be made as efficient as a money that costs much labor, the first should have the preference. Cheapness, however, is not esesntial. The same is true of steadiness of value—it is admirable, but not essential. Gold, silver, paper, cattle, furs, every money that has ever been used has been subject to more or less variation in value.

### INTRINSIC VALUE.

There is a common notion that money must have or ought to have what is called "intrinsic value." The idea is that paper is not real money but only "representative" money, representative of gold or silver, or some "real" money made out of some material having an inherent value of its own, which sustains its purchasing power independently of any legal-tender quality. "Representative" money is supposed to be defective unless it can be exchanged upon demand for a stated weight of gold or silver or other money possessing inherent or intrinsic value. It is thought by some that it is only by such convertibility that paper money can retain its value, and it is further said that nothing destitute of intrinsic value can be real money, because nothing without value of its own can measure the values of other things. We have to use length to measure length, capacity to measure capacity, and value to measure value. Whatever we measure must be measured by a unit of the same nature as itself. (See Prof. Bowen's Pol. Econ., p. 293.)

Let us examine the last point first: (1) It is not quite true that whatever we measure must be measured by units of its own nature. For example, with a thermometer we measure heat by units of length.

(2) As we have seen when speaking of the second function of money, values are not measured by anything inherent in the thing used as money, but by comparison of the relations between money and the commodity to be measured—with the relation betwen money and commodities in general. Strictly speaking, money *does not measure* the value of commodities, but only *enables* us to measure it by means of a double comparison, giving us the exchange power of the commodity in terms of commodities in general, which exchange power constitutes the value of the commodity.

(3) To say that we must have value to measure value does not prove that we must have "intrinsic" value in order to perform the measurement. It is not utilities that are measured by money, but exchange values. We don't measure intrinsic values with money, nor measure by intrinsic values. We can't measure exchange values by intrinsic values unless by intrinsic values we mean exchange values; and exchange value arising from the use of an article as money will do as well for purposes of measurement as exchange value arising from its use in the arts or in any other relation to human need. A bit of stamped paper used as a medium of exchange fulfills as valuable a purpose, is just as useful, as a bit of iron fashioned into a spade, or a bit of silver stamped into the shape of a spoon, or a bit of gold made into a breastpin. A piece of paper that will exchange for commodities, services, taxes, etc., has exchange value as truly as corn, cotton, cattle, silver or gold.

(4) To give a paper dollar exchangeable value it is not necessary to make it convertible into gold or silver, but only, by law or usage, to make it generally receivable in payment of debts, taxes, etc. Dr. C. F. Taylor, of Philadelphia (whose admirable "Monthly Talks" in The Medical World contain some of the best and clearest statements of great questions that are to be found in our literature), has many times exposed the fallacy of the "intrinsic value" hypothesis, and shows that *receivability* is much more important than convertibilty. On p. 525 of The Medical World for December, 1897, is printed a letter from Secretary of the Treasury, L. J. Gage, to Dr. Taylor, in which the Secretary says:

"While the Government does not specifically redeem either silver dollars or silver certificates in gold, *it receives them* the same as gold (i. e., at face value) *in payment of all debts due to the United States.* This amounts to a practical daily redemption of such dollars and certificates in large amounts."

(5) Examine one of our silver certificates, of which there are several hundreds of millions in circulation. You will find that it is not redeemable in gold, but only in silver worth at this time less than half the face value of the certificate—less than fifty cents on the dollar; yet the certificate passes at its full face value because everybody knows it has receivability—because it is redeemable in services, and commodities and settlement of debt.

(6) The case is the same with the silver dollars themselves; it is not their intrinsic value that makes them pass at par, for their intrinsic value is less than half the par. It is the fact that they are receivable for the same things that gold dollars are receivable for—the fact that they will do the *money work*, the exchange service that gold will do. It is that fact that keeps their value level with gold, and would keep it so even if the silver in them were not worth one cent to the hundred.

(7) Even in the case of gold, the intrinsic value of the material, the value it would have as a commodity for use in the arts, the value it has independently of what comes to it by reason of its use for monetary purposes, is comparatively small, and is not the value that is used in money measurements.

Silver fell in value from 70 to 50 cents in a few days when the Indian mints were closed to it, and its demonetization in Germany, France, the United States and other countries has reduced the value of $371\frac{1}{4}$ grains (the weight of silver in a dollar) from its former level of 100 cents to its present level of 35 cents. If all the countries that still use silver for money were to demonetize it, there is no doubt that its value would sink much lower yet, and it is safe to say that at least two-thirds of the value silver possessed in 1873 was derived from its use as money; its mere commodity value, its intrinsic value, was less than one-third of its exchange value when it was a full legal-tender money and the mints were open to its coinage.

If silver had been made the sole money metal, and if gold had been demonetized by the leading nations in 1873 and following years, there can be no doubt that the value of gold would have fallen very greatly for the same reason that silver has fallen, viz., the diminution of demand without a corresponding diminution of supply. The main demand, or the main element in the demand, for both gold and silver in 1873, was the monetary demand—the demand for them to be used as media of exchange in the growing commerce of the nations. If this main element in demand were removed without contemporaneous and equal failing of the mines, the value must fall by the inevitable working of the law of demand and supply. Under given conditions of mining output, etc., the exchange value of a metal used as money will have a tremendous fall if it ceases to be used as money.

The exchange value of gold, thru which it measures values and performs the functions of money, is, therefore, not inherent or intrinsic at all, but is a consequence of its use as money, its receivability in exchanges and settlements, together with the limitation of its volume by natural or artificial causes. Anything that by law or custom has equivalent receivability, and whose volume is similarly limited by nature or by man, will have the same value for monetary purposes. Men do not, as a rule, take gold in commerce because of any use they have for the gold as such, but simply because they know they can pay their debts and taxes with it, and obtain for it food, clothes, shelter, pictures, books, transportation, education, labor—any commodity or service in the market. Anything else that will do these things will be taken by merchants, manufacturers, laborers, etc., just as eagerly as gold (perhaps more eagerly if more convenient to carry, keep and send), and anything will do these things if it is portable, durable and hard to counterfeit, limited in volume and made a full legal tender for all debts and dues public and private. Even counterfeit dollars, metal or paper, circulate as well as gold dollars so long as people do not know they are counterfeits; so long as the people think they have a right to circulate, and therefore possess the quality of general receivability, they will buy as much as gold. A genuine dollar that has the right to circulate possesses permanently the quality that a counterfeit possesses while it is masquerading as genuine money, and the people are ignorant of its lawless character.

(8) History and experience in our own time abundantly confirm the statements just made. In the first chapter we have seen that the financial history of England, France, Austria, the United States, Venice and Brazil shows many instances of the maintenance of the value of money without metallic redemption or basis, the independent paper or bank currency being kept at par or even above par with gold, not by promising to pay gold for it, not by promising to pay anything for it, but by promising that it should be *received*, and by limiting its volume—the two elements which must exist in the case not only of paper but of gold, or silver, or anything else that is to serve as money.

In 1873 the Netherlands rejected silver at their mints, and also refused for two years to coin gold. During that time their exchanges increased till the money volume became so limited relative to the demand that the whole coinage went to a premium above bullion; the coins would buy much more metal than they contained. "The gold necessary to make 9½ florins would buy silver enough to make 11 silver florins, yet 11 silver coined florins would buy gold bullion enough to make about 12 gold florins." That is, a silver coined florin would buy about 9 per cent. more gold than was in a gold florin, and would buy as much silver as was contained in 1.4 silver florins. (Hon. Henry Winn, Faneuil Hall Address, October 7, 1891, p. 10, and Amer. Mag. of Civics, December, 1895, p. 580.) Our own silver dollar will at present buy silver bullion enough to make nearly three silver dollars. The nickel with which we pay street railway fares will buy enough of the metal on which the coin is stamped, enough "nickel," to make 6 or 8 nickels—the metal in the coin is worth less than a cent, yet the coin passes for 5 cents gold value, and neither it nor the silver dollar is redeemable in gold.

The city of St. Joseph, Mo., in recent years has used an independent paper currency for local purposes which was receivable for taxes, and being limited in volume kept its value perfectly. Many of our counties have done and are doing the same thing.

Persons who have not studied the subject or thought much of it, on hearing about independent paper, are apt to declare that, history or no history, it is perfectly clear to them that the Government cannot create value, and that paper without gold or silver behind it must be worthless. They fail to recognize that the paper has the whole field of service and commodities behind it, and that they are making a pun on the word value. Suppose the Government cannot, by stamping paper, give it the *intrinsic* value possessed by gold; it can give the same *exchange* value, and it is the exchange value that makes gold money.

The Government can give even intrinsic value of a certain kind to practically worthless paper by stamping it and limiting the number of pieces; men will pay far more than the legal-tender value of such pieces in order to possess them as curiosities or art treasures. For example, rare postage stamps, Columbia coins, old currency, etc.

It is clearly absurd to say that the Government cannot give value to paper. An individual can do it, why not a nation? A deed has value, and a note, and a bit of manuscript. Tennyson could make a sheet of paper worth $1,000 by writing a few verses upon it. A postage stamp has value, and is just as good as gold or silver all over this country, altho it is "irredeemable" in coin—redeemable in service only. Anything that is useful has value. The difference between gold money and paper money is not that gold has value and paper has none, but that the gold money has a value aside from its character as money. It has another utility and therefore another source of value, while paper in general has only value as money, because it has only that one utility (or rather its other utilities are insignificant in comparison with its money utility bulk for bulk). But in that utility it is as useful as gold, and therefore has the same value for money as gold, and frequently more.

It will not do to point to the French assignats, the Continental money, and the Confederate script, and conclude that paper money will not keep its value. They lost value because of the relaxation of limitation on their volume; and experienced extinction by the failure of their legal-tender quality thru withdrawal, or the downfall of the Governments that established them. No number of failures where the essential conditions of money, legal tender and limitation, were not fulfilled, can go any distance at all toward proving that intrinsic value is necessary, especially in the light, not merely of one, but of many cases where independent, inconvertible, non-intrinsic money has kept its value by the fulfillment of the said conditions.

Nearly all economists, and *all* the great economists agree in affirming that intrinsic value is not requisite to money. John Stuart Mill says (Polit. Econ., Book iii, chap. 13, §1):

"After experience had shown that pieces of paper, of no intrinsic value, by merely bearing upon them the written profession of being equivalent to a certain number of francs, dollars or pounds, could be made to circulate as such, and to produce all the benefit to the issuers which could have been produced by the coins they purported to represent; governments determined to try whether they could not make a piece of paper issued by them pass for a pound, by merely calling it a pound, and *consenting to receive it in payment of the taxes.* And such is the influence of almost all established governments, that they have generally succeeded in attaining this object: I believe I might say *they have always succeeded for a time, and the power has only been lost to them after they had compromised it by the most flagrant abuse.*"

Ricardo and our own Francis Walker, two of the greatest economists that have ever lived, give special emphasis to the case of coins which have lost much of their intrinsic value by abrasion or clipping or sweating, or by the original abstraction of a certain portion of the metal at the mint, to cover expenses of coinage or for the profit of the Sovereign, and both Ricardo and Walker affirm that "in no case will depreciation (of money value) result unless the coin be supplied in excess." (Walker, Money, p. 196; Ricardo, Polit. Econ. Discussion of Seigniorage, and Reply to Bosanquet, pp. 95-6.) Ricardo says: "However debased a coinage may become, it will preserve its mint value; that is to say, it will pass in circulation for the intrinsic value of the bullion which it ought to contain, provided it be not in too great abundance."

Many times Sovereigns have debased the coin of the realm for their private gain, abstracting a part of the gold or silver, and the coin has circulated just the same as before. King John of France was especially noted for this. But the idea has not been confined to crowned heads. The merchants of New York stated to Lord Cornbury that

"The people of Boston publicly and avowedly have practiced to clip and file all the small current money along the continent, to 25 per cent. loss, which practice and the unlawful profit coming thereby, did encourage enough to make it their business to carry it thither and return it again to us and our neighbors, where it passed for the same value as formerly." (Documentary History of New York.)

In his "Report on the Mint," Alexander Hamilton speaks of "the new dollar" as being 5 per cent. less valuable intrinsically than the old dollar, and yet circulating together with the old at a par. Our present silver dollar presents a seigniorage of 65 per cent. Gresham's law that inferior money will drive out and replace the superior only applies where there is an excess of money above the needs of the community. If sufficiently limited in quantity, both will circulate at or even above par in bullion. (See Walker, Money, p. 194; Ricardo's reply to Bosanquet, p. 95; Case of the Netherlands above, etc.)

General Walker says (Money, p. 277):

"Several expressions of Mr. Ricardo have already been quoted to the effect that a bank-note may be regarded as a coin upon which the seigniorage is enormous, extending to its whole nominal amount. While some exception might possibly be taken to this statement regarding a bank note (on account of the bank reserves which may be regarded as entering into the cost of maintaining the notes), there can be none to its application to independent govermnment paper. We said that, by Mr. Ricardo's reasoning, a seigniorage of 10 per cent., or even of 50 per cent., on coin would not alter the purchasing power of each piece, provided only the pieces were not supplied in excess of the amount of money of full value which would circulate as the community's distributive share of the world's stock of money.

"No more, if we suppose the seigniorage to be carried out to 100 per cent., and instead of debased coin, pieces of paper to be issued, costing so little in their production that, for purposes of economical reasoning, we may say they cost nothing, would the purchasing power of each piece be diminished provided the pieces were not issued in excess. Upon this point there is substantial unity among economists."

Pages 288 et seq. by a careful analysis of the facts and principles of exchange Walker shows that intrinsic value is not necessary to money. On page 297 he quotes Wilson as saying that *"The gold is no more essential to the guinea than the brass or ivory of the ruler is to its inches."*

In his Political Economy, §213, General Walker (tho favoring bimetallism and not independent paper) says:

"It is undoubtedly true, as Prof. Bonamy Price asserts, that 'experience has proved that it (paper money) need not of necessity suffer any depreciation of value.'" (Principles of Currency, Price, p. 156.)

General Walker continues: "On a point so vital it may be well to add authority to reason, especially as current American literature misrepresents the real purport of economic opinion on this subject."

"Mr. Thomas Tooke, the most eminent economic statistician of the world, explicitly and repeatedly states that depreciation is not a necessary consequence of inconvertibilty.

"Mr. James Wilson, founder of the London *Economist*, and a statesman and financier of wide experience, declares that if the amount of inconvertible paper be properly regulated, 'there is no reason whatever why such notes should suffer depreciation.'" (Capital, Currency and Banking, p. 42.)

M. Courcelle-Seneuil, an eminent French writer on finance,

speaking of inconvertible paper says: "The value of such money, resulting solely from its use, is limited by that use. If the issues are moderate, paper money will be able to have the same value as metallic money." (Operations de Banque, p. 370.)

I have made use of three names of the first rank in the economics of finance. Let me now quote once more from *"the most illustrious writer known to monetary science."*

"The whole charge for paper money," says Mr. Ricardo, in his Political Economy, "may be considered as seigniorage. Tho it has no intrinsic value, yet by limiting its quantity its value in exchange is as great as an equal denomination of coin, or of bullion in that coin. *It is not necessary that paper money should be payable in specie to secure its value; it is only necessary that its quantity should be regulated.*"

Wm. G. Sumner, Yale Professor of Political and Social Science, in his "History of American Currency," p. 249, quotes the report of the English Bullion Committee to the effect that "The value of an inconvertible currency depends on its *amount* relatively to the needs of the country for a circulating medium."

And Professor Sumner declares that "The doctrines of the Bullion Report have been tested by experience of their opposites and of themselves, and they are no longer disputable. They are not matters of opinion or theory, but of demonstration. They are ratified and established as the basis of finance."

#### THE ONLY ESSENTIAL ATTRIBUTES

are general receivability,[8] and limitation of volume either by nature or man. Indeed, since general receivability in exchange cannot exist in respect to any article in the absence of limitation upon the quantity of it in circulation, we may con-

---

[8] "It is the disposition or the indisposition of the great majority of the community to receive it in payment which settles the question whether a particular commodity shall become money or not. The willingness of the mass of the people to receive one article rather than others in payment for whatever they have to sell, furnishes the prime, the one essential condition of a true money." (Walker, Money, pp. 24-5.) In primitive societies the willingness generally arises by the slow growth of usage. In civilized societies the willingness arises by definite act of the Government, establishing the legal tender and maintaining it by enforcement in the courts, and by reception for public dues.

sider receivability the sole essential test. An article may be limited without being generally receivable in exchange, but it cannot be generally receivable in exchange unless it is limited. If it comes to be generally receivable and should afterwards become absolutely unlimited it will cease to be receivable. If alchemy should be so wonderfully successful that mountains of dirt could be turned into gold by a wave of the hand, people would not use gold as a medium of exchange any more than they would use mud now. They might use stamped gold, however, because the quantity of that could easily be limited. Receivability in exchange implies limitation, so that receivability covers both essentials and may be taken as the index of both.

Anything that the people are willing to take in exchange for commodities and services and in payment of debts, so that the taker knows he can in his turn use the same thing to pay his debts and to purchase commodities and services from others, will answer for money. It may be very poor money; it may not possess the other attributes needful for efficient performance of the various functions of money; but it can act as a medium of exchange and roughly perform all four resulting functions. In other words, it can be money, if by custom or law the mass of the people are willing to receive it in payment. We have found communities using corn, leather, cattle, bullets, notched sticks, iron, copper, gold, silver, paper, bank accounts, and they would use any reasonably convenient thing upon which the Government put the stamp of legal tender, receiving it for duties and taxes, and enforcing it in the courts as a valid payment of debt for its face value.

### STEADINESS OF VALUE.

Next in importance to the essential quality of legal tender or general receivability, is the attribute of stable value. Indeed this attribute, tho not essential to the existence of money, is absolutely essential to just and equitable money. By steady money I mean money of constant purchasing power; money that will buy the same average quantity of commodities and services this year that it did last year; money that gives its possessor the same command over the world of exchange at all times.⁰ If a dollar gives its owner more power of purchase than formerly, or less power, it has changed its value. The holder can get more or less for it than before, and it becomes a false standard of payment, and a dangerous regulator of industry and wealth distribution. If prices rise, the dollar has less purchasing power than before; if prices fall, the dollar has more purchasing power than before. In order that the purchasing power of the dollar may remain the same, the general level of average prices must neither rise nor fall. A steady currency is one that maintains general prices at a constant level. A money that does not accomplish this is dan-

---

(⁰) It is sometimes said that money should be constant with labor—that a dollar should always buy the same quantity of labor. A bill has even been proposed providing for the issue of labor dollars by the Government at the rate of $2.50 per day of 8 hours unskilled labor, the Government to redeem the money on demand in unskilled labor at the same rates. (Labor as Money, by John O. Yelser.) It has been suggested that labor is intrinsically the most proper measure of value, on the ground that one day's ordinary exertion of one man may be looked upon as always to him the same amount of effort or sacrifice. (See Adam Smith's Wealth of Nations, Bk. 1, Chapter XI; John Stuart Mill's Polit. Econ., Bk. III., Chapter XV., Sec. 2; Ricardo's Works, III.; D. A. Wells "Recent Economic Changes," p. 225.) While labor for labor, and even day for day is a very admirable principle of distribution which in a co-operative brotherhood might be incorporated in the money system see Our Country's Need, Parsons, p. 12 et seq.), yet it by no means follows that it could properly become the monetary basis to-day. (Ibid., and J. Allen Smith's remarks in "Annals, etc.," supra, pp. 10-12.) In the first place, labor day for day does not truly represent exchange values nor real values. The product of a day's work by a savage in the wilds of Africa, or the product of a lazy Italian in a street sweeping gang in one of our cities is not the equivalent for the product of a day's work by a fine mechanic or an efficient farmer, a wise statesman, a successful inventor or an eminent physician. Moreover, the value even of unskilled labor in the same country is continually changing. A new invention may double the product of a day of unskilled labor. It is absurd to say that the double product is worth no more than the former product. The truth is that the day's labor is twice as valuable as before, and a dollar regulated by the labor unit, maintaining a constant relation with the day's work, would double in value under such circumstances. So long as the competitive system continues, and values rest upon demand and supply, a labor unit can hardly represent them truly. To regulate money by a labor unit under competition would be about as unjust as the present method of nonregulation. The creditor who lent $1,000 or 1,000 days work for two years or ten years might at the end of that time receive 1,000 days work of vastly increased efficiency—days whose product might be double the product of the days he lent. In other words, the whole benefit of inventions and improvements would go to the creditor class, whereas it is much more equitable to give the benefit of improvements to the burdened debtor class, as would happen were the dollar kept steady with commodities. If debtors have to pay back an equivalent in commodities, then every improvement in production makes it easier for them to pay their debts, and does this without the slightest injustice to the creditors who receive the same number of dollars of the same purchasing power as those they lent; i. e., they receive back the same command over the world that they gave, whereas if the dollar is regulated by the labor day, each dollar repaid may buy two or three times as much wealth as the dollar lent.

The labor dollar means the fall of prices, and this, under competition, means panic and depression. If the dollar is kept steady with the labor day, then the progress of invention would produce a series of industrial crises. When a day's work created twice as much product as formerly, the labor dollar would buy twice as much; that is, prices would have fallen to one half. Every increase in the productivity of labor would reduce prices in proportion and the worst variety of money fluctuation would become a perpetuity.

gerous and unjust. Rising prices cheat the creditor classes, and award to labor less than its share of the total product. Falling prices cheat debtors, displace labor and crush industry into the dust. Fluctuating prices produce periodical panics. The only way to give the creditor just what he lent, no more, no less, and the only way to be secure against panic and depression under a competitive system of industry, is to keep prices level. And the only safe or honest dollar is the dollar that will do this; the dollar that has a constant and unchanging purchasing power; that will buy the same average amount of commodities at one time as another.[10]

---

(10) Ricardo says: "All writers on the subject of money have agreed that uniformity in the value of the circulating medium is an object greatly to be desired. A currency may be considered as perfect, of which the standard is invariable, which always conforms to that standard, and in the use of which the utmost economy is practised. * * During the late discussions on the bullion question, it was most justly contended, that a currency to be perfect should be absolutely invariable in value." (Proposals for an economic and secure currency, Sections 1 and 2.)

Locke says that money "as the measure of commerce ought to be kept as steady and invariable as may be." (Address of the Master of the English Mint in 1816.)

Jevons holds: "It is evidently desirable that the currency should not be subject to fluctuations of value. The ratios in which money exchanges for other commodities should be maintained as nearly as possible invariable on the average." (Money and the Mechanism of Exchange, p. 38.)

Fonda observes that "invariable value is the great requirement for both the functions: 'a measure of value' and 'a standard of deferred payments.'" (Honest Money, p. 28.)

Professor Sherwood remarks: "The ideal that we want so far as price adjustment is concerned, is to keep prices stable, so that a contract which is payable in one year from now can be paid with just the amount of commodities which will then represent the value stated in the contract of to-day. * * * "That is what we want, a stability of prices that persists from one year to another and from one generation to another, * * a currency which shall expand with the expansion of trade and commerce and development generally; a currency which shall not be lagging behind the commerce and development of the country and hindering that development, and a currency which shall not, by being too rapidly increased, lead to excessive speculation and to loss." (History and Theory of Money, p. 225.)

J. L. Laughlin, head professor of political economy in the University of Chicago, says: "The highest justice is rendered by the state when it exacts from the debtor at the end of a contract the same purchasing power which the creditor gave him at the beginning of the contract, no less, no more."

"The value of money does not remain the same for any length of time; and the precious metals cannot serve as a proper measure of value during a long term of years. * * One way suggested to get a standard of payment for long contracts is by a device known as the multiple standard. A long contract, like a government or railway bond, ought not to be settled by paying back the amount of gold or silver borrowed, but by giving the lender a sum which would at the time of payment, purchase the amount of commodities for which the money loaned could have been exchanged at the time that it passed from the lender to the borrower." (History of Bi-Metallism in the U. S., pp. 70 to 76.)

R. B. Chapman, for many years financial secretary to the government of India, remarked to the British Gold and Silver Commission, January 27, 1888: "To my apprehension, a steady standard of value is absolutely necessary for the purposes of commerce; and if stability of standard is lost, commerce is paralyzed."

President E. B. Andrews says on p. 135 of his "Institutes of Economics": 'It (money) is a more perfect measure the more steady and invariable it is as to its own value. It inevitably shrinks in value so soon and about in proportion as it is multiplied beyond the requirements of exchange."

## MOVEMENT OF THE MONEY VOLUME.

The value of money, that is, the general level of prices, can be controlled by controlling the volume of the currency. Prices can be made to rise by increasing the volume of money in circulation, and prices can be made to fall by decreasing that volume.[11] Contrariwise, a fall of prices otherwise caused

---

[11] Some writers appear to think that the volume of money has no relation to prices. They say that the volume of money may increase very much without affecting prices, while on the other hand prices may rise or fall thru the movement of credit without any change in the volume of legal tender money, and from these facts they conclude that the money volume has no controlling influence on prices. But this conclusion is not justified by the premises. A given movement of the money volume may not ALWAYS cause prices to move any more than gravitation will always cause a body to fall, or than an electric current will always cause a trolley car to move. It depends upon the circumstances of the case HOW MUCH CURRENT will be required before the car will move, and HOW MUCH CHANGE in the money volume must be made in order to cause a movement of prices. If population and business are growing as fast as the money volume, or if people accustom themselves to using more money in doing the same business, paying cash more frequently and relying on credit less, there may be a large accession to the money volume without a rise of prices.

The fact that a shrinkage of credit may cause a fall of prices without any change having taken place in the volume of legal tender money shows that there are other causes of fluctuating prices besides a movement of the legal tender money volume, but does not prove that such movement is not also a cause of price change; indeed it proves the opposite, for a shrinkage of credit is equivalent to a contraction of the currency—it is a shrinkage of that which in a certain field has acted in the place of legal tender money, and its failure enlarges the business to be done with legal tender money, which, if the volume of the latter remains the same, amounts to a contraction relatively to the work it has to do. As a matter of fact the volume of legal tender in circulation is apt to shrink along with credit, thru the hoarding of money in time of danger.

We know from history that the movement of money does cause a corresponding movement of prices. The influx of the precious metals following the discovery of Mexico and Peru increased the volume of money in Europe 500%, and prices rose to a degree estimated at 200 to 400 per cent, notwithstanding the growth of population, and expansion of the business to be done with money. (See Economic Studies, Vol. I, No. 1, Amer. Econ. Assoc.; and Mulhall's Hist. of Prices, tables in the back of the book.) So in the middle of this century the discovery of gold in California and Australia increased the money volume and lifted prices very materially. On the other hand the contracton of the currency in England after the Napoleonic wars, and in this country after the Rebellion, produced a serious fall of prices, as we have seen.

It is sometimes said that credit will expand to take the place of money, so that a decrease of the currency does not necessarily affect prices. This may be so in some cases, but as a rule it is, as President Walker remarks, "a question whether the operations of credit are not less active, rather than more active, when contraction of the currency is going on than when the currency is undergoing a moderately progressive increase." (Economic Studies, Vol. i., No. 1, pages 44-5.) Contraction depresses business, and men are less willing to give credit, more insistent on cash, when trade is bad and danger is ahead, than when business is brisk and the sea is smooth. Walker, Price and other leading economists declare that the credit system may modify but does not destroy the relation between currency volume and price, there being a large field of exchange in which cash is required.

There is no precise quantitative relation between money movement and price movement because of the interference of other forces; neither is every price movement due to money movement. The truth is simply that a SUFFICIENT movement of the money volume will cause a movement of prices, and that when a price change is produced by another cause a SUFFICIENT counter movement of the money volume will cancel the change. A sufficient upward movement would be one large enough to overcome opposing resistances, like shrinkage of credits, etc., and saturate business with cash up to the point people care to use it, and introduce an excess of currency beyond this point of saturation. That excess would move prices. A sufficient downward movement would be one not met by increase of credit or other substitute, and not accompanied by a corresponding shrinkage of business.

may be checked and expunged by an increase in circulation, and a rise of prices can be overcome by contraction of the currency. With sufficient foresight a threatened rise or fall of prices could be *prevented* by a movement of the money volume contemporaneous with the action of the cause threatening to produce the rise or fall.

Under a strong and stable government able to enforce its legal-tender laws, the most important monetary fact is the movement of the volume of the currency; control of this movement means control of prices, and the control of prices means the power to increase or diminish the weight of public

---

Attention is sometimes directed to per capita circulation as a matter of importance. But within wide limits it is a matter of no consequence. Nations have adjusted themselves successfully to $3 or $4 per capita and to $35 or $40. But the MOVEMENT from one per capita to another, especially if it be from a large per capita to a small one, while the business to be done with money is all the time increasing, may be a matter of the most vital moment.

The conclusion that the money volume has a determining influence upon prices is simply one application of the law of supply and demand, and is affirmed by all the leading economists.

Professor Alfred Marshall, the highest living English authority in political economy, says: "I accept the common doctrine that prices generally rise, other things being equal, in proportion to the volume of money. * * I include paper money." (Testimony before the Herschell Commission, No. 9929-32.)

Pres. F. A. Walker, the highest authority on this side of the water upon the question of finance, writes (Sec. 218, Polit. Econ.): "Mr. Ricardo has rightly said that, by limiting the supply, any degree of value can be given to the money of a country, be it of gold and silver, or of paper;"—giving us in a single sentence his own conclusion and that of Ricardo, whom he calls "the most illustrious writer known to monetary science."

Pres. Walker wrote very strongly on this subject in his "Relation of Changes in the Volume of the Currency to Prosperity." (Economic Studies, Vol. I., No. 1, April, 1896, Amer. Econom. Assoc.)

Professor Sumner (Hist. Amer. Currency, p. 221) speaking of irredeemable paper, says: "The whole story which precedes, goes to show that the value of a paper currency depends on its amount. At the time of issue, or during a war in which the issuer is engaged, it depends in some degree on his credit; but when it settles down in peace as the normal medium of exchange, its value comes to depend purely on its amount. This amount of course is relative to the requirements of the country for the purpose of performing its exchanges."

David Hume says in his Essay on Money: "It is the proportion between the circulating money and the commodities in the market that determines prices."

John Stuart Mill says (Polit. Econ. III., 8, Secs. 2, 3,; and III., 13, Sec. 1.): "The value or purchasing power of money depends in the first instance on demand and supply. * * In point of fact, money is bought and sold like other things, whenever other things are bought and sold *for* money. Whoever sells corn, or tallow, or cotton buys money. Whoever buys bread, or wine or clothes, sells money to the dealer in those articles. * * If there were less money in circulation in the community, and the same amount of goods to be sold, less money would be given for them, and they would be sold at lower prices. * * That an increase of the quantity of money raises prices, and a diminution lowers them, is the most elementary proposition in the theory of currency. * * The immediate agency in determining the value of money is its quantity. If the quantity, instead of depending on the ordinary motives of profit and loss, could be arbitrarily fixed by authority, the value would depend on the fiat of that authority. The quantity of a paper currency not convertible into the metals at the option of the holder can be arbitrarily fixed, especially if the issuer is the sovereign power of the state. Wherefore the value of such a currency is entirely within the control of the government."

(See the closing paragraphs of the preceeding section on "Intrinsic Value.")

and private debts, to govern the distribution of wealth, to command prosperity or panic. A matter of such moment should not be left to chance or private manipulation. A money of *elastic* volume, carefully regulated in the public interest, is essential to prevent oppression and gambling, to maintain a constant average of general prices, keep the value of money steady, and make the dollar a perfect medium of exchange, a reliable measure and means of storing value, an honest standard of deferred payments doing injustice neither to debtor or creditor, and a safe regulator of industry and distributor of wealth.

### WHAT MONEY SHOULD BE ADOPTED?

There are few if any more important questions before the American people to-day. The Gold Standard, the Bimetallic Standard and the Multiple Standard are the systems chiefly spoken of, and the only ones that have sufficient support in reason to make it worth while to consider them.[12] The gold standard makes the dollar conform to the value of a given weight of gold. The bimetallic standard subjects the dollar to the controlling influence of gold and silver, giving it sometimes the value of one metal, and sometimes of the other, such value being always limited however by the monetary potentiality of the other metal, and amounting, if long periods are considered, to the average value of the two metals. The multiple standard requires the dollar to conform itself to the average value of commodities in general, so that its purchasing power may remain constant. The average value of commodities, and the increase or diminution of the money volume necessary to cancel or prevent a rise or fall of the average level of prices, are determined by methods that will be described in the next chapter.

It is clear from the discussion preceding this section that steadiness of value in the monetary unit is of the very highest importance to justice and prosperity, and necessary to the due performance of the functions of money. And it is equally clear that steadiness of value cannot be attained with either

---

[12] See above for discussion of the labor standard.

the gold or the bimetallic standard. Even if the Government owned all the mines in the country, it could not stop Wall Street from cornering gold, or prevent scheming syndicates from draining the treasury, or shut out the perturbing influence of foreign markets, mines and financial politics. In general, bimetallism is superior to monometallism. Two metals are better than one, less easily cornered, less affected by the accidents of production, less liable to sudden and wide fluctuations from any cause, but the difference is slight as is clearly shown by the facts platted in diagram below. As a general rule it is evidently better to base the money unit on two commodities than on one, as the average of two commodities will be likely to represent all commodities or general purchasing power more nearly than either one of the two.[13]

However much of an improvement two commodities may be over one as a basis for the money unit, it is manifest that two are not so good as 100 or 200 or 500. We cannot rely upon two to represent all so fully as we can rely upon 100 or 200 or 500, or upon the all itself.

So long as no attempt is made at a wise public control of the movement of the money volume in the interest of justice and industrial well-being, so long as Congress neglects the duty of regulating money imposed upon it by the Constitution, so long as the volume and value of money is left to nature and conspiracy and foreign emergencies, so long will gold and silver be rightly used instead of independent paper; the *rude regulation* of Nature's restrictions on production, with all the perturbations of competition, conspiracy, etc., *is better than no regulation;* but so soon as *the necessity of replacing chance and private manipulation with intelligent regulation on scientific principles for the public benefit comes to be understood,*[14] just that soon does it become clear

---

[13] This likelihood is by no means a certainty. Silver, for example, might keep prices nearer level than gold, or gold and silver together; the white metal's variations from the general average of all commodities being less than those of gold; and the average of the flustuations of gold and silver, the nearer the true level than gold alone, is not so near as silver. It is very doubtful, however, if this would continue to be true if the monetary demand were thrown upon silver. The case would be clearer with cotton and leather, leather varying much less from the average commodity level than cotton. (See diagrams below.)

[14] This is the vital point in the monetary problem of the day. There must be intelligent control of money in the public interest in order to stop panics, do justice between debtor and creditor, and regulate the distribution

that gold and silver must be abandoned as monetary bases, and reliance placed on independent paper carefully regulated in volume so that its value may remain constant, representing from month to month and year to year the same average amount of commodities in general, retaining the same power of purchase in peace or war, in good mining or bad, and ridding the nation of the pestilence of falling prices. Such regulation is hardly possible with a money based on gold and silver, because the sources of supply and causes of variation would be in large part beyond the control of the Government. No one people could hope to stem the tide of the world. If gold and silver appreciated abroad for a considerable time and to a considerable degree, we would simply lose all our gold and silver if we tried to keep our prices steady with coin and convertible paper,[15] and be compelled at last to rely upon independent paper. Even if due regulation of metallic money, or currency based on metallic money, were a possibility, it would still be undesirable not merely because of the added difficulties it would involve, but because of the needless expense of using costly materials for a service that can be performed as well or better with cheap materials. In other words, money should be intelligently regulated anyway, and if it is intelligently regulated, independent paper is preferable to monometallism or bimetallism, because it is cheaper and less open to disturbing influences beyond the control of the Government.

We have said that bimetallism is but little better than monometallism. In detailed proof of this we present the following diagram from Professor Alfred Marshall, bringing the lines to date and adding the Professor's comments.

---

of wealth. Men favor metallic money because they think in terms of present methods. Gold is better than limitless issues of paper; little regulation is better than none, bad regulation is better than no regulation, but good and sufficient regulation is better than either. It will not do to say that money cannot be wisely regulated in the interests of the people. It has been done (See Chap. I) and can be done with great perfection and certainty by methods developed by modern economics. (See next chapter.)

[15] Convertible paper is open to even more variations than metallic money itself. It may at any time through industrial disturbance or other cause be called upon to toe the mark with gold, and follow wherever it goes, and it may between whiles enjoy little excursions of its own away from the value a metallic currency would have; a phenomenon arising from the friction or inertia usually attending convertibility which permits an "over-issue" of the "convertible" notes. (See Walker "Money," pp. 479-484. Prof. Sumner Hist Amer. Currency p. 186.)

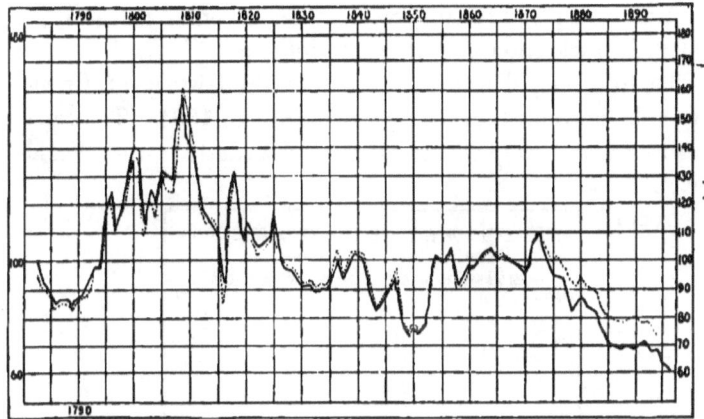

"The *dark curve* shows the variations of the index number which represents the average prices of the leading wholesale commodities during the last hundred years, estimated in *gold alone;* while the *dotted curve* shows the same index number estimated in terms of *the two metals,* gold and silver in equal shares. On comparing these, we find that the fluctuations shown by the second curve are not very much less than those shown by the first; and, what is of even more significance, that the fluctuations in the index number during the period when the gold value of silver was nearly stationary are greater than they have been since 1873, when its value has been much disturbed."[16]

"There is no security that the yield of the silver mines will be great when that of the gold mines is small; history shows that the probability is the other way, in the ratio of 3 to 2. The production of gold has been changing in the opposite direction to that of silver during about 160 out of the last 400 years; during the remaining 240, the two productions have been either increasing together or diminishing together."[17]

The truth is that gold and silver belong to the same class, and are much more likely to vibrate together than two commodities of a more different nature. If we are to confine our-

---

[16] Prof. Marshall, Contemporary Review, Vol. 51, Mar., 1887, p. 360.
[17] Ibid, p. 359.

selves to two commodities it would be better to choose so that both would not belong to the class that is subject to the law of diminishing return nor very similar in other respects, so that their fluctuations might offset each other.

The following diagram from Mulhall's History of Prices shows the movement of money from 1841 to 1884. The solid line represents English prices and the dotted line World prices.

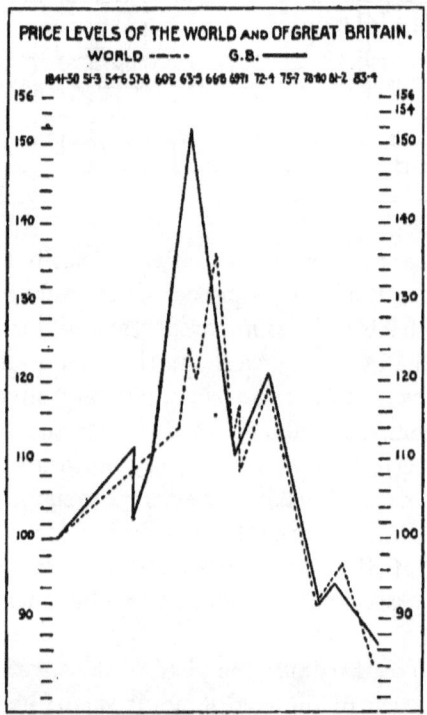

The rise and fall of prices since 1846 is shown in the following tables. Dr. Sauerbeck and Dr. Soetbeer (two of the most eminent statisticians in Europe), The London "Economist," the Report of the Finance Committee of the United States Senate, 52d Congress, on "Wholesale Prices, Wages and Transportation," commonly known as the "Aldrich Report," and "The American," edited by the distinguished economic writer, Wharton Barker, are the authorities. Palgrave's table is a recast of a portion of the Economist figures, each commodity being "weighted," i. e., entered in the estimate of average prices according to its importance relatively to the other commodities, instead of entering each commodity as the equal of every other, as is the case in most of the tables, — the average being obtained by taking the sum of the prices of all the commodities without weighting, and dividing by the number of commodities.

The Economist list is not considered wholly satisfactory because the number of commodities is small (22), and 4 of them are either raw cotton or cotton manufactures, which rose 300 or 400 per cent. during the war. It is all right to include erratic elements in due proportion—the same proportion that occurs in the total of commercial products—but 4 skyrockets in 22 products is too high a ratio.

The Aldrich Report bears many marks of careless work[18] (perhaps by the clerks employed to handle the enormous body of data obtained by the committee), and for the "weighted" column only the relative importance of the various *groups* of articles is used, so that altho the number of commodities is large (223), the results are not considered by economists to be as reliable as the averages of Sauerbeck and Soetbeer. The first two columns of the Aldrich table give the actual prices, paper prices during the war and until 1879, then gold prices. The last two columns show gold prices all the way thru, the paper prices of 1862 to 1879 being reduced to terms of gold at the premium then existing. The prices thus obtained do not exactly represent the course that a continuous gold standard would have taken because speculation in gold widened the distance between it and paper, lifting the yellow plaything, and putting gold prices during and after the war below the normal gold level as indicated by the movement of price levels in other countries during this period. In the first and third columns of the Aldrich table we have the relative prices

---

[18] One of the most striking illustrations of the imperfect methods employed in the Aldrich Report is the fact that in obtaining average wages, the wages of a few foremen were added together and divided by the number of foremen (4, for example) to get the average pay of a foreman ($5 a day, for example). Then the wages of perhaps 100 workmen were added and divided by the number of workmen, giving perhaps $1.00 for the average. Finally, the foremen's average ($5) and the workmen's average ($1) were added together and the sum ($6) divided by 2, giving $3 (in this example) for the average wages on the whole of the data concerned, whereas the true average would be $1.15.

calculated as a simple average of all the commodities. In the second and fourth columns, the relative price resulting from giving each commodity its due weight according to its consumption. Rent, insurance, charity, etc., had to be omitted. The shorter lists used in calculating the tables include such commodities as coffee, sugar, tea, wheat, corn, oats, cotton, wool, silk, flax, indigo, timber, tallow, leather, copper, iron, lead, tin, etc. The long list of the Aldrich report contains 8 groups of commodities: food,[19] cloths and clothing, fuel and lighting, metals and implements, lumber and building materials, drugs and chemicals, house furnishing goods, and miscellaneous articles. A number of items are considered under each group. The committee ascertained from statistics of 2,561 normal families that the expenditure for food is 41 per cent. of the total expenditure, clothing 15 per cent., rent 15 per cent., fuel 5 per cent., light 1 per cent., house furnishing 2.5 per cent., insurance 1.5 per cent., taxes 1.15 per cent., tobacco 1 per cent., intoxicants 1.68 per cent., amusements .92 of 1 per cent., religion .92 of 1 1.68 per cent., other amusements .92 of 1 per cent., religion .92 of 1 per cent., charity $\frac{1}{4}$ of 1 per cent., books and newspapers 1 per cent., illness and death 3.35 per cent., other purposes 15 per cent. Not being able to measure the changes of rent, insurance, etc., the committee confined its table of prices and averages to the 8 groups above named which represent 68.6 per cent. of the total expenditure of the average family.

In using the tables it must be remembered that each statistician arbitrarily places the location of the 100 level; he may take any year as the standard and call its index number 100. The index numbers of the other years will then differ from 100 in the same ratio that their prices differ from prices of the standard year.

The Sauerbeck list has been extended from 1895 to 1897 by applying the percentages of fall shown by the American table, which has been used in extending the Economist list from 1891 as given in the Aldrich Report.

---

([19]) To show the character of the groups we give the main elements of the first group: beans, bread (10 varieties, including Boston crackers, oyster crackers, shipbread, etc.), butter, cheese, coffee (Rio), eggs, cod, salt, mackerel, (3 nos), rye, flour, dried apples, raisins, lard, yellow corn meal, bacon, beef (joints), ribs (salt), ham (sugar cured), lamb, mutton, pork, fresh milk, molasses (New Orleans prime), rice (California prime), salt (5 sorts), nutmegs, pepper, corn starch.

## TABLE XIII.

| SAUERBECK. 1867-1877=100. Simple Average. English prices. 45 commodities. | SOETBEER. 1847-1850=100. Simple Average. Hamburg prices 100 commodities, and Eng. export prices 14 commodities. | ECONOMIST LIST. 1845-1850=100. Simple Average. English prices. 22 commodities. |
|---|---|---|
| 1846 .... 89 | 1847.... ⎫ | 1845.. ⎫ |
| 1847 .... 95 |  to  ⎬ 100 |  to  ⎬ 100 |
| 1848 .... 78 | 1850.... ⎭ | 1850.. ⎭ |
| 1849 .... 74 |  |  |
| 1850 .... 77 |  |  |
| 1851 .... 75 | 1851.... 100.21 | 1851.... 104 |
| 1852 .... 78 | 1852.... 101.69 | 1852.... 93 |
| 1853 .... 95 | 1853.... 113.69 | 1853.... 108 |
| 1854 .... 102 | 1854.... 121.25 | 1854.... 122 |
| 1855 .... 101 | 1855.... 124.23 | 1855.... 118 |
| 1856 .... 101 | 1856.... 123.27 | 1856.... 123 |
| 1857 .... 105 | 1857.... 130.11 | 1857.... 132 |
| 1858 .... 91 | 1858.... 113.52 | 1858.... 119 |
| 1859 .... 94 | 1859.... 116.34 | 1859.... 115 |
| 1860 .... 99 | 1860.... 120.98 | 1860.... 121 |
| 1861 .... 98 | 1861.... 118.10 | 1861.... 124 |
| 1862 .... 101 | 1862.... 122.65 | 1862.... 131 |
| 1863 .... 103 | 1863.... 125.49 | 1863.... 159 |
| 1864 .... 105 | 1864.... 129.28 | 1864.... 172 |
| 1865 .... 101 | 1865.... 122.63 | 1865.... 163 |
| 1866 .... 102 | 1866.... 125.85 | 1866.... 162 |
| 1867 .... 100 | 1867.... 124.44 | 1867.... 137 |
| 1868 .... 99 | 1868.... 121.99 | 1868.... 122 |
| 1869 .... 98 | 1869.... 123.38 | 1869.... 121 |
| 1870 .... 96 | 1870.... 122.87 | 1870.... 122 |
| 1871 .... 100 | 1871.... 127.03 | 1871.... 118 |
| 1872 .... 109 | 1872.... 135.62 | 1872.... 129 |
| 1873 .... 111 | 1873.... 138.38 | 1873.... 134 |
| 1874 .... 102 | 1874.... 136.20 | 1874.... 131 |
| 1875 .... 96 | 1875.... 129.85 | 1875.... 126 |
| 1876 .... 95 | 1876.... 128.33 | 1876.... 123 |
| 1877 .... 94 | 1877.... 127.70 | 1877.... 123 |
| 1878 .... 87 | 1878.... 120.60 | 1878.... 115 |
| 1879 .... 83 | 1879.... 117.10 | 1879.... 101 |
| 1880 .... 88 | 1880.... 121.89 | 1880.... 115 |
| 1881 .... 85 | 1881.... 121.07 | 1881.... 108 |
| 1882 .... 84 | 1882.... 122.14 | 1882.... 111 |
| 1883 .... 82 | 1883.... 122.24 | 1883.... 106 |
| 1884 .... 76 | 1884.... 114.25 | 1884.... 101 |
| 1885 .... 72 | 1885.... 108.72 | 1885.... 90 |
| 1886 .... 69 | 1886.... 103.99 | 1886.... 92 |
| 1887 .... 68 | 1887.... 102.02 | 1887.... 94 |
| 1888 .... 70 | 1888.... 102.04 | 1888.... 101 |
| 1889 .... 72 | 1889.... 106.13 | 1889.... 99 |
| 1890 .... 72 | 1890.... 108.13 | 1890.... 102 |
| 1891 .... 72 | 1891.... 109.19 | 1891.... 102 |
| 1892 .... 68 |  | 1892.... 97 |
| 1893 .... 68 |  | 1893.... 96 |
| 1894 .... 63 |  | 1894.... 89 |
| 1895 .... 62 |  | 1895.... 89 |
| 1896 .... 60 |  | 1896.... 89 |
| 1897 .... 59 |  | 1897.... 86 |

## TABLE XIV.

| PALGRAVE. 1865-69=100. Economist prices. 22 commodities. | | | THE AMERICAN, OCT. 16, 1897. Jan. 1, 1891=100. Simple average, 100 commodities. | | | |
|---|---|---|---|---|---|---|
| | Simple average. | Weighted average. | | | | |
| 1865.... | 110.6 | 107.5 | 1891 | Jan. 1.... | 100. | |
| 1866.... | 111.3 | 110.6 | | Apr. 1.... | 101.96 | 98.74 |
| 1867.... | 98.0 | 99.0 | | July 1.... | 98.28 | |
| 1868.... | 90.1 | 93.5 | | Oct. 1.... | 94.71 | |
| 1869.... | 90. | 89.2 | 1892 | Jan. 1.... | 93.12 | |
| Average | 100. | 100. | | Apr. 1.... | 92.87 | 95.6 |
| 1870.... | 91. | 90. | | July 1.... | 92.85 | |
| 1871.... | 90. | 93. | | Oct. 1.... | 93.60 | |
| 1872.... | 97. | 100. | 1893 | Jan. 1.... | 98.42 | |
| 1873.... | 102. | 104. | | Apr. 1.... | 99.75 | 95.77 |
| 1874.... | 100. | 108. | | July 1.... | 93.39 | |
| 1875.... | 95. | 97. | | Oct. 1.... | 91.43 | |
| 1876.... | 93. | 99. | 1894 | Jan. 1.... | 87.59 | |
| 1877.... | 94. | 100. | | Apr. 1.... | 84.70 | 84.87 |
| 1878.... | 87. | 95. | | July 1.... | 84.40 | |
| 1879.... | 76. | 82. | | Oct. 1.... | 82.81 | |
| 1880.... | 87. | 89. | 1895 | Jan. 1.... | 79.74 | |
| 1881.... | 81. | 93. | | Apr. 1.... | 82.59 | 83.31 |
| 1882.... | 83. | 87. | | July 1.... | 86.05 | |
| 1883.... | 80. | 88. | | Oct. 1.... | 84.88 | |
| 1884.... | 75. | 80. | 1896 | Jan. 1.... | 85.29 | |
| 1885.... | 70. | 76. | | Apr. 1.... | 81.29 | 80.93 |
| | | | | July 1.... | 78.81 | |
| | | | | Oct. 1.... | 78.34 | |
| | | | 1897 | Jan. 1.... | 79.95 | |
| | | | | Apr. 1.... | 79.38 | 79.63 |
| | | | | July 1.... | 76.33 | |
| | | | | Oct. 1.... | 82.88 | |

## TABLE XV.

#### THE ALDRICH REPORT.
#### 1860=100.
#### U. S. Prices, 223 Articles.

|  | Actual Prices. | | Gold Prices. | |
|---|---|---|---|---|
| Year. | Simple average. | Weighted average. | Simple average. | Weighted average. |
| 1840 | 116.8 | 97.7 | 116.8 | 97.7 |
| 1841 | 115.8 | 98.1 | 115.8 | 98.1 |
| 1842 | 107.8 | 90.1 | 107.8 | 90.1 |
| 1843 | 101.5 | 84.3 | 101.5 | 84.3 |
| 1844 | 101.9 | 85.0 | 101.9 | 85.0 |
| 1845 | 102.8 | 88.2 | 102.8 | 88.2 |
| 1846 | 106.4 | 95.2 | 106.4 | 95.2 |
| 1847 | 106.5 | 95.2 | 106.5 | 95.2 |
| 1848 | 101.4 | 88.3 | 101.4 | 88.3 |
| 1849 | 98.7 | 83.5 | 98.7 | 83.5 |
| 1850 | 102.3 | 89.2 | 102.3 | 89.2 |
| 1851 | 105.9 | 98.6 | 105.9 | 98.6 |
| 1852 | 102.7 | 97.9 | 102.7 | 97.9 |
| 1853 | 109.1 | 105.0 | 109.1 | 105.0 |
| 1854 | 112.9 | 105.0 | 112.9 | 105.0 |
| 1855 | 113.1 | 109.2 | 113.1 | 109.2 |
| 1856 | 113.2 | 112.3 | 113.2 | 112.3 |
| 1857 | 112.5 | 114.0 | 112.5 | 114.0 |
| 1858 | 101.8 | 113.2 | 101.8 | 113.2 |
| 1859 | 100.2 | 102.9 | 100.2 | 102.9 |
| 1860 | 100.0 | 100.0 | 100.0 | 100.0 |
| 1861 | 100.6 | 94.1 | 100.6 | 94.1 |
| 1862 | 117.8 | 104.1 | 114.9 | 101.6 |
| 1863 | 148.6 | 132.2 | 102.4 | 91.1 |
| 1864 | 190.5 | 172.1 | 122.5 | 110.7 |
| 1865 | 216.8 | 232.2 | 100.3 | 107.4 |
| 1866 | 191.0 | 187.7 | 136.3 | 134.0 |
| 1867 | 172.2 | 165.8 | 127.9 | 123.2 |
| 1868 | 160.5 | 173.9 | 115.9 | 125.6 |
| 1869 | 153.5 | 152.3 | 113.2 | 112.3 |
| 1870 | 142.3 | 144.4 | 117.3 | 119.0 |
| 1871 | 136.0 | 136.1 | 122.9 | 122.9 |
| 1872 | 138.8 | 132.4 | 127.2 | 121.4 |
| 1873 | 137.5 | 129.0 | 122.0 | 114.5 |
| 1874 | 133.0 | 129.0 | 119.4 | 116.6 |
| 1875 | 127.6 | 128.9 | 113.4 | 114.6 |
| 1876 | 118.2 | 122.6 | 104.8 | 108.7 |
| 1877 | 110.9 | 113.6 | 104.4 | 107.0 |
| 1878 | 101.3 | 104.6 | 99.9 | 103.2 |
| 1879 | 96.6 | 95.0 | 96.6 | 95.0 |
| 1880 | 106.9 | 104.9 | 106.9 | 104.9 |
| 1881 | 105.7 | 108.4 | 105.7 | 108.4 |
| 1882 | 108.5 | 109.1 | 108.5 | 109.1 |
| 1883 | 106.0 | 106.6 | 106.0 | 106.6 |
| 1884 | 99.4 | 102.6 | 99.4 | 102.6 |
| 1885 | 93.0 | 93.3 | 93.0 | 93.3 |
| 1886 | 91.9 | 93.4 | 91.9 | 93.4 |
| 1887 | 92.6 | 94.5 | 92.6 | 94.5 |
| 1888 | 94.2 | 96.2 | 94.2 | 96.2 |
| 1889 | 94.2 | 98.5 | 94.2 | 98.5 |
| 1890 | 92.3 | 93.7 | 92.3 | 93.7 |
| 1891 | 92.2 | 94.4 | 92.2 | 94.4 |

The ups and downs of prices shown in these tables and especially the long descents are sufficiently startling, but they soften the real facts because they show only the *averages* for each year, and do not exhibit the maximum or minimum price attained during the year. Here is a very suggestive table from p. 336 of the Aldrich Report.

### TABLE XVI.

#### FLUCTUATION OF PRICES.

#### 1860-1869.

|  | Maximum. | | Minimum. | |
| --- | --- | --- | --- | --- |
|  | Year. | Price. | Year. | Price. |
| United States...... | 1864 | 172.9 | 1861 | 98.2 |
| England ........... | 1864 | 144.8 | 1868 | 99.3 |
| Hamburg ......... | 1864 | 137.8 | 1861 | 99.3 |
| France ............ | 1864 | 128.6 | 1868 | 94.5 |

#### 1870-1879.

|  | Maximum. | | Minimum. | |
| --- | --- | --- | --- | --- |
|  | Year. | Price. | Year. | Price. |
| United States...... | 1872 | 126.5 | 1879 | 86.7 |
| England ........... | 1873 | 114.6 | 1879 | 80.7 |
| Hamburg ......... | 1872 | 116.9 | 1878 | 92.5 |
| France ............ | 1872 | 104.6 | 1879 | 76.4 |

#### 1880-1891.

|  | Maximum. | | Minimum. | |
| --- | --- | --- | --- | --- |
|  | Year. | Price. | Year. | Price. |
| United States...... | 1880 | 100.5 | 1886 | 80.4 |
| England ........... | 1880 | 92.2 | 1886 | 73.3 |
| Hamburg ......... | 1880 | 91.1 | 1886 | 74.8 |
| France ............ | 1880 | 79.2 | 1886 | 69.3 |

#### 1860-1891.

|  | Maximum. | | Minimum. | |
| --- | --- | --- | --- | --- |
|  | Year. | Price. | Year. | Price. |
| United States...... | 1864 | 172.9 | 1886 | 80.4 |
| England ........... | 1864 | 144.8 | 1886 | 73.3 |
| Hamburg ......... | 1864 | 137.8 | 1886 | 74.8 |
| France ............ | 1864 | 128.6 | 1886 | 69.3 |

What would we think of a measure that would be 172 inches long in 1864 and then shrink to 80 inches in 1886, and to 60 inches in 1897? If we took the maximum and minimum actual prices instead of gold prices, the contrast would be greater still, a contrast of 280 to 60 in round numbers.

What would we think of a yard stick that would expand to more than four times its former length, so that a piece of cloth that measured a yard by its test a generation ago would measure less than a quarter of a yard to-day—only 8 inches at the lowest point this year? No doubt some creditors are willing to receive 4 yards for every one they lent, but what is the effect on the debtor?

So far as we have dealt with fluctuations of *price*. Gold has been deemed the standard and the variations in the price of a given quantity of commodities has been recorded. Now let us take commodities as the standard and record the variations of gold from the commodity base. That this is the true method is clear upon plain common sense, upon scientific principle and upon authority.

The object of commerce is not to get gold. In 999 out of a thousand sales the vendor does not want gold or silver. The dollar is not sought by him for the sake of the 23.22 grains of gold in it. Most of the dollars he gets contain no grains of gold at all, but are made of paper. He does not think of asking for gold, and would deem it a burden if he were required to take large payments in gold. His object is to exchange his commodities for other commodities, and he takes money because it is a convenient means of making that exchange. The *purpose* of money is not to convey a certain weight of gold, 23 grains to the dollar or any other number of grains to the dollar, but *to transfer a purchasing power* equal to that of the goods which are being paid for, or the loan that is being liquidated. The receiver of the dollar takes it because it will buy the means of life and happiness—commodities in the broad sense. The dollar is taken as the representative of the means of living, the representative of commodities; and in order that it may be a true representative it must be based on commodities and kept in harmony with them.

The real standard of values is command of the means of life, and not a grain of gold which may at one time have twice the command over the means of life that it possesses at another time.

The purpose of money being the transfer of equivalences in purchasing power—equivalences of command over commodities in general—equivalences in exchangeable value, it is clear that the base or standard should be something that is constant in exchangeable value; and the only thing that is thus constant is a composite of all commodities. No one commodity, nor two, nor three commodities can be relied on to be constant in exchange value, or have the same command over life and the world; but the *average of all commodities* (in the broad sense) will do this. The sum of the internal exchange values of any list of commodities is a constant quantity. Take leather, corn and iron, for example, and suppose that last month 100 units of leather exchanged for 100 units of corn, or 100 units of iron, we may represent the exchanges thus:

100 iron (spades e. g.) would buy........ { 50 corn.
and 50 leather.

100 leather (shoes perhaps) would buy.. { 50 corn.
and 50 iron.

100 corn would buy ..................... { 50 leather.
and 50 iron.

Sum of exchange values ................ 300

Now suppose the iron loses 20 per cent. of its exchange value by reason of cheaper production perhaps. Then corn and leather will gain in exchange power exactly as much as iron loses. Iron will buy less corn and leather, but corn and leather will buy more iron than before. This command over iron increases in the same ratio that iron's command over them diminishes, and the sum of the internal exchange values remains the same as before, the table taking this form:

100 iron will buy ..................... { 40 corn.
and 40 leather.

100 leather will buy .................. { 60 corn.
and 50 iron.

100 corn will buy ..................... { 60 leather.
and 50 iron.

Total of exchange values ................ 300

Iron having lost one-fifth of its power can only buy 40 corn and 40 leather, which leaves 60 corn for leather to buy and 60 leather for corn to buy. As the relations between corn and leather have not changed, it takes 60 leather to buy 60 corn, and leather has 40 left which buys 50 iron. In the same way corn buys 60 leather and 50 iron, and the sum of the *internal* exchange values of the group is 300 as at first. The external exchange values, the exchange relation between this group and other commodities may not remain constant, but if *all* commodities (in the broad sense including services and all purchaseable things) are included in the list, all exchange values then become internal. Wherefore a list including all commodities is the constant in exchange which science seeks. A composite including a large number of commodities carefully selected so as to fairly represent all classes of purchaseable things is much nearer the real base and infinitely more to be relied upon than any one or two commodities. A composite commodity standard is the true base from which to measure the variations of gold and every other commodity.

To common sense and reason we may add authority to the point that commodities are constant. John Stuart Mill says: "There is such a thing as a general rise of prices. All commodities may rise in their money price. But there cannot be a general rise of values. It is a contradiction in terms. A can only rise in value by exchanging for a greater quantity of B and C; in which case these must exchange for a smaller quantity of A. All things cannot rise relatively to one another. If one-half of the commodities in the market rise in exchange value, the very terms imply a fall of the other half; and reciprocally, the fall implies a rise. Things which are exchanged for one another can no more all fall, or all rise, than a dozen runners can each outrun all the rest, or a hundred trees all overtop one another."

Robert Giffen, the great English statistician, speaking of the commodity lists of Sauerbeck, Soetbeer, The Economist, etc., says that even shorter lists carefully selected would answer, and declares that "Viewing a long period dynamically it is beyond all question that the commodities are compara-

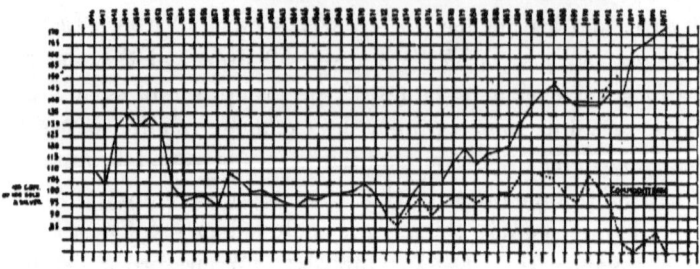

DIAGRAM VI.
VARIATIONS IN THE VALUE OF GOLD AND SILVER
THE RELATIVE AMOUNTS OF COMMODITIES NECESSARY TO BUY 100 GRAINS OF GOLD IN DIFFERENT YEARS,
PLATTED FROM THE DATA OF SAUERBECK AND THE AMERICAN. THE DOTTED LINE REPRESENTS SILVER.

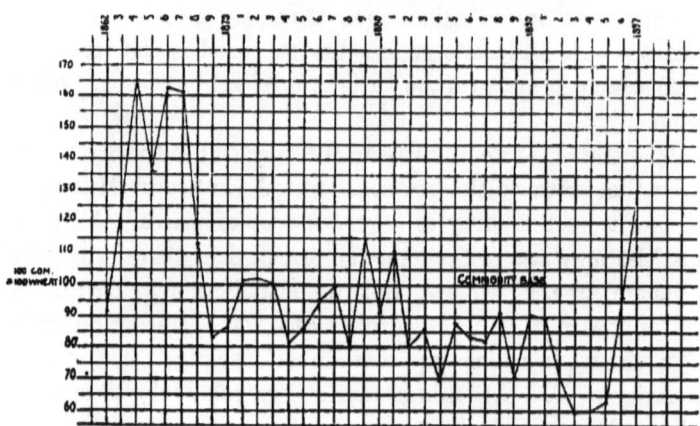

DIAGRAM VII.
VALUE OF WHEAT IN TERMS OF COMMODITIES
THE AMOUNT OF COMMODITIES NECESSARY TO BUY 100 UNITS OF WHEAT.
IN 1873 & 1877 100 UNITS OF WHEAT WERE EQUIVALENT TO 100 UNITS OF
COMMODITIES BY THE ALDRICH WEIGHTED STANDARD.

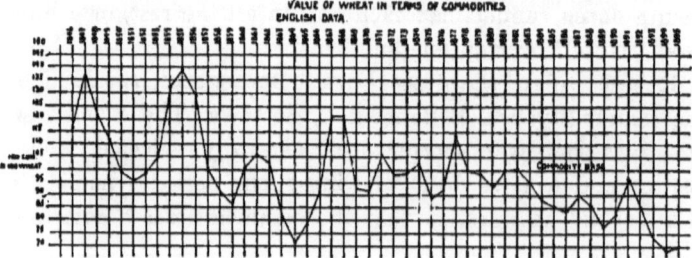

DIAGRAM VIII.
VALUE OF WHEAT IN TERMS OF COMMODITIES
ENGLISH DATA

# THE BEST MONEY. 117

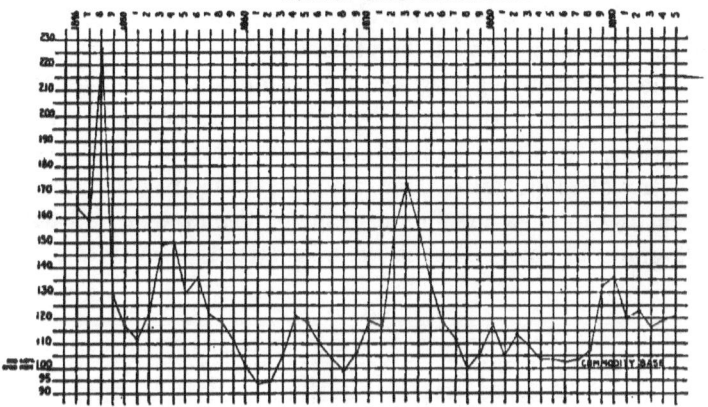

DIAGRAM IX
VALUE OF IRON IN TERMS OF COMMODITIES
RELATIVE NUMBER OF UNITS OF COMMODITIES NECESSARY TO BUY 100 UNITS OF IRON
IN DIFFERENT YEARS BY SAUERBECK'S DATA

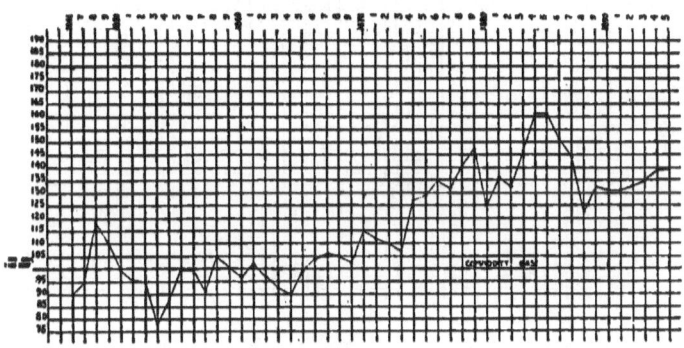

DIAGRAM X
VALUE OF BEEF IN TERMS OF COMMODITIES
RELATIVE NUMBER OF UNITS OF COMMODITIES NECESSARY TO BUY 100 UNITS OF BEEF IN DIFFERENT YEARS BY SAUERBECK'S DATA.

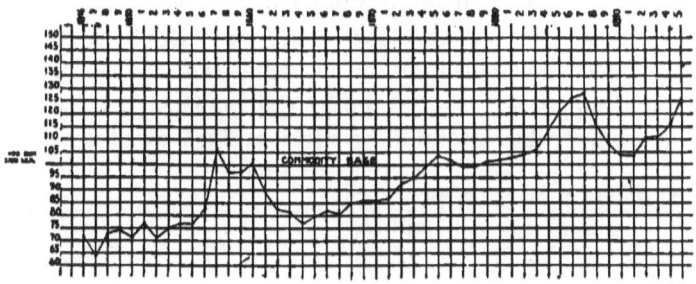

DIAGRAM XI.
VALUE OF LEATHER IN TERMS OF COMMODITIES
RELATIVE AMOUNTS OF COMMODITIES IN GENERAL NECESSARY TO BUY 100 UNITS OF LEATHER
IN DIFFERENT YEARS. SAUERBECK'S DATA.

118    PHILOSOPHY OF MONEY.

tively steady, and only money changes."[20] That is, even a small group of commodities well selected will keep quite close to the real standard, the all-commodities base, very much closer than the money of the present day.

The accompanying diagrams take commodities as a base and record the variations of gold.[21] The usual method is to register prices, i. e., the amount of money necessary to buy a given quantity of commodities. Here we reverse the process and represent the relative amounts of commodities necessary to buy 100 grains of gold. That is, we take a fixed quantity of gold

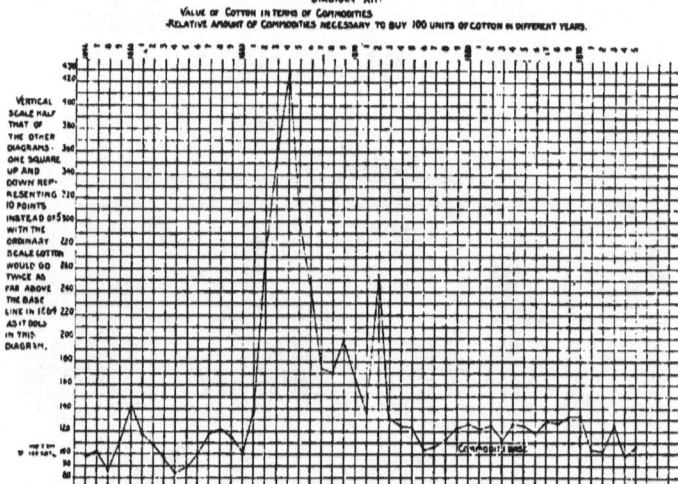

and mark the variations of its value in commodities. No one who will glance at the diagrams can entertain the idea that gold or silver or any one of the commodities dealt with could possibly be a fair representative of the commodity base, or a just and proper basis for money intended to transfer equivalences in commodities, or command over the means of life and happiness. Neither gold or silver money, nor any money convertible into gold or silver at fixed weights so as

---

[20] Growth of capital, p. 61.
[21] We have had the diagrams made from the data of Sauerbeck, the Aldrich Committee and The American. In some cases the maker used the Aldrich trnnslation of Sauerbeck to the 1860 base together with Sauerbeck's general price levels as given in the Journal of the Royal Statistical Society.

to be dependent upon them or tied to their values, could be relied on to have a constant purchasing power, or truly represent the all-commodity base. The only rational money is an independent[22] currency based on a composite commodity standard.

An independent money regulated by a composite commodity standard would not only be vastly superior to our present money in steadiness of value; it would be superior also in respect to every other attribute and function of money.

In general receivability our paper ranks higher than gold. Mr. Eltweed Pomeroy, President of the National Direct Legislation League, writing in the Arena for September, 1897, says on p. 321: "To-day the civilized world has settled on paper as the best form of money. During the money famine of 1894 in New York City, gold coin commanded a premium of 1 per cent. over bullion, silver coin of 2 per cent., and paper of 4 per cent., showing that paper was preferred to metallic money." And silver certificates with no "intrinsic" equivalent back of them were as eagerly sought and at as high a premium as gold notes or any other paper. It was *money*, not gold, the merchants wanted, and paper was the most convenient form of it. Even the banks abandon metal in time of panic, and the Government abandons it in time of war. If we have to resort to paper whenever the financial situation is difficult, why not keep it all the time? If it will answer for the most complex and dangerous periods, surely it will do so for the easy times, and will save all the jolts and derangements that so often accompany the transition from one sort of money to the other.

It is decidedly expensive to use gold for a service that paper can perform. It is unwise to dig silver and gold out of the ground at enormous cost in order that the precious

---

[22] It might be redeemable in gold or silver or both AT THE CURRENT MARKET PRICES of those metals without being DEPENDENT. The essential matter is that the value of the currency should not be dependent on the value of the metals in such a way as to be in danger of following them in their wobbles, instead of remaining constant with the commodity base. Convertibility by weight, so that a dollar means so many grains of gold, no matter what the purchasing power of these grains may be, is necessarily destructive of steadiness in the dollar; but convertibility into gold at the amount a commodity based dollar would buy at the time is not a dependence, but only a convertibility of the kind that exists in respect to any other commodity in the market. Such a provision however would be of doubtful wisdom.

product may be used for a purpose that can be answered as well or better by a product that is almost costless. Paper at less than 1 cent an ounce will do the work of money better than gold worth more than $20 an ounce. Is it not folly to coin the gold and bury it in vaults, or scatter it over the world in the fine dust that wears from its surface as it passes from hand to hand and counter to counter? Better reserve the gold for purposes paper cannot serve—beautiful watch-cases, fine table service, etc., where it will last practically forever.

Dr. C. F. Taylor throws a strong light on this point when he says that the present idea of money "is like writing a deed to a house on a plate of gold of equal value with the house. It is an enormous waste. Money is a title to wealth; and money made of gold and silver is just like titles to property written on gold and silver."[23]

In elasticity an independent regulated paper would be incomparably superior to money on a metallic base. The metal base is subject to nature's limitations, and restrains in greater or less degree the flexibility of the whole currency based upon it, while an independent paper possesses any degree of flexibility that may be required. As the value of money depends upon its volume, this quality of elasticity is of the first importance. A money whose volume is subject to other control than that of the agents of the sovereign people cannot be expected to respond to the needs of the people, and expand or contract as occasion may require to keep the dollar steady. In 1894 European banks of issue increased their hoardings of gold by 176 millions, an amount that exceeded the whole worlds supply for 3 years, after deducting enough for the arts.[24] That one fact speaks volumes. With independent paper they might hoard all they pleased and its place could be easily supplied. There could be no corners, no Black Fridays, no endless chains of Treasury withdrawals and bond issues.

In portability gold can make no pretence of rivalry with paper. To carry $100,000 in gold a merchant would require

---

[23] Medical World, August, '97, p. 349.
[24] Hon. Henry Winn, Amer. Mag. of Civics, December, '95, p. 578.

a team; but in paper he can carry it in his pocket without trouble.

In regard to counterfeiting, Del Mar says: "The silk threaded distinctive fibre paper, the water marks, the printing in colors, the highly artistic vignettes, the geometrical lathe work, the numbers, the signatures and other mechanical safeguards of the modern paper note render it far more difficult to imitate than coin."

In respect to the regulation of industry and the diffusion of wealth no money based on one or two commodities can be trustworthy, because such money cannot avoid rising and falling in value. The disasters of rising and falling prices are inevitable with a metallic money or a metallic base. It will not do to charge these disasters to the abuse of the credit system. It is true that expanding credit has often much to do with the rise of prices, and shrinking credit with their fall. But it is the business of a rational money to correct and steady credit—absent itself when credit is over-brisk, and be present in force when credit retires from active business. This, gold fails to do. It is brisk when credit is brisk and absent when credit is absent—just the opposite of what it ought to do. Moreover "The abnormal expansion of credit is itself an effect which must be ascribed to the gold standard."[25] Gold causes or permits prices to go up. If it becomes more plentiful in relation to business it may *cause* a rise of prices. If it remains stationary in quantity while expanding credit or diminishing business produce a rise of prices, then it *permits* the rise. It is the business of a true money not to vary in value—it should keep itself at a constant level, and to do this it must keep average prices at a constant level. It must not merely refrain from causing a rise or fall—it must not *permit* a rise or fall. If credit unduly expands gold should contract sufficiently to balance the excess, prevent a rise and keep prices level. If credit shrinks unduly, gold should expand enough to prevent a fall of prices. But gold does not act that way. It frequently causes a change of the price level,

---

[25] Prof. J. Allen Smith, Annals Amer. Acad. P. & S. Sc., March, '96, p. 19. (See also p. 17.)

and rarely or never prevents one. It adds its own weight to increase the vibrations of credit instead of balancing them. A movement of gold, or business, or credit makes prices fall. Does gold expand to restore the balance? No! It goes into hiding, still further diminishing the money volume, causing a further fall of prices, which results in another shrinkage of credit, more hoarding of gold, a new fall of prices, and so on. Every round of the disaster is emphasized and intensified by gold instead of being checked by it. On the other hand, if a movement of gold or business or credit causes a rise of prices, a rapid expansion of credit is apt to result. Men are willing to trust on a rising market, for times appear to be prosperous and profits are large. The expansion of credit still further lifts the value of goods and lowers the value of gold. The higher the prices of goods, the more gold a certain quantity of goods will bring; the less the value of gold. The more dollars you have to give for a sack of flour, the fewer the pounds of flour a dollar will buy. So that rising prices mean depreciating gold. Does gold do anything to prevent its depreciation when credit expands unduly? No. It is apt to intensify its humiliation. It comes out of its hiding places, for hoarding does not pay on a rising market. The volume of money is thus still further increased. Prices rise higher, credit expansion is again stimulated, which produces a new rise of prices and fall of gold, and so on in a seamless circle of rising prices, expanding credit, falling gold, till a crash comes, or the expansion is checked by prudence, or lack of materials, or foreign conditions, and for it all gold is the responsible party because it is the business of a true money to prevent rising prices, which at each step provoke a new inflation of credit. The fact that gold is subject to such variations, no matter what the cause may be, shows that it is not a good standard.

If in contemplation of all the great advantages of independent paper based on a composite commodity standard, you ask why it is that gold is still the foundation of our finances, the answer is two-fold: (1) The gold standard is very valuable to creditors and bankers, and to the men who devote themselves to the cornering of money and the capture of millions by watching or controlling the movement of gold values. In one of the flurries a shrewd New Yorker made two millions at a single deal on gold the Government had contracted to him at a fixed price; and recently a New York syndicate multiplied this figure by four on a bond contract with the Treasury. The people thus interested in gold and its fluctuations have a great deal of power at Washington. (2) A really complete and scientific plan for a regulated paper based on commodities is of very recent date, and as yet few people have become acquainted with the merits of the system.

In the following chapter we will try to explain the details of such a plan.

# CHAPTER III.

#### THE MULTIPLE STANDARD.

From what precedes it appears: First. That a steady money, a dollar of constant purchasing power, is a matter of the highest importance to justice, prosperity, development, civilization. Second. That metallic money is not steady, and any plan to make it steady would be very difficult if not impossible to execute. Third. That the value of independent National paper can be regulated without difficulty, its volume being under the control of the issuing government, wherefore by intelligent regulation in the interests of the public, it can easily be kept at a uniform level so that it will always represent substantially the same amount of commodities in general.

The problem is to replace the single standard, and the double standard by the *multiple standard*—to base the dollar not on one commodity, nor on two, but so far as possible on the whole mass of commodities, using the word in its widest sense to include goods, services, privileges and all manner of purchaseable things.[1] The ideal basis of value is the whole

---

[1] The Multiple Standard appears to have been first proposed by Joseph Lowe, in 1822, in his "Present State of England," which contains a very able treatise on the variation of prices, state of the currency, etc. His idea was to use the standard in long time contracts. He proposed that persons should be appointed to collect information concerning the prices of staple articles. Having regard to the comparative quantities of commodities consumed in a household, he would frame a table of reference, showing in what degree a money contract must be varied so to make the purchasing power uniform. Jevons, in his "Money and the Mechanism of Exchange," after outlining Lowe's plan substantially as above, mentions Mr. G. Poulett Scrope as having independently proposed a similar scheme 11 years later, in his "Inquiry Into the Nature of a Just Standard of Value," his "Principles of Political Economy," p. 406, and "Political Economy for Plain People," p. 308. The plan was taken up by Mr. G. R. Porter in 1838, in "The Progress of the Nation." The Multiple Standard has also been advocated by Count Soden and Prof. Roscher, of Germany, Prof. Walras, of Lausanne, Prof. Jevons Pres. F. A. Walker, Prof. Simon Newcomb, Prof. Alfred Marshall, President E. B. Andrews, Pres. Thos. E. Will, Hon. Henry Winn, Prof. Frank Parsons, A. I. Fonda, Prof. J. Allen Smith, Dr. C. F. Taylor and Eltweed Pomeroy.

The earlier writers confined themselves to suggesting the use of the multiple standard as the basis of payment in long time contracts. The idea of controlling the movement of the money volume so as to keep the dollar in harmony with the commodity standard does not appear to have occurred even to Prof. Jevons or Pres. Walker. Profs. Walras, Newcomb, Will, Andrews and the last six writers named above have advocated, not merely the use of a commodity base as a standard for deferred payments, but the

mass of commodities. The best practicable basis is the largest number of commodities that can be handled with definiteness and accuracy. The nearest to all commodities is a large number of commodities.

In order to substitute intelligent public control for chance and private scheming, it is only necessary:

Incorporation of the multiple standard in the monetary system and the regulation of money in conformity to that standard. Prof. Newcomb's article in the North American Review for September, 1879, was a very valuable contribution to the subject. He wished, however, to continue the use of gold and silver, making the currency redeemable not in a fixed weight of metal, but in such quantity as should at the time possess a purchasing power equal to the unit value of the multiple standard.

Pres. Andrews, in the first edition of "An Honest Dollar," 1889, followed Prof. Walras in advocating the regulation of the currency by the issue or withdrawal of token silver coins, or silver certificates. Gold was to continue to be the money base, paper dollars being redeemable in a fixed weight of metal, but the value of gold to be kept in harmony with a multiple commodity standard by increasing or diminishing the volume of the currency, thru the use of call bonds. Prof. Marshall, in the Contemporary Review for March, 1887, suggests the plan of using an inconvertible paper money kept in harmony with the multiple standard by the Government's buying consols (bonds) to enlarge the circulation when falling prices show that the money volume is too small, and selling consols when the circulation needs to be contracted. He also suggests a plan for applying the multiple standard to the regulation of a convertible currency. The paper sovereign to be based on the commodity unit, but redeemable in half a standard unit's worth of gold bullion plus half a unit's worth of silver bullion at the market value of those metals at the time. So far as I know, Professor Marshall was the first to suggest the use of an inconvertible currency in connection with the multiple standard. On this side of the water, I believe, the Hon. Henry Winn was the first to conceive the idea of an independent national paper based on the multiple standard. He worked it out without knowing of Marshall's suggestion, and outlined it in a speech in Fanueil Hall in 1891, when he was Peoples' Party candidate for Governor of Massachusetts. In December, 1895, he published in the American Magazine of Civics one of the most valuable discussions of the Multiple Standard that we possess. In a series of lectures given in Boston in 1894, Thos. E. Will, now President of Kansas State Agricultural College, advocated a government paper money regulated by a multiple standard. Speaking of the assertion that government paper money would not be safe—that it would be "dangerous for the government to issue promises to pay and call them money." Professor Will said with fine irony: "Instead of this the banks should issue their promises to pay and call them money. Bank promises would be perfectly sound and trustworthy for the reason that they would rest on government bonds. What is a government bond? Answer: A government promise to pay. Hence a government promise when called a greenback is utterly untrustworthy, but, a bank promise when based on a government promise called a bond is perfectly secure." In "Our Country's Need," (1894), Sec. 21, I advocated substantially the same plan that is elaborated in the present volume. In 1895, Mr. A. I. Fonda, in "Honest Money," strongly urged the claims of inconvertible multiple standard money, arguing pp. 157-8, that "Since the value of the circulating medium—the money—depends on supply and demand, the supply should be so controlled that the value of the money would always correspond with that of the standard adopted; and since paper money is the cheapest, the most convenient, and the only money entirely free from outside influences affecting its volume and value, our currency should be a paper money."

The most profound discussion of the subject that has yet appeared is contained in the article of Prof. J. Allen Smith in the "Annals of the American Academy of Political and Social Science," March, 1896. The Professor proves the case for an independent National paper money regulated in volume by the government, so that its value shall remain substantially constant with a carefully selected multiple standard. Dr. C. F. Taylor, during the last two years, has urged the same idea in his pungent "Monthly Talks" in the Medical World, and in The Arena, September, 1897, Mr. Eltweed Pomeroy, President of the National Direct Legislation League, published a spirited popular argument for the same plan. The unanimity with which thoughtful men adopt the independent multiple standard paper system as soon as it is thoroly understood by them is a powerful evidence of the wisdom of the plan. (See further, Chapter IV.)

First. To replace our bank bills and convertible notes with independent paper money issued by the National Government as full legal tender for all debts and dues, public and private, with no promise to pay gold or silver, no promise to *pay* anything, but only a promise to receive it at its face for taxes, duties and all public dues, and to see that it is received at par in settlement of private debts, which promises being enforced by public opinion and the courts confer upon the paper the fundamental attribute of general receivability or legal-tender quality.

Second. A commission of eminent men should be appointed who would watch the course of prices in the chief markets of the country, tabulate the results and publish them monthly, weekly, or at whatever interval might be specified by law. They would report to the Secretary of the Treasury any movement in the level of general prices, together with their estimate of the amount of increase or decrease in the volume of the currency necessary to steady prices and bring them again to a normal level.

Third. The requisite expansion or contraction of money volume could be effected in several ways. The best methods that have been suggested are the use of call bonds, the buying and selling of securities, the establishment of a sliding scale of interest on government loans, and the inter-adjustment of taxation and public expenditure.

If more money is paid out by the Government in its ordinary expenses or for special public improvements than is taken in by taxation, the volume of the currency is increased and prices raised, or a fall cancelled; while on the other hand if the taxes are made larger than the expenditures, the volume of money is decreased and prices lowered, or a rise counteracted.

A method requiring less time to produce is effects, and therefore affording greater elasticity to the monetary system would be the issue of one or two hundred millions of *call bonds* payable at the pleasure of the Government, interest to cease on call. The currency could be contracted by selling such bonds, and expanded by calling them in, wherefore the

Government, by issuing and recalling bonds, would be able to control the money-volume.*

Another plan would be for the Government to add to the currency volume by going into the market and buying up good securities: National, State, and municipal bonds, railway and telegraph securities, real estate, etc., or other property obtainable with the highest advantage and safety,—such property to be sold when the currency needed contraction. This would act with great rapidity and would have the further advantage that, the Government would buy on a falling market and sell on a rising market, yielding incidentally a revenue that might be sufficient to cover all the expenses of collecting the data, etc., and leave a margin of profit besides.

A fourth method would be for the Government to loan money on good security, U. S. bonds, State and municipal bonds, land, buildings, deposits of gold and silver, perhaps even first class paper and personal property in case of special need. If such loans were made at an interest varying with the movement of prices, the volume of the currency would probably receive all needed regulation automatically. The law would fix a sliding scale of interest to be paid to the Government on such loans, arranging said scale so that the rate of interest should rise, perhaps in geometric ratio, as prices rose above the normal level, and fall in corresponding ratio as prices fell.† The result would be that money would be plentifully borrowed on a falling market when money is scarce, and the new influx would lift prices again, while on a rising market interest would pile up at too rapid a rate for debtors, and loans would be paid back to the Government, thereby contracting the currency and checking or cancelling the rise of prices.

Thus by taxation and expenditure, lending and borrowing,

---

*If the bonds were made payable on demand it is probable that they could be made to act *automatically* to prevent any serious fluctuation. (See discussion, p. 178.)

†See Fonda's *Honest Money*, p. 166 (McMillan & Co., 1895). Fonda would use existing banks as distributing agencies for the Government loans, guarding against monopoly by providing that the loans should be open to all on equal terms and making the list of acceptable securities as wide as possible consistent with safety. It is perfectly practicable to use existing banks, but it would be much better to establish a system of Postal Banks and use them as agencies in all the monetary transactions of the Government. (See *infra* 178.)

buying and selling, the Government could regulate the volume and consequently the value of money. All the methods mentioned have their advantages, and might be used in combination. The law should make it the positive duty of the Secretary of the Treasury to maintain as nearly as possible a uniform level of prices.

To aid him in doing this, he would obtain information in regard to the acreage of various crops, condition of the crops from time to time in all parts of the country, the out-put of various kinds of mines, the building and operation of various kinds of factories, etc., and publish such information at frequent intervals. He would also consider the probable foreign demand for various products, the actual movements of prices, as recorded by the Commission, etc., etc.

In obtaining the periodic record of average prices the Commission should take as wide a range of purchaseable things as possible. It might not be possible at first to include such items as rent, insurance, taxes, education, medical attendance, legal advice, domestic service, transportation, etc., but it seems clear that an effort should be made to do so as soon as a body of data sufficient to give a definite character to these items can be collected. Rent, insurance, taxes, labor, etc., are things that almost everyone has to buy, and if they are not included in the estimate a change in them may seriously alter the ordinary purchasing power of the dollar. By ascertaining every year or every few years the total rents paid, and the total acres and total rooms rented, a rough indication of the general movements of rents could be obtained, and in the intervals the item of rent could be deemed a constant quantity, or modified in accordance with the observed relation between its movement and that of the growth of population and other varying conditions. In case of insurance and taxes it is easy to obtain a reasonably reliable average. The last census shows that $100 of property insurance costs about $1 in the United States. Similar methods may be employed in dealing with the average cost of labor and services of various sorts.

Until such items as those discussed in the last paragraph become more definite and generally understood than at present, and the multiple system is fully established in the public confidence and comprehension, it would be best to use only commodities capable of easy and accurate definition as to quantity and quality. It would be better to sacrifice completeness, at first, for the sake of perfect clearness and defiiteness, and eliminate every item the correctness of which could not be easily tested by the people. One or two hundred representative commodities could be selected from the price lists published by the trade journals, and a careful record kept of their prices at New York, Chicago, Philadelphia, Boston, New Orleans, San Francisco, etc., and the average price of each commodity for each week placed in the table of standard prices. The sum of these averages divided by the number of commodities would give the price level for the week on the plan of simple averages. It would be better in many respects however to give each commodity a *"weight,"* or importance in the calculation in proportion to its importance in the expenditure of the average family.[2]

It is obvious that to allow a change in the price of indigo, silk, wine, or nutmegs to affect the composite standard and the

---

(*) While it is true that a large number of commodities weighted according to their relative importance is the ideal requirement, it is also true that a very substantial degree of accuracy may be obtained without weighting and without anything like an exhaustive list of commodities. In other words, the prices of all commodities vary substantially in the same way as the prices of any considerable number of commodities representing the various groups. And the result of a simple average is but slightly different from the result of a weighted average. Mr. Sauerbeck says: "I have checked my figures to some extent by calculating also according to quantities (consumed) and found that the change in prices was, if anything, more important than is actually shown by my ordinary index numbers; but that it did not differ materially." (Testimony before English Gold and Silver Commission, December 8, 1886, Sec. 905.) Palgrave's table given in the preceeding chapter shows the same thing. The Aldrich weighted figures vary more from the simple average, but there is reason to doubt the scientific validity of the methods, and even the accuracy of that report.

The fact that the average prices of all commodities vary in about the same way as the average prices of a considerable number judiciously selected is shown by the substantial agreement in the results of taking different sets of commodities. The fall of prices from 1875 to 1885,

- As judged by the 22 commodities of the Economists Table was............................. 24½ per cent.
- As judged by the 45 commodities of Sauerbeck's table ................................................ 24½ per cent.
- As judged by the 114 articles of Soetbeer's Table 19.6 per cent.
- As judged by the 22 articles of Palgrave's Table.. 22. per cent.
- As judged by the 223 articles of the Aldrich Tables ................................................ 25. per cent.

Divide the total by the number of groups—  5)115.6

The fall as judged by average of all the groups.. 23.1 per cent.

The very slight difference between the results of different sets of commodities estimated by different men and on prices obtained in different markets, is a fact worthy of most careful consideration, as is also the equally interesting fact that the average of all the tables, 23.1 per cent. is much more closely represented by either of them than by gold, which is 23 points away; while even the Hamburg group is only 3½ points off.

value of the dollar equally with a change in the price of beef, butter, leather, wheat, corn, cotton, etc., is to depart from the purpose of keeping the dollar constant in its power of making the purchases usually made with it, so that it will mean always the same thing to the average user of it—the same instrument with the same ability to do what he wants to do with it—the same command over what he wishes to obtain.

The average family spends at least 100 times more for wheat than for indigo, so that indigo should have only one-hundredth part as much weight or influence as wheat in making up the standard.

The following table shows the opinions of various writers as to the weight that should be given to different articles:

TABLE XVII.

|            | Jevons. | Edgeworth. | Giffen. | Sauerbeck. | Soetbeer. | Mulhall. | Average. |
|---|---|---|---|---|---|---|---|
| Butter*    | 35   | 75   | 75   | 30   | 45   | 80   | 57   |
| Sugar      | 35   | 25   | 25   | 55   | 45   | 15   | 33   |
| Wine       | 35   | 25   | 25   | ..   | 70   | 45   | 40   |
| Wool       | 35   | 25   | 25   | 75   | 20   | 20   | 33   |
| Silk       | 35   | 25   | 25   | 10   | 20   | 15   | 22   |
| Tea & coffee. | 35 | 25 | 25   | 20   | 20   | 15   | 23   |
| Wheat      | 35   | 65   | 50   | 110  | 45   | 100  | 67   |
| Barley     | 35   | 65   | 50   | 55   | 45   | 35   | 47   |
| Oats       | 35   | 65   | 50   | 60   | 20   | 50   | 47   |
| Metals     | 70   | 50   | 50   | 15   | 40   | 80   | 51   |
| Coal       | ..   | ..   | 100  | ..   | ..   | 40   | 70   |
| Indigo     | 35   | 1    | 10   | 5    | 20   | 1    | 12   |
| Flax       | 35   | 3    | 30   | 10   | 20   | 5    | 17   |
| Palm Oil   | 35   | 1    | 10   | ..   | 20   | 1    | 13   |
| Timber     | 70   | 30   | 30   | 20   | 70   | 60   | 47   |
| Leather    | 70   | 25   | 25   | 20   | 70   | 40   | 62   |
| Meat       | 110  | 100  | 100  | 155  | 90   | 120  | 113  |
| Cotton     | 110  | 30   | 25   | 100  | 20   | 20   | 51   |
| Sundries   | 150  | 365  | 370  | 260  | 320  | 258  | 195  |
| Total      | 1000 | 1000 | 1000 | 1000 | 1000 | 1000 |      |

*Butter includes also cheese and milk.

The earlier writers appear to have drawn broad lines without detailed investigations of relative consumption. Mulhall observes that four writers took no account of coal. There seems to have been no good reason for inserting indigo and palm-oil, which are items of trifling value, while fish, lard, rice, potatoes, and other important articles are omitted. Another feature that seems inexplicable is, that four of the above writers give barley the same relative importance as wheat, whereas the latter, according to statistics of consumption, should have three times the weight of the former. A similar remark applies to oats, which should stand for only half the value of wheat.

The Aldrich Committee made a strong effort to arrive at accurate conclusions respecting the relative consumption of various commodities by the average family. Table XVIII. from p. 61, of Vol. 1, of the said Report gives the average consumption of 2,561 "normal" families, and Table XIX, from pp. 62-3, shows the average consumption of various articles by 232 families.

TABLE XVIII.
Proportions of 10,000.

| | |
|---|---|
| Rent | 1,506 |
| Food | 4,103 |
| Fuel | 500 |
| Clothing | 1,531 |
| Light | 90 |
| All other purposes | 2,270 |
| Total | 10,000 |

TABLE XIX.
GROUP FOOD.

| | Per family. | Proportion of 10,000 |
|---|---|---|
| Beef | $40.95 | 1,561 |
| Hog products | 17.20 | 655 |
| Meat (kinds not specified) | 16.10 | 614 |
| Poultry | 2.78 | 106 |
| Fish | 2.97 | 113 |
| Eggs | 8.28 | 316 |
| Milk | 15.02 | 572 |
| Butter | 29.04 | 1,107 |
| Cheese | 1.73 | 66 |
| Tea | 4.51 | 172 |
| Coffee | 13.97 | 532 |
| Sugar | 16.69 | 636 |
| Molasses | 1.44 | 55 |
| Lard | 5.27 | 201 |
| Flour and meal | 28.62 | 1,022 |
| Bread | 11.42 | 436 |
| Rice | .62 | 24 |
| Fruit | 8.80 | 332 |
| Potatoes | 11.92 | 454 |
| Vegetables (kinds not specified) | 12.55 | 479 |
| Vinegar, pickles, condiments | 1.86 | 71 |
| Food (not specified) | 12.47 | 476 |
| Total | 262.42 | 10,000 |

## TABLE XIX—Continued.

### CLOTHING.

|  | Per family. | Proportion of 10,000 |
|---|---|---|
| **Husband:** | | |
| Coats, vests, trousers, overcoats.. | $14.11 | 1,407 |
| Boots and shoes | 4.71 | 470 |
| Hats | 1.73 | 173 |
| Underclothes | 2.75 | 274 |
| Shirts | 1.49 | 149 |
| Miscellaneous | 9.01 | 898 |
|  | 33.80 | 3,371 |
| **Wife:** | | |
| Dresses, cloaks and shawls | 8.26 | 824 |
| Boots and shoes | 3.56 | 354 |
| Underclothes | 2.55 | 254 |
| Miscellaneous | 8.39 | 836 |
|  | 22.76 | 2,268 |
| **Children:** | | |
| Coats, etc. | 6.10 | 608 |
| Dresses, etc. | 6.59 | 657 |
| Boots and shoes | 7.76 | 774 |
| Hats | 2.78 | 277 |
| Underclothes | 2.96 | 295 |
| Shirts | .31 | 31 |
| Miscellaneous | 17.25 | 1,719 |
|  | 43.75 | 4,361 |
| Grand total | 100.31 | 10,000 |

### MISCELLANEOUS EXPENSES.

|  | Per family. | Proportion of 2,270 |
|---|---|---|
| Taxes | $8.34 | 115. |
| Insurance | 10.98 | 151. |
| Organizations | 4.82 | 66. |
| Religion | 6.71 | 92. |
| Charity | 1.77 | 24. |
| Furniture and utensils | 18.36 | 253. |
| Books and newspapers | 7.27 | 100. |
| Amusements | 6.68 | 92. |
| Intoxicants | 12.14 | 168. |
| Tobacco | 7.71 | 107. |
| Illness and death | 24.36 | 335 |
| Other purposes | 55.64 | 767. |
|  | 164.78 | 2,270 |

It would be a simple matter to request families and individuals to send in sworn statements of the relative amounts annually spent by them for different purposes. And these data, together with the figures of total product, plus imports and minus exports, and the records of wholesale and retail rates would, in the course of a few years, afford a very accurate idea of the relative expenditure for various commodities both at wholesale and retail. It will not be best to rely on wholesale prices alone. Retail prices are steadier than wholesale, and it is retail rates that the average buyer has to pay. Retail prices largely govern the household expenditure of the average family, and should have due weight in the standard, as well as the wholesale rates involved in the expenditures of merchants and business men.

Our standard then is to be made up (1) of the largest practicable number of commodities (using the word in its broad sense), (2) weighted according to importance in ordinary consumption. We are to prefer (3) commodities largely bought and sold. (4) Commodities that are independent of each other.. (5) Commodities capable of accurate definition as to quantity and quality. (6) Commodities regularly quoted in the public prints. (7) Our commodities should be taken partly from the class that is subject to the law of diminishing return and partly from the class not subject to this law, the choice being made so as to fairly represent each class in the proportion it bears to total consumption. (8) Commodities whose prices vary much must be taken as well as those that vary little, for men and women have to use their dollars to buy both, and dollars are not steady in their purchasing power unless they are steady in reference to the average of all the purchasing to be done with them. Moreover a commodity whose price varies greatly may be nearer steady with average commodity values than a commodity whose price varies little. Slight variation of price (on the gold basis, as at present) means that the commodity moves with gold, and that means that the commodity does vary greatly from the general commodity base. The moon does not vary in distance from the earth so much as Venus, but it varies in its distance from the sun much more widely than Venus. (9) Prices must be registered in all the principal markets of the country. And (10) the averages for the chosen commodities must be tabulated and published periodically.

Let us now select a dozen commodities and illustrate the working of the multiple standard. Suppose that, on the average of ordinary expenditures for every $100 spent for beef, pork, mutton and other meats, $75 are spent for butter, cheese, milk and cream, $20 for sugar, $20 for tea and coffee, $50 for wheat, $25 for oats, $20 for fruit, $60 for coal, $30 for leather, $20 for cotton, $30 for wool, $50 for iron, steel, lead, copper, tin, silver, gold, etc., and $50 for wooden utensils, furniture, etc. In the first column we write the names of the commodities or groups of commodities selected for the standard; in the second column we place the numbers just mentioned representing the relative importance of the said commodities in average consumption; in the third we write the prices of the commodities per unit of volume or weight; and in the fourth column we write the weights or volumes that would be required at the said prices to equal the amounts in the second column. For example, if the market price of meat averages $10 per hundred weight it would require 10 hundred weight to amount to the $100 spent for meat, wherefore 10 cwt. is the item in the fourth column opposite meat. In the same way, if $50 represents the relative amount spent for wheat, and wheat is $1 a bushel, the quantity of wheat bought will be 50 bushels.

TABLE XX.
MULTIPLE STANDARD.

| 1 | 2 | 3 | 4 |
|---|---|---|---|
| Meat | $100 | $10. per cwt. | 10 cwt. meat. |
| Butter, milk, etc.. | 75 | 15. per cwt. | 5 cwt. dairy products |
| Sugar | 20 | 4. per cwt. | 5 cwt. sugar. |
| Coffee and tea | 20 | 20. per cwt. | 1 cwt. coffee & tea. |
| Wheat | 50 | 1. per bush. | 50 bushels wheat. |
| Oats | 25 | 1.5 per cwt. | 17 cwt. oats. |
| Coal | 60 | 3. per ton. | 20 tons coal. |
| Leather | 30 | 20. per cwt. | 1½ cwt. leather. |
| Cotton | 20 | 10. per cwt. | 2 cwt. cotton. |
| Wool | 40 | 40. per cwt. | 1 cwt. wool. |
| Metals | 50 | 2.5 per cwt. | 20 cwt. metals. |
| Wood | 50 | 25. per cwt. | 2 cwt. wood. |
| | $540 | | |

The quantities in the fourth column with their total value $540 constitute the composite or multiple standard.[4]

---

[4] Different units of weight and measure are used to show that no uniformity in this respect is requisite. Some of the items in this table are

These quantities are made the standard just as the law now makes 23.22 grains of gold the standard for a dollar. In the real work of the Commission the prices of the third column, instead of being the current rates at the time of putting the system into effect, might be the averages for 5 or 10 years so as to bring the dollar to a level representing its past average for the time during which existing debts and obligations were contracted.[5]

The Multiple Standard being made and published as above suggested, let us now make up our first report on the condition of prices and the currency. We place in column A the quantities from column 4, Table XX, which compose the standard. In column B we write the average prices obtained from the market records of New York, Chicago, etc., during the past month. In column C appear amounts obtained by multiplying the quantities of column A by the prices of column B.

TABLE XXI

| A | B | | C |
|---|---|---|---|
| Meat, 10 cwt. | $9 | per cwt. | $90 |
| Dairy, 5 cwt. | 14 | per cwt. | 70 |
| Sugar, 5 cwt | 4 | per cwt. | 20 |
| Coffee and tea, 1 cwt. | 20 | per cwt. | 20 |
| Wheat, 50 bush. | 0¾ | per bush. | 37.5 |
| Oats, 17 cwt | 1 | per cwt. | 17 |
| Coal, 20 tons | 4 | per ton. | 80 |
| Leather, 1½ cwt | 22 | per cwt. | 33 |
| Cotton, 2 cwt | 10 | per cwt. | 20 |
| Wool, 1 cwt | 38 | per cwt. | 38 |
| Metals, 20 cwt | .2 | per cwt. | 40 |
| Wood, 2 cwt | 26 | per cwt. | 52 |
| | | | $517.5 |

definite and simple, but others are complex. The item "metals," for example, is made up of iron, steel, lead, tin, copper, zinc, gold, silver, etc. If tin be taken as the unit of consumption, zinc will be about 5, lead and copper each 20, iron 600, silver 1-10, and gold 1-100, so that altho gold costs thirty thousand times as much as iron, yet as there is 60,000 times as much iron used as gold, the effect of iron upon the metal average is double that of gold. Meat, dairy products and other items are also composite. For the sake of easy checking by the public it would be best to require the Commission to state each separate item, pig iron, gold, silver, lead, beef, pork, mutton, granulated sugar, etc., clearly defining the precise grade of quality of every item. We have bunched some items in order to save space and avoid too much detail.

(⁵) It would be best also to consider retail prices and the distribution of final expenditure as well as wholesale prices and relative wholesale expenditure or proportional amounts of total product, or else transportation and the cost of distributing products should be entered as specific items with their due weight. The price and relative importance of commodities at retail could be entered in the table along with the price and relative importance of the same commodities at wholesale, the retail and wholesale items being weighted so as to have the same relation to each other that exists in the retail and wholesale trade. It has been customary to rely on wholesale prices alone; but this does not seem wise or just.

A comparison of the footing of column C with the total value in the original or standard table (XX) shows that the price level of the standard commodities has fallen from $540 to $517.5—$22.5 or 4.46 per cent. below the normal level. Interest would therefore fall a notch or two at the Postal Savings Banks, or the Government would buy securities, or call in and pay off some bonds; or if interest were left to private adjustment, it would go up and Goverment bonds would begin to come in of themselves. Any one of these moves would increase the volume of money and tend to bring prices up to the normal level again. Precisely how much increase of volume would be necessary to effect a given alteration in the price level under given conditions could only be ascertained by experience.

At the end of the second month we would make out another table, and if the price level were still below the normal level we would further increase the money volume. If prices had gone above the normal we would decrease it. And so month after month we would check the rise or fall of prices and keep the dollar very close to the line, now a little above, now a little below, but never soaring into the clouds or falling thru long years of ruin and despair.

Every year or so the weighting of the standard commodities should be tested, and if it is found that their relative importance has changed, the weighting should be corrected.

It is entirely possible to adjust our standard table so that the normal sum of values shall be an even number like $100,000 or $100 or $1. For example, take Prof. Smith's table of total annual product of corn, wheat, cotton, oats, silver and gold and the wholesale value of each.

TABLE XXII.

| P<br>Commodity | Q<br>Quantity. | R<br>Wholesale.<br>Price. | S<br>Wholesale.<br>Value. |
|---|---|---|---|
| Corn | 1,600,000,000 bush. | $0.50 per bush. | $800,000,000 |
| Wheat | 500,000,000 bush. | 1.00 per bush. | 500,000,000 |
| Cotton | 3,500,000,000 lbs. | .10 per lb. | 350,000,000 |
| Oats | 625,000,000 bush. | .40 per bush. | 250,000,000 |
| Silver | 70,000,000 oz. | 1.00 per oz. | 70,000,000 |
| Gold | 1,450,676 oz. | 20.68 per oz. | 30,000,000 |
| Total | | | $2,000,000,000 |

Now suppose we wish to make a composite standard that will have a value of $100. The value of corn in column S is eight-twentieths or two-fifths of the total value of all the products represented. Corn would, therefore, occupy two-fifths of the standard, or $40 (two-fifths of $100 the total value to be covered by the standard). Wheat is five-twentieths or one-fourth of the total in column S, wherefore giving wheat the same relative importance in the standard that it has in the table of annual production and consumption, it would appropriate one-fourth or $25 of the $100 chosen for the standard total. Treating the other commodities in the same way, and dividing the value of each that enters into the standard by the price of each per bushel, pound or ounce, we get the quantity of each that enters into the standard.

TABLE XXIII.

| U | V | W | X |
|---|---|---|---|
| Commodity | Value of it that enters the standard. | Price. | Quantity that enters the standard. |
| Corn | $40 | $0.50 per bush. | 80 bush. corn. |
| Wheat | 25 | 1.00 per bush. | 25 bush. wheat. |
| Cotton | 17.5 | .10 a lb. | 175 lbs cotton. |
| Oats | 12.5 | .40 per bush. | 31¼ bush. oats. |
| Silver | 3.5 | 1.00 per oz. | 3½ oz. silver. |
| Gold | 1.5 | 20.68 per oz. | 34 1-3 grs. gold. |
| Total | $100 | | |

At the end of each month or tabular period we take the standard quantities in column X, multiply by the new average price per bushel, pound or ounce, which emerges from the records of the month, and add the products to find how much, if any, the average level of prices has varied from the $100 normal value of the standard. These processes carried out, not merely with half a dozen or a dozen commodities, but with one or two hundred well chosen items, would afford a rational basis for a scientific money system.

### MASSACHUSETTS MULTIPLE MONEY.

It is interesting to know that Massachusetts, more than a century ago adopted a multiple standard as the basis of notes issued to settle balances due to the State's quota of the Continental Army. The law regulated the value of the notes by the value of a composite standard composed of fixed quantities of corn, beef, wool and sole leather. The standard adopted was 5 bushels of corn, *plus* 68 4-7 pounds of beef, *plus* 10 pounds of sheep's wool, *plus* 16 pounds of sole leather, *equals* £130.

On the following page is a fac-simile of one of the notes issued in 1780.[6]

### OBJECTIONS.

The chief objections likely to be raised against the Multiple Standard are political, international, or selfish. To the claim that it is dangerous to entrust the Government with the power of regulating the currency, we reply:

First: That the power is already entrusted to the Government; and not only that, but the decisions of the Supreme Court make it clear that the trust is a mandatory one. The Federal Constitution makes it the duty of the National Government to regulate the currency, and a trustee does not fulfil his duty unless he uses the best available means to carry out his trust. Not only does the Government *possess* the power of issuing and regulating money, but it has exercised the power to great advantage, even tho the plan adopted was far from perfect. The war paper was a marked success. Only when we began to retire it in order to go back to gold did disaster overtake us.

Second. The *automatic* action of the system will of itself keep the variations of prices within narrow limits. Even if no official were empowered to increase or diminish the currency, the new standard would be a great gain.

Third. The *publicity*, *definiteness* and *importance* of the standard and its operation would constitute a strong protection against fraud. As Hon. Henry Winn says: "The commission would hang out a barometer of monetary value whereby all men could see, not only what the government ought to do, but what it was actually doing, and whether it was acting

---

[6] The note itself is the property of Hon. Henry Winn, and was by his courtesy reproduced in The Arena for September, 1897, in illustration of a paragraph in Mr. Eltweed Pomeroy's article in that number of the magazine.

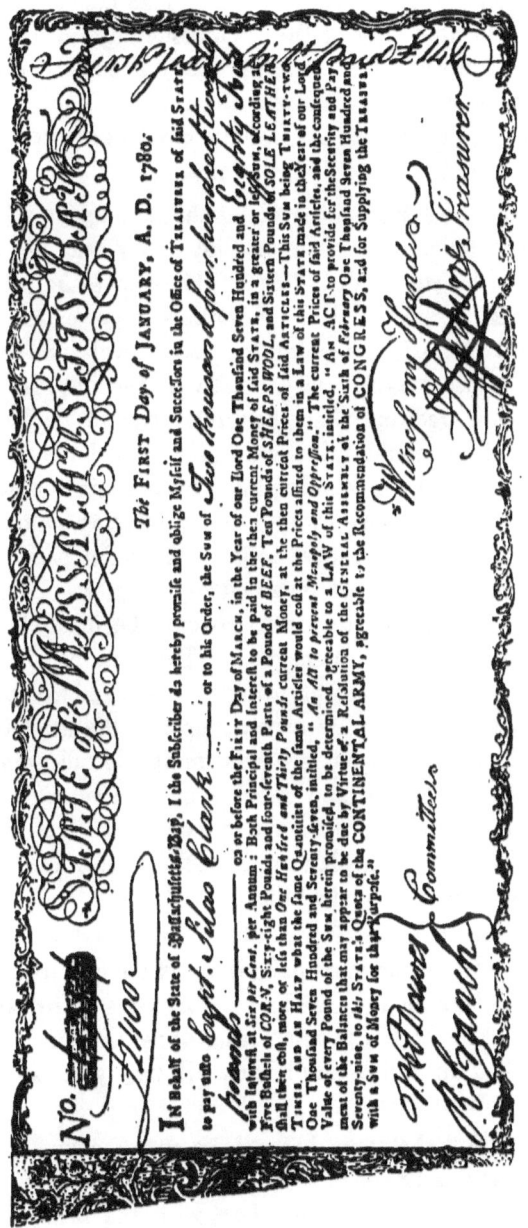

honestly. There could be no fraud in that barometer, for every trade paper gives the prices, and any man could detect an error in the printed data of the commission, and discover the true index number. That a people accustomed to a price barometer, and knowing that it ought and could be kept close to 100, would permit their money, as ours has, to grow so bad that it would stand at 170, or 200, is almost unthinkable."

Fourth. It could be enacted that debts should be payable at standard values, no matter whether the money was at, or above, or below the standard. This would remove the principal motive that executive officers and others in power might have to fail in their duty of keeping the dollar level. Such a provision would also make it very greatly to the interest of both debtors and creditors that the dollar should be kept normal, since neither could gain by an abnormal dollar, and the settlements would be much simplified by keeping the dollar steady. These great classes would therefore bring a strong pressure to bear in favor of a level dollar. A similar pressure would come from those who receive and pay salaries. If the dollar went below the line, the former would be injured; if above, the latter would be damaged. The said provision would further have the effect of bringing the standard into court, and subjecting it and its management to the most intense scrutiny. The provision, however, might detract somewhat from the smoothness and facility of commerce, and would, we think, be quite unnecessary in view of the fact that the automatic features of the plan would at the most, leave but a very narrow margin to official action.

Fifth. No monetary control would be exercised by the Government that is not far more dangerous where it is to-day. No public control of money can be so dangerous as private control. The agents of the people acting under definite provisions of law, and under the public eye, will surely do better than chance and Wall Street.

Another objection that may be made is that the multiple standard (especially if linked with a system of Postal Savings Banks as it ought to be) will interfere with the profits of private banking. This objection is likely to be far the most difficult to overcome. In fact it is the only one that has any real vitality or resisting power. And the answer that private interests must yield to public is not apt to be satisfactory to the men whose private interests are affected. These men have a powerful grip on affairs of state, and their opposition is no child's play. All private profits on the circulation of bank notes will cease, and the Postal Banks will be so much safer than private banks that they may absorb a large proportion of deposits. This fact, together with loans at low interest, and the facilities and safety of transmitting money thru an institution with an office in every town and having the entire wealth and power of the nation back of it, would be likely to considerably diminish the business of private banks, and might, in the course of a few years, make private banking quite unprofitable. The Multiple system could be adopted without Postal Banks and would then very slightly affect the legitimate business of private banks. This might be a good way at first, but to bring the plan to its full perfection Postal Banks must be ultimately established, and it is not improbable that we may in fact get the Postal Banks before we achieve the Multiple Standard; and if so, their establishment will greatly facilitate the introduction of the Multiple Standard. Beyond question there is force in the objection that a good money system would be dangerous to the banks. But the all sufficient answer is that individual profit must yield to the public good.[7] If the matter be examined on a plane above mere dollars and cents, the Multiple Standard will benefit even the bankers; for as men and citizens their interests are identical with the welfare of their country.

The objection chiefly relied on in the public utterances of those who oppose an independent money, is that the discontinuance of a metallic standard would disturb our international relations, and injure our foreign commerce, it being affirmed that to carry on foreign trade to good advantage requires a money that will pass in Europe. As a matter of fact, however, foreign payments are not made in money,[8] and if

---

[7] Justice Strong delivering the opinion of the U. S. Supreme Court in the famous Legal Tender Cases, said "A new tariff, an embargo, a draft, or a war may inevitably bring upon individuals great losses; may, indeed,

they were, it is probable that our independent paper would be taken in Europe at its face value, less brokerage and transportation, just as readily as our metallic money. Practically the whole of our foreign commerce is carried on by means of bills of exchange. Balances are settled with commodities; when gold is used it is used as a commodity, not as money; as bullion, not as coin. It could be used in the same way, no matter what sort of a home-currency we had. If it could not be had in this country, a cargo of wheat, beef, cotton, or other commodity could be sent over the sea, sold in Europe for coin or bullion or bills, and the debt settled with that. Such shipments of commodities are the fundamental facts in international commerce. It is upon such facts that bills of exchange are based. Foreign exchanges would go on all right without an ounce of gold. We were on a paper base for 17 years during and after the war, and our merchants did not mention any inconvenience resulting therefrom in their trade with other nations. Russia is on a paper basis now, but her commerce is not disturbed by that fact. Silver countries trade with gold

---

render valuable property almost worthless. They may destroy the worth of contracts. But whoever supposed that because of this, a tariff could not be changed, or an embargo enacted, or a war declared." (12 Wallace at 551.) The Justice also instanced the damage that may be done to creditors by passing a bankrupt act (p. 549). We might mention the grant of a franchise that partly or wholly destroys the value of a former grant or business. When a bridge or railway franchise is not expressly made exclusive, a new bridge or railway may be built or authorized by the state, tho the value of the former franchise is thereby completely destroyed. (Charles River Bridge v. Warren Bridge, 7 Pick., 344; 11 Peters, 420, 536, 546, 549; Turnpike Co. v. State, 3 Wallace, 210.)

(⁹) Mr. Fonda says in "Honest Money:" "International trade is an exchange of commodities; not, to be sure, a direct barter, but an indirect one. * * It would make no difference in the foreign trade of any country if it did not possess an ounce of gold or of silver, or whether its money was based on gold or was inconvertible paper." Walter Bagehot, in "A Universal Money," says that the rates of exchange are not determined by the nature of the currency, but by the relative AMOUNTS of the settlements to be made in each direction between the two countries. "If France and America had the same currencies as England, it would still happen, as now, that bills on Paris or New York would be at a discount or a premium. The amount of money wishing to go eastward across the Atlantic, and the amount wishing to go westward, would then, as now, settle how much was to be paid in London for bills on New York, and how much was to be paid in New York for bills on London." In the Medical World for October, '97, Dr. C. F. Taylor says: "With paper money on a multiple standard our foreign exchanges would be conducted just as they are now. * * The value of each commodity would be calculated on the basis of its real value, first in the medium of its own country, and then translated into the other according to the exchange value, which is governed by laws of comparative values, and is never difficult to discover. Bills of exchange are emitted by dealers in foreign exchange, on the basis of the comparative value of the two mediums, each in its own country. Our money, of whatever kind, is worth in a foreign country just what it is worth here. less brokerage and transportation."

In his "Recent Economic Changes," Mr. David A. Wells cites the testimony of members and directors of English Chambers of Commerce to the effect that there is no difficulty in negotiating exchange or conducting foreign trade between silver countries and gold countries.

countries without any difficulty. The rates of exchange vary somewhat from time to time, but so they do between New York and London, which have the same standard, and between Great Britain and Australia, which not only have the same standard, but the same money unit.

Even if it were true that independent money would be detrimental to foreign commerce, the objection would have but little weight as against the advantage of such money to domestic commerce, since the latter forms 96 per cent. of our total business against only 4 per cent. foreign trade.

The truth is that an independent money, instead of being a disadvantage in respect to our foreign relations, would be of the greatest service in shutting out foreign panics, and freeing us from the disturbing influence of changes in foreign markets, mines and Governments. The disastrous crises of 1825 and 1837 came to us from over the sea. It was the fall of prices and failure of banks in Great Britain that deranged our finances. We were on a metallic base. The appreciation of the metallic standard there caused an appreciation of it here, and money became harder to get, instead of taking the place of retiring credit. But in 1866 a very severe panic occurred in England without affecting our industries to any perceptible degree, because we were on an independent paper basis, and a change in English prices and the value of the English standard did not disturb the value of our currency at all. Hon. Henry Winn, in a magazine article soon to appear, has a fine passage on this point, which he has kindly allowed me to quote. "To-day every foreign panic or corner in gold, every state buying to hoard, draws away gold from our money volume and deranges by fluctuation in price our domestic exchanges. We remember how prices tumbled and we were thrown into panic conditions thru sympathy with London when the Barings failed in 1890. But in 1866 when we were on an independent paper standard, a panic fell on London so much more severe that the bank act was suspended for the Bank of England. It sent up the price of gold here of course, but it caused hardly a ripple in our domestic trade. Martin, in his 'History of the Boston Stock Market,' boasts that in June, 1866 money stood at 5 to 6 per cent., actually 1 per cent. cheaper than the month before, and was 'abundant while the bank rate in London was 10 per cent.[9] and a panic in the market.' The lowest quotations for railroad stock were far higher than the year before, and the dividends of Massachusetts factories showed wonderful prosperity."

In the very matter, therefore, mainly relied on for the support of the gold standard, we find that independent paper is superior. It would be an excellent thing to have an international money, *if* the various nations involved would adopt the multiple standard; but until that time arrives there will be an immense advantage in having a separate standard—a standard that will keep on the even tenor of its way regardless of foreign crises and contingencies. We must never forget that the fundamental fact, the prime requisite, the crucial test of good money is steadiness of value. As Professor Smith remarks, "No argument for international money is sound which fails to recognize that the first requisite of a good monetary system is steadiness of value."

### ADVANTAGES.

The Multiple Standard will be just.

It will not defraud labor.

It will not defraud debtors.

It will not defraud creditors.

It will stop the waste of digging gold for a use that paper can serve at almost no cost.

It will free $1,200,000,000 of the people's capital that is now locked up in metallic money. This gold and silver could be used in productive industry, or sent away to buy American securities held abroad, and pay American debts in foreign countries, relieving us of a considerable burden of interest, increasing the volume of money and raising prices across the water, whereby a better market would be made for our products, and a bit of the prosperity that comes with the impetus of rising prices would be introduced into Europe.

---

([9]) The ordinary rate of the Bank of England is 2 or 3 per cent.

It would check gambling and speculation. No more rocking of our finances by the cornering of gold. No more long, steep slopes of rising prices, nor financial precipices, with their catastrophes to honest industry and engorgements of parasites and beasts of prey.

It would not build a new bonded debt thru an endless chain of withdrawing gold from the Treasury with Greenbacks, paying it in again for bonds, and again withdrawing it till the Government has to issue more bonds to get it back, and so on.

It would not subject the Government to the ignominy of hiring a foreign syndicate to maintain the treasury reserve, and "preserve the faith of the nation."

It would not make the war debt heavier after more than two-thirds of it had been paid than it was at the close of the struggle.

It would ease the burdens of debt without injustice to the creditor, by enabling the debtor to avail himself of inventions and improvements in production instead of bestowing the whole advantages of social progress upon the creditor, as gold with its falling prices does now. To give the benefit of improved production to the active instead of the passive classes is not unjust, but very distinctly just.

It would recognize the vast importance of the movement of the money volume, by means of which average prices may be made to rise or fall, or remain stationary, and it would subject this movement to intelligent control in the public interest instead of leaving it to chance and private manipulation.

It would provide a practically invariable standard of value, and a medium of exchange whose variations of value would be slight. The trifling departures of the dollar one way or the other from the standard in the intervals between the tabular reports would be like the swelling and shrinking of a steel ruler under changing temperatures, and could not accumulate or go far enough to materially affect the truth of its measurements in exchange, the settlement of debt, etc.

It would afford a money in accord with common sense and scientific principles—a currency capable of performing *all* the functions of money with *reasonable perfection*.

It would favor prevision, and so increase the steadiness of business. The movement of prices in the fall caused by the annual movement of the crops and the settlement of the year's accounts could be anticipated and prevented by an increase of the currency volume in September or October, on the same principle that a wise manufacturer prevents overpressure on his engines and workmen by using more machines and employing a larger force when he has more work to do.

It would prevent panics. There would still be individual failures and possibly local flurries, but no panics. A panic is the product of fear. Something makes men suspect credit, and it shrinks. Cash instead of becoming more plenty than usual to fill the place of the departed, takes flight itself. It becomes difficult to get money even at ruinous interest. To pay their debts merchants slaughter prices, and widespread ruin follows the fall. We all know the story. It is lack of elastic money that turns the failure of a few speculators into a national disaster. Under the Multiple Standard the Government will stand ready at all times to furnish any amount of money necessary to prevent the fall of prices. There will be no money famine, no big interest, no need for men really sound to sell at a loss. The very knowledge that the Nation will issue funds and lend money at a reasonable interest in any needful quantity will prevent the fear and distrust of the future, which makes men " rush into the market and outvie each other in selling goods at a loss."

It will benefit all classes of the community except the wreckers and parasites.

It will carry out the constitution, destroy a dangerous special privilege, and return to the sovereign people as a real possession, one of the most important of sovereign powers, the power of issuing and regulating the money of the country.

It will be as good in war as in peace. The multiple dollar would not go to foreign parts in time of danger, but it would stay at home, equip our armies, and go with the cannon to the front of the fight.

It would free our financial system from the baneful influence of foreign disturbances. Not only would we be safe from foreign panics and the vicissitudes of foreign mines and markets, but the ups and downs of foreign legislation would affect us but slightly as compared with the present.

It would operate as a beneficient influence in the regulation of industry and the distribution of wealth. Neither landlord nor tenant, laborer nor employer, capitalist nor entrepreneur would be deceived or defrauded by it. It would beget neither feverish excitement nor despair, but the calm serenity that comes with certainty of prevision. The man of enterprise could invest his money, employ his workmen, and make his contracts with assurance that his calculations would not be brought to nought and his enterprise be wrecked by an unforseen change in the value of money.

It would greatly increase the wealth of our people, not merely by saving the waste of digging gold for monetary use and part of the waste of speculation, but by putting a stop to the disastrous panics and depressions that now cripple our productive industries.

Finally the Multiple Standard would have a beneficient influence morally and socially. Its tendency would be to turn men from feverish speculation, and to relieve in some degree the pressure of financial anxiety for the future. It would tend to remove one of the great antagonisms of interest in society. Social cohesion would be promoted, and a frame of mind developed more favorable to thought, to art, to quiet home life, to development of man and society on planes above the level of dollars and cents. It would cancel some of the causes that are producing undue accumulation of wealth and power in the hands of a moneyed aristocracy, would tend toward democracy and the diffusion of wealth. It would dispose of one of the great questions that are absorbing the attention of the people, and so make room for discussion of other weighty problems awaiting decision. In every way it would tend toward justice, harmony. equality and progress.

# CHAPTER IV.

### THE AUTHORITIES.

Distinguished leaders of thought, eminent economists, illustrious statesmen, renowned jurists and famous financiers have affirmed the principles on which this book is based. The need of a better monetary system rests upon two propositions.
1. The great importance of steady money—the moral and economic need of a dollar of unchanging power of purchase.
2. The unsteadiness of gold and silver.

These two facts are affirmed or admitted by all the leading authorities.

The claims of the Multiple Standard rest upon three propositions.
1. The importance of steadiness.
2. The unsteadiness of a metallic standard.
3. The steadiness of a composite commodity standard.

This third proposition is also admitted or affirmed by all authorities to whom the thought of a composite standard has presented itself.

The establishment of a money that shall remain constant in its purchasing power requires the co-ordination of the dollar and the multiple standard—the incorporation of the said standard in the monetary system as the basis of the circulating medium, and involves four propositions.
1. The importance of steadiness.
2. The unsteadiness of the precious metals.
3. The steadiness of the multiple commodity standard.
4. The practicability of keeping the dollar in harmony with the multiple commodity standard by careful regulation of the money volume.

The fourth proposition, like the third, is affirmed or admitted by all authorities conversant with any of the methods of regulation proposed in the last chapter. The earlier writers dealing with the money question before the fourth proposition had been worked out, do not take the final step, and some of the later writers, tho recognizing the fourth proposition, think the time has not yet come to apply it, because they deem the Government as yet unfit to be trusted with such work. This plea was answered in the third chapter, but even if there were no answer to it, even if there were no way of checking the work so that it would be safe in the hands of Government officials to-day, still the plea would have no force as against the multiple money system as such, but only against its immediate adoption. It would only afford an additional reason to put forth every effort for the purification of Government so that it may be fit to administer a rational system of finance.

Many of the authorities who have most fully discussed the Multiple Standard, have been quoted in the third chapter. We will confine our attention now to the views of some of the most widely known thinkers who have not been dealt with sufficiently in previous chapters.

### PRESIDENT WALKER.

The late General Francis A. Walker, President of the Massachusetts Institute of Technology and former Chief of the Census, was the leading American economist, and our foremost writer on monetary science. His text-books are used in Oxford on an equality with the writings of Professor Alfred Marshall.

President Walker says: "It is evident that to enable an article to perform the function of a standard for deferred payments, a certain steadiness in value is essential." ("Money," p. 36.) "The object of a standard for deferred payments being to secure the payment, at the maturity of obligations, of substantially the same purchasing power that was in contemplation of the parties at the formation of the contract, it is conceivable that a paper money might be so regulated as to preserve a more uniform value, from generation to generation, than the precious metals have maintained during any considerable period of the world's history. We have seen that that is the weak point of the precious metals in their use as money." (Ibid., p. 377.)

"The production of the precious metals is of the most spasmodic character. At times, a flood of gold, or of silver, or of both, has poured from newly-opened mines, as after the discovery of the mines of Potosi in 1545, and of the mines of California almost coincidently with those of Australia, in 1849-51; at times, on the other hand, mining industry has almost wholly ceased, either from the exhaustion of known deposits, or as the result of war or civil disturbance. Such a cessation of mining industry followed the invasion of the Roman Empire by the Teutonic tribes. The series of revolutions and insurrections in the Spanish States, beginning in 1809, destroyed the mining machinery, scattered the mining populations, and closed the mines of regions which had previously been among the most prolific sources of the world's supply of metallic money." (Pol. Ec., p. 141.)

President Walker then speaks of the comparative steadiness of agricultural products, showing that there is much reason to regard "Bread-corn as, in truth what Francis Horner pronounced it to be, 'the real and paramount standard of all values.'" A remark which must be taken with some qualifications, but which is very forcible and covers an important truth. President Walker continues: "The superior stability of value of the cereals, thru long periods of time, has led to the suggestion that, in the case of contracts extending over considerable terms of years, grain should be adopted as the standard for determining the obligations of the debtor, the rights of the creditor." (Pol. Ec., p. 142.)

Locke favored this idea in his paper on "The Value of Money," and the principle has been put to practical use in the corn-rents so long in use in England, and which have proved so much more stable in value than money. "We are forced to admit," says Prof. Jevons, "that the statesmen of Queen Elizabeth were far-seeing when they passed the act which obliged the colleges of Oxford, Cambridge and Eton to lease their lands for corn-rents. The result has been to make those colleges far richer than they would otherwise have been, the rents and endowments expressed in money having sunk to a fraction of their ancient value." ("Money," p. 159.)

After speaking of these corn-rents, President Walker remarks that a proposition has been made by Jevons and others to establish a multiple or tabular standard by joining a great number of articles together so that their individual value variations may offset each other, whereby the undeserved losses resulting to debtors and creditors from changes in the precious metals may be avoided. ("Political Economy," § 191.)

Discussing the proposed Multiple Standard, General Walker affirms that, "Certainly, as Prof. Jevons says, such a standard would add a wholly new degree of stability to social relations, securing the fixed income of individuals and public institutions from the depreciation which they have often suffered." ("Money," p. 161.)

"Certainly the need of such a standard of deferred payments is most imperative in the case of those who are not in the way of repairing any losses they may suffer thru fluctuations in the value of money, upon whom the full effects of depreciation fall directly and remain without relief." (Pol. Ec., p. 374.)

"The effect of the introduction of the tabular standard would be to decide how much money at that date constituted the equivalent in the power to purchase the necessaries, comforts and luxuries of life, of the money which would have been paid had the sale been for cash. In short, it is a means of giving and taking credit without receiving an unearned advantage or suffering an undeserved injury thru fluctuations in the value of money." (Pol. Ec., p. 373.)

President Walker, while thus pronouncing in favor of the Multiple Standard as a basis for deferred payments, does not appear to have considered the question of regulating the volume of money so as to keep the dollar in harmony with the said standard. This final element not entering his thought, he was a bi-metallist, advocating the use of the Multiple Standard in deferred payments.

### PRESIDENT ANDREWS.

E. Benjamin Andrews, the honored President of Brown University, is one of the best known economists on this side of the water. In his Institutes of Economics, section 87, he says: "The best monetary systems yet used are very imperfect, permitting the most unhappy fluctuations in the purchase-power of their units, discouraging enterprise and robbing now debtors, now creditors! Bi-metalism would relieve, yet only temporarily. The time must come when Governments will be authorized (i) to watch, thru competent commissions, for each rise or fall in the value of money (fall or rise of general prices), and (ii) to correct the same by expanding or contracting the circulation."

In his "Honest Dollar," 1889, pp. 8-39, President Andrews says: "Money, besides furnishing our system of value-denominations, measures value, serves as a reservoir of value, and as a standard for deferred payments. To fulfill ideally any one of the last-named offices it must preserve its general purchasing power unchanged. Increase in the value of money robs debtors. * * * Decrease in the value of money robs creditors. * * * It is very often taken for granted that the gold dollar must be an honest dollar, and one may hear this alleged in the same breath with the admission made by all, that money is good in proportion to its stability of value. The two positions are of course contradictory, except upon the pretense, which no well-informed person will offer, that gold never appreciates or depreciates. * * * Gold is produced under the law of diminishing return, and hence must in the long future grow more and more scarce, its cost of production greater and greater, while most of the commodities trafficked in by means of money are not under this law, are to grow cheaper and cheaper forever, and almost none are so completely in the clutch of the law as gold is.

* * * The fall of prices since 1873 has been a terrible calamity, but it has occurred in spite of us, and here we are. The evil, as a whole, a general rise of prices would not correct, but only repeat. We have struck a new base line of prices; let us plant ourselves upon it, and see to it that we are not forced to change again, whether up or down.

"If the rehabilitation of silver as full legal tender would fully and finally keep change of prices from recurring, I would advocate it in spite of its immediate injustice. But it certainly would not.

The relief would be partial and temporary. We should never be certain that maximum and minimum total production of metal would synchronize respectively with maximum and minimum need, while we should be certain that in the long run production must fall behind need. * * *

"So Mr. Giffen concedes, Contemp. Rev., vol. xlvii, pp. 800 seq. Cf. Robertson, Westm. Rev., Oct. 1880. Cf. also Contemp. Rev., vol. 51, p. 359, note. More instructive than all these are the critical views of America's chief geologists and metallurgists, set forth in Consular Report No. 87, December, 1887. They nearly all agree with the well-known conclusions of Suess, in his *Zukunft des Goldes*. N. S. Shaler thinks that the output of both gold and silver must henceforth gradually decrease, and that 'gold is more likely to become an article of increased cost within the coming half century than any other metal,' tho we are 'liable to many sudden increments in the production thereof.' J. D. Hague is of opinion that while gold may slightly increase in yearly supply, silver can hardly fail to go the other way. R. H. Richards concludes almost exactly with Shaler. J. S. Newberry utters, as the result of his long experience, the conviction that our production of both gold and silver has passed its maximum, and that in future we cannot expect a yield of more than perhaps one-half the greatest annual product of gold. Not only America's but 'the world's stock of gold will gradually decline from the diminished supply, the increased consumption in the arts, the abrasion of coin, etc.' The outlook, he thinks, is much the same for silver.

"R. H. Inglis Palgrave, in his memorandum printed as Appendix B. to the final Report of the (1886) British Commission on the Depression of Trade and Industry, says that even now, in spite of its wide demonetization, the employment of silver for coinage purposes appears to exceed the net production."

After discussing at length the history of gold fluctuations, President Andrews says: "Is this plague necessary? Must it be perpetual? Is the commercial world, the entire money-using world, to be forever tormented with this accursed up and down in the purchasing power of money * * * *

"Are we to despair of stability in general prices? I believe not. I am impressed with the practicability of preserving prices permanently at whatever level they have at any time assumed, by swelling or contracting the volume of money in circulation, on some such plan as has been outlined by Professor Walras, of Lausanne. The method would involve (1) the critical, official ascertainment of the course of prices; (2) the use of some form of subsidiary full legal tender money; and (3) the injection of a portion of this into circulation or the withdrawal of a portion therefrom, according as prices had fallen or risen. * * * *

"The universally conceded equity of a composite value-standard would in this way be incorporated in the monetary system itself, and would spread to all the exchange transactions of the nation. The very knowledge of an existing purpose thus to regulate would do much to regulate.

"Walras's project differs from this as follows: He would work *a priori*. He judges that the volume of commerce, the volume of money, and the relation between the two can all be so closely figured out and followed that threatened changes in general prices may be forecast and prevented. I would be less presumptuous, and apply the needed corrective in an *a posteriori* way."

President Andrews advises the use of call bonds as the best means of regulating the volume and value of money. His preference would be, not to discard the precious metals, but to buy silver and coin it and issue silver certificates, adding to or subtracting from their volume in circulation by calling in or selling the bonds. His reason for continuing the use of metal as a backing for the currency is the additional security thereby obtained. But the danger is, that convertibility into gold or silver at fixed weights would subject the currency to disturbing influences that would make it impossible to keep the dollar steady, and the silver backing, moreover, appears to be an entirely useless expense. (See Chaps. 2 and 3.) President Andrews admits that if we are to continue the use of gold and seek to steady its value by means of the Multiple Standard and regulation of the money volume, an international agreement would be necessary.

### PROFESSOR MARSHALL.

Prof. Alfred Marshall, of Cambridge University, England, is the leading English writer on Political Economy since Mill." In an article in the Contemporary Review for March, 1887, he says: "The precious metals cannot afford a good standard of value." He then says in substance that bi-metallism would tend toward greater steadiness than monometallism, but would not go very far, for at best it would substitute the mean between two fluctuating supplies in place of one fluctuating supply. He believes, however, that bi-metallism is the next step in the direction of a steadier money. After speaking of Ricardo's plan for using a paper currency, based not on coin, but on stamped gold bars weighing 20 ounces each, he outlines a bi-metallic scheme consisting of paper money redeemable in gold and silver, 56½ grains of gold plus 1130 grains of silver to the pound. The holder of a pound note could not demand full payment in gold nor full payment in silver, but must take part of each in a fixed ratio. One of his reasons for advocating this plan, Professor Marshall says, is the fact that "It is a movement in the direction in which we want to go, of a tabular standard for deferred payments."

In the same article Professor Marshall discusses the regulation of the money volume in order to keep the dollar in harmony with the "unit" value of a multiple standard. He does not appear to think that the time has come for a practical realization of such regulation, but his remarks are important and suggestive, especially when viewed in the light of the words above quoted from him. He says:

"Mr. Walras has proposed to steady the value of gold by issuing or withdrawing token silver coins according as gold rose or fell in value. His scheme is able and ingenious. But as he admits, it would, like any other scheme for regulating the value of gold and silver, require an international agreement. And I do not see how this could be managed, because, to say nothing of minor difficulties, there cannot be a common unit of purchasing power for all countries. Every plan for regulating the supply of the currency, so that its value shall be constant, must, I think, be national and not international.

"I will indicate briefly two such plans, tho I do not advocate either of them. On the first plan the currency would be inconvertible. An automatic Government Department would buy consols for currency whenever £1 was worth more than a unit, and would sell consols for currency whenever it was worth less. Those who had to pay balances to foreign countries would buy gold or silver in the open market; they would be certain of getting in exchange for this money gold and silver that had a fixed purchasing power in England. The researches of Mr. Palgrave and Dr. Soetbeer show that a unit of fixed purchasing power in England would give a more nearly uniform purchasing power in any other civilized country than would an ounce of gold or an ounce of silver. On the whole, this currency would, I believe, give more stability to our foreign trade than our present one.

"The other plan is, that of a convertible currency, each one pound note giving the right to demand at a Government office as much gold as at that time had the value of half a unit, together with as much silver as had the value of half a unit. The necessary provisions for keeping a proper reserve of gold and silver would be a little intricate, but would involve no great practical difficulty. Under either of these plans, contracts for deferred payments might be made fairly well in terms of the currency."

### PROFESSOR JEVONS.

W. Stanley Jevons, Professor of Political Economy in Owen's College, Manchester, Eng., has a worldwide reputation as one of the foremost writers on monetary science. His writings are used as text-books in universities and colleges all over the English-speaking world.

In his "Money and the Mechanism of Exchange," written in 1874-5, he says:

"It is evidently desirable that the currency should not be subject to fluctuations of value. The ratios in which money exchanges for other commodities should be maintained as nearly as possible invariable on the average." (P. 38.)

Speaking of the plans of Lowe, Scrope, and others, for a tabular or multiple standard of value to be used as the basis of settlement in long contracts, Jevons says:

"Such schemes for a tabular or average standard of value appear to be perfectly sound and highly valuable in a theoretical point of view, and the practical difficulties are not of a serious character. To carry Lowe's and Scrope's plans into effect, a permanent Government commission would have to be created, and endowed with a kind of judicial power. The officers of the department would collect the current prices of commodities in all the principal markets of the kingdom, and, by a well-defined system of calculations, would compute from these data the average variations in the purchasing power of gold. The decisions of this commission would be published monthly, and payments would be adjusted in accordance with them. Thus, suppose that a debt of one hundred pounds was incurred upon the 1st of July, 1875, and was to be paid back on 1st of July, 1878; if the commission had decided in June, 1878, that the value of gold had fallen in the ratio of 106 to 100 in the intervening years, then the creditor would claim an increase of 6 per cent. in the nominal amount of the debt.

"At first the use of this National tabular standard might be permissive so that it could be enforced only where the parties to the contract had inserted a clause to that effect in their contract. After the practicability and utility of the plan had become sufficiently demonstrated, it might be made compulsory, in the sense that every money debt of, say more than three months' standing, would be varied according to the tabular standard, in the absence of an express provision to the contrary. (Pp. 330-1.)

"The space at my disposal will not allow me to describe adequately the advantages which would arise from the establishment of a National tabular standard of value. Such a standard would add a wholly new degree of stability to social relations, securing the fixed incomes of individuals and public instiutions from the depreciation which they have so often suffered. Speculation, too, based upon the frequent oscillations of prices, which take place in the present state of commerce, would be to a certain extent discouraged. The calculations of merchants would be less frequently frustrated by causes beyond their own control, and many bankruptcies would be prevented. Periodical collapses of credit would no doubt recur from time to time, but the intensity of the crises would be mitigated, because as prices fell the liabilities of debtors would decrease approximately in the same ratio." (Pp. 332-3.)

### PROFESSOR SIMON NEWCOMB.

The writings of this distinguished educator having received no attention in previous chapters beyond a bare mention, we may briefly summarize here his valuable article in the North American Review for September, 1879. The Professor says that notwithstanding the wonderful progress of civilization, we have not improved on the money of Abraham. This is partly because the fluctuations of money escape our notice. Our whole education leads us to look on the dollar as absolutely invariable. It is like the earth. We do not see it move. The sun and stars appear to move round the world, and commodities appear to move while gold stands still, whereas in both cases the actual fact is the reverse of appearances. "The dollar of to-day is worth twice as much as was that of 15 years ago." And we have every reason to anticipate the slow advance of a gold famine. If new sources of supply are discovered, it will only delay a little the inevitable famine (unless the chemists learn to *make* gold and then the standard will become worthless for the opposite reason.) The Professor says that the Multiple Standard has not received the attention it deserves and continues thus: (Pp. 231-5.)

"An invariable standard is better than either a depreciating or an appreciating one. * * * That a standard of value with the use of which no such thing as general fluctuations in price should be possible, is one of the greatest social *desiderata* of our day, no one will deny.

"What we want is a dollar of uniform value, as measured by the average of commodities."

"The legal-tender dollar shall be defined as a quantity of something, no matter what, sufficient to purchase in the public markets, at average wholesale prices, a definite collection of commodities."

"The first and most obvious method of attaining the object is to issue a paper currency which shall be redeemable, not in gold dollars of fixed weight, but in such quantities of gold and silver bullion as shall suffice to make the required purchases."

### RICARDO.

President Walker, and other great economists, regard Ricardo as the most illustrious of all writers upon finance. In his "Proposals for an Economic and Secure Currency," 1816, Ricardo says, Secs. 1 and 2:

"All writers on the subject of money have agreed that uniformity in the value of the circulating medium is an object greatly to be desired. Every improvement, therefore, which can promote an approximation to that object, by diminishing the causes of variation, should be adopted. * * * A currency may be considered as perfect, of which the standard is invariable, which always conforms to that standard, and in the use of which the utmost economy is practiced. * * * During the late discussions on the bullion question it was most justly contended that a currency to be perfect, should be absolutely invariable in value.

"No plan can possibly be devised which will maintain money at an absolutely uniform value, because it will always be subject to those variations to which the commodity itself is subject, which has been fixed upon as a standard. While the precious metals continue to be the standard of our currency, money must necesssarily undergo the same variations in value as those metals."

Ricardo did not deem it impossible to attain a steady money because of any failure to recognize the principles on which the value of paper money depend. In his Political Economy, §125, he says:

"It is on this principle that paper money circulates: the whole charge for paper money may be considered as seigniorage. Tho it has no intrinsic value, yet, by limiting its quantity, its value in exchange is as great as an equal denomination of coin, or of bullion in that coin."

Ricardo further says: "A regulated paper currency is so great an improvement in commerce that I should greatly regret if prejudice should induce us to return to a system of less utility. The introduction of the precious metals for the purposes of money may with truth be considered as one of the most important steps towards the improvement of commerce and the arts of civilized life. But it is no less true that, with the advancement of knowledge and finance, we discover that it would be another improvement to banish them again from the employment to which, during the less enlightened period, they had been so advantageously applied." ("Works" by McCulloch, p. 404.)

Again he says: "It is not necessary that paper money should be payable in specie to secure its value; but only that its quantity should be regulated according to the value of the metal which is declared to be the standard." (Ricardo's "Plan for the Extinction of Bank Notes.")

Tho fully recognizing the imperfections of the precious metals, Ricardo proposed to use gold as the standard of value for want of a better. The use of a composite commodity standard did not occur to him. If he had thought of that, his principles would inevitably have led him to a system substantially like the one proposed in this book, for that standard supplies the one additional element he said was necessary to make a perfect money.

### PETER COOPER.

This great New York financier believed in honest money and urged his countrymen, after the war, not to abandon the paper basis, but to use an independent National currency and regulate its volume. Peter Cooper, Horace Greely and Henry Carey Baird advocated a paper money issued by the Government and convertible into United States bonds bearing low interest. The mutual convertibility would prevent any great excess or dearth of money.

Cooper said in substance (Letter on the Currency, N. Y., Phila. Library, 20527, O. 11, Pamphlet): "Experience has shown that individuals or corporations cannot be trusted with the power of issuing money. Governments are the safest depositories of the power. Value has hitherto been measured by its exchangeableness with gold, but this is subjecting paper to the laws of barter. It presumes that Governments can control what is uncontrollable, namely, the amount of gold that may, at any time, be in a country.

"To fix upon an arbitrary and fluctuating standard, such as the worth or exchangeable value of a gold dollar, is as uncertain as to take any other permanent product of human labor, such as a bushel of wheat or a pound of cotton. But how shall Government give an exchangeable value to a paper currency? Can it do so by a standard which is beyond its control, and which naturally fluctuates?

"This is the unsound state which possesses the minds of our people and of our politicians.

"We must come out of this unreasonable condition, or we shall be subject, for all time, to these periodic disturbances of our money and currency which bring such widespread ruin and distress on our commercial industries, and work, on the part of the Government, positive and cruel injustice. The remedy seems to me to be very plain. *First.* We must put this whole power of coining money or issuing currency, as Thomas Jefferson says, where, by the Constitution, it properly belongs',—entirely in the hands of our Government. We must trust our Government with this whole function of providing the standards and measures of exchange as we trust it with the weights and measures of all trade. The more stake the people have in the wisdom and honesty of the administration of the Government, the more watchful and firm they will be in its control."

"*Secondly.* We must require the Government to make this currency at all times, and at the option of the individual, convertible. But the currency must be convertible into something over which the Government has entire control, and to which it can give a definite as well as a permanent value. This is its own interest-bearing bonds."

If money were scarce, interest would rise and bonds would come in for translation into currency. If money were plenty, interest would fall and it would be profitable to invest in bonds again, thus diminishing the volume of the currency. If the Government may "call" the bonds in, they become a still more plastic means of reguation. (See Chap. III.)

### THE UNITED STATES SUPREME COURT.

In the Legal Tender Cases, the United States Supreme Court made some very significant remarks concerning intrinsic value, monetary standards, the advantages of paper money, the necessity of sustaining the debtor interest and not allowing it to be crushed under the weight of appreciating money, etc. The Court said: "Whatever power there is over the curency is vested in Congress. If the power to declare what is money is not in Congress, it is annihilated. (12 Wallace, 545).

"No one ever doubted that a debt of one thousand dollars, contracted before 1834, could be paid by one hundred eagles coined after that year, tho they contained no more gold than ninety-four eagles such as were coined when the contract was made, and this, not because *of the intrinsic value of the coin*, but because of its LEGAL VALUE. The eagles coined after 1834 were not money until they were authorized by law, and had they been coined before, without a law fixing their legal value, they could have no more paid a debt than uncoined bullion, or cotton, or wheat. (12 Wallace, 548-9).

"The coinage acts fix its unit as a dollar; but the gold or silver thing we call a dollar is, in no sense, a standard of a dollar. It is a representative of it. (12 Wallace, 553).

"The debtor interest of the country represents its bone and sinew and must be encouraged to pursue its avocations." (12 Wallace, 564).

The opinion of the Court in respect to the advantages of paper money, has been quoted in the first chapter and need not be here repeated.

In the same cases (12 Wallace, 557, 568), the Court used the following language in respect to the value of paper money:

"Dr. Franklin, in a letter to a friend, dated from Paris, in April,

1779, after deploring the depreciation which the Continental currency had undergone, said: "The only consolation under this evil is, that the public debt is proportionately diminished by the depreciation; and this, by a kind of imperceptible tax, every one having paid a part of it in the fall of value that took place between the receiving and paying such sums as passed thru his hands.' He adds: 'This effect of paper currency is not understood this side of the water. And indeed the whole is a mystery even to the politicians, and how we have been able to continue a war for four years without money, and how we could pay with paper that had no previously fixed fund appropriated specially to redeem it. This currency, as we manage it, is a wonderful machine. It performs its office when we issue it; it pays and clothes troops, and provides victuals and ammunition.' (Franklin's Works, Vol. 8, p. 329). In a subsequent letter of 9th October, 1780, he says: 'They (the Congress) issued an immense quantity of paper bills, to pay, clothe, arm and feed their troops and fit out ships; and with this paper, without taxes for the first three years, they fought and battled one of the most powerful nations of Europe.' (Franklin's Works, Vol 8, p. 507).

"It is well known that for over twenty years, from 1797 to 1820, the most stringent paper money system that ever existed prevailed in England, and lay at the foundation of all her elasticity and endurance.

"It is unnecessary to refer to other examples. France is a notable one. Her assignats issued at the commencement and during the Revolution, performed the same office as our Continental bills; and enabled the nation to gather up its latent strength and call out its energies. Almost every nation of Europe, at one time or another, has found it necessary or expedient to resort to the same method of carrying on its operations or defending itself against aggression."

### WILLIAM JENNINGS BRYAN.

In his California speeches, as reported in the Denver "New Road," of July, 1897, Mr. Bryan admitted that neither gold nor silver represents an honest dollar. "An honest dollar," said he, "is a dollar that will always buy the same amount of products; and if such a dollar could be constructed, a man would not be called upon in ten years to pay back a debt in dollars worth four times the dollar he borrowed; neither would he be enabled to pay off a debt with dollars four times as cheap as the dollar he borrowed." The report continues: "Mr. Bryan advocates a paper dollar based upon ten leading products of the nation, and when he does so he recommends the most scientific money the world ever saw. Given a dollar based upon oats, corn, wheat, rye, petroleum, pork, cotton, sugar, tobacco and coal, the value of which would be controlled by the average of these commodities, would give us 'an honest dollar.' "

### WENDELL PHILLIPS.

The great anti-slavery orator, one of the greatest orators and one of the truest friends of the people that has ever lived, regarded the emancipation of the country from the despotism of an unjust currency as *the vital issue* after slavery was abolished. In 1878, he said: ("Who shall Rule Us, Money or the People," by Wendell Phillips. Boston, 1878. Rand, Avery & Co.) "I shall vote for General Butler because he represents the determination of the people to take the currency out of the control of money-kings. * * * When slavery was abolished—when it was settled that the capitalist should no longer own the laborer—all labor, black and white, North and South, was lifted to the level of *wages*. Of course every wage-laborer desired a fair division of the joint product of labor and capital. Horace Mann said (substantially): 'Yankee ingenuity has increased production tenfold, but we have made hardly one step forward toward a fair division of that product.'

"In our effort to secure a fairer division, we soon saw that the *dollar* in which labor was paid was one of the most important, if not the most important, element in the solution of this problem. In other words, we saw it was currency which, rightly arranged, opened a nation's well-springs, found work for willing hands, and filled them with a great return, while honest capital, daily larger and more secure, ministered to a glad prosperity; or it was currency, wickedly and selfishly juggled, that made merchants bankrupt, and starved labor into discontent and slavery, while capital added house to house, and field to field, and gathered into its miserly hands all the wealth left in a ruined land.

"The first question, therefore, in an industrial nation, is, where ought the control of the currency to rest? In whose hands can this almost omnipotent power be trusted? Every writer on political economy, from Aristotle to Adam Smith, from Ricardo to Calhoun, allows that a change in the currency alters the price of every ounce and yard of merchandise and every foot of land. Whom can we trust with this despotism?

"At present the banks and the money-kings wield this power. They own the yardstick, and can make it shorter or longer as they please, and when they will. They own the pound-weight and can make it heavier or lighter as they choose.

"This explains the riddle, so mysterious to common men, why those who trade in money always grow rich, even while those who trade in other things go into bankruptcy.

"This is the issue of to-day. *Who shall make the yardstick?*

"Mr. Schurz, my friend Mr. Blaine, Mr. Secretary Sherman, fancy we are discussing what the money shall be made of; whether paper or metal. Not yet, gentlemen. The question is not what the money shall be made of: the question to-day is, *Who shall make the Money; Banks, or the Government? Money-Kings or the people?* As Ewing said, last August, 'The practical money question in the United States is not whether the currency shall be coin or paper, but *who shall issue the paper money, and how shall its volume be determined?*' By and by, after we have settled this first point, we will discuss that second one. To-day we are fighting to secure what Jefferson, in 1813, advised that 'the circulation be restored to the nation to whom it belongs.'

"This is the reason why the banks and money-kings hate this movement so bitterly, and pour out their money like water to kill it. They feel and know it is a hand-to-hand fight between themselves and the people—one of the last battles between aristocracy and democracy. The most cunning weapon they use is that of confusing the question, in order to hide the real issue, which is simply: Shall the Nation make its own currency, or put itself under the guardianship of capital—sheep in the keeping of wolves?"

In another address (Wendell Phillips on the Currency, a pamphlet in the Boston Public Library), Phillips said: "England and France—the two nations to which gold naturally and almost inevitably runs, since they are credit States—have been obliged to resort to paper currency upon every emergency. The specie bank of England, since she was remodeled in 1844, has thrice been obliged to beg the Government to save her from suspension. If England, the richest nation in the world, the reservoir and refuge of coin, cannot without subterfuge, support one specie paying bank in London, the world's business centre, how can we expect to hoard gold enough to form a real basis for two thousand banks scattered over the continent?

"Gold is no trustworthy standard of value. During the rebellion gold—measured by the prices of twenty of our great staples—varied more than any of them did, except cotton, the cause of the war.

"Now while gold has thus varied during the last ninety years, there is in England one commodity which never changes: that is consols and shares in the Bank of England; which practically are public funds, since they are in effect guaranteed by the nation. From 1789 to 1875, both inclusive, the average price of a consol was £81. If, as Jevons says, from 1809 to 1849 gold more than doubled in value, the consol never changed; its average price those forty-one years was just what it was before and after, that is, £81. If, as Jevons and Fawcett say, since 1809, gold has fallen one-quarter, consols have not fallen. So of the bank shares; the interest on their selling price from 1789 to 1872 was the slightest trifle above four per cent. During the forty-one years (1809-1849) that Jevons says gold rose to double, the interest was just the slightest trifle below four per cent (4.04 in one case, 3.94 in the other.) During these last twenty-five years, when gold has fallen one-quarter, the interest on a bank share is 3.67 per cent.

"Now, let men explain the unchanging values of these stocks as they please, their unchanging value remains a fact. Remember what these last 84 years have done and seen—the French Revolution and Napoleon Wars, Waterloo, paper money, riots, famines, California, the Crimean War, the Franco-Prussian War, steam, the use of cotton, extension of the ballot, the telegraph, and our rebellion. Still, thru all, the ebb tide and the flood, the sunshine and the tempest, the funds of England have steadied with unchanging keel. What explains it? Their basis is a government bond, at a low rate of interest, but *sure* as 'death and taxes.'

"Taking note of this, we propose to found our National currency on a Government bond, bearing a low rate of interest. Why should not our bond be as unvarying as that of England? She is encompassed by troubles and dangers, half a dozen warlike rivals, and constant risk of international complications. We have a clear sky, and the ocean for a wall of defence. Why should not our bond be better than hers? \* \* \*

"The moment you leave a simple barter, that moment the power to inflate begins. This power must always reside in civilized States which have ceased to use barter. The only real question is, *where* shall it be trusted? Under our present system it rests in the hands of the bank directors. Ricardo and all other writers allow that those who increase and diminish, at their pleasure, the currency (not note currency merely, but discounts, checks, credits, notes and coin) have the power to change prices at their will. To-day, our bank directors have this power. The New York City banks increased this currency $2,957,200 in one month, September, 1874, and decreased it $5,000,000 in one week of March, 1875. They thus changed the value of every commodity in that city. To inflate in the same proportion, Congress must pour out and keep out $50,000,000 a week. \* \* \*

"They (the people) will keep it in the form of bonds, or draw it forth in greenbacks, as the hour dictates. They will decide, under this elastic system, how much currency is needed by a nation, not rich, but widely scattered and marvellously busy; one whose harvests can feed the world, and her mines supply it with metal and coal; while rivers and mountains and thousands of miles divide prairie and seaport, plantation and spindle, mine and forge. Indeed, this movement is a revolt against a system of finance which rests the power of inflation in the hands of a few hundred bank directors, and let's them play with values at their pleasure. This movement is in its essence the assertion that when our fathers settled it that the people were competent to govern themselves, they meant to include among the points as to which they were competent, the question of finance, as well as marriage, crimes, real estate, wills, and other matters of government. This movement is a revolt against the notion that in ordinary matters the people can govern themselves, but on questions of finance they must be kept under perpetual guardianship, and be the wards of rich men."

### BENJAMIN FRANKLIN.

In Chapter I., we have already seen that the great philosopher and patriot of Revolutionary days was a strong believer in paper money of limited volume. We will not requote, but merely add one further brief citation.

"Paper money," says Franklin, "well founded, has great advantages over gold and silver, being more light and convenient for handling large sums, and not likely to have its volume reduced by demands for exportation. No method has hitherto been formed to establish a medium of trade equal in all its advantages to bills of credit made a general legal tender." ("Works," Vol. IV., p. 2. The passage is frequently quoted. Wendell Phillips, Peter Cooper, the United States Supreme Court and many other authorities cite Franklin's views on the money question with hearty approval.)

### THOMAS JEFFERSON.

The father of Democracy clearly saw that the money system of the country should belong to the sovereign people and not to the sovereign banks.

"Bank paper must be suppressed, and the circulating medium must be restored to the nation to whom it belongs. It is the only fund on which they can rely for loans; it is the only resource which can never fail them, and it is an abundant one for every necessary purpose. Treasury bills, *bottomed on taxes*, bearing or not bearing interest, as may be found necessary, thrown into circulation will take the place of so much gold or silver, which last, when crowded, will find an efflux into other countries, and thus keep the quantum of medium at its salutary level.

"No method has hitherto been formed to establish a medium of trade equal in all its advantages to bills of credit made a general legal tender." (Jefferson's Works, Vol. VI., p. 199).

Jefferson saw that money should be public, independent, regulated. In 1776 he wrote the Declaration of Independence for American manhood, proclaiming the truth that American citizens ought to be free from the rule of European monarchs. And if he were living to-day, he would write a Declaration of Independence for the American dollar, proclaiming the truth that American money should be freed from the despotic rule of the square mile of London, which controls the financial policy of the world. Indeed, the new Declaration is necessary for the fulfillment of the first, for American citizens cannot be free from European rule so long as American dollars are subject to foreign control.

### ABRAHAM LINCOLN.

In a letter to Col. Edmund Taylor, December, 1864, President Lincoln said: "Chase thought it a hazardous thing, but we finally accomplished it, and gave to the people of this Republic the greatest blessing they ever had—their own paper to pay their own debts."

# APPENDIX A.

## PENNSYLVANIA CURRENCY.

(See reference, page 14.)

In 1697 silver was plentiful in Pennsylvania, but by 1719 payments for imports and payments to the foreign proprietors had stripped the colony of its coin,[1] and the people had to carry on the principal part of their commerce by barter. In 1723 the Assembly ordered the issue of £15,000 in paper money, £11,000 to be loaned to the people on real estate security, the balance to be issued against taxes. The loans were to be at 5 per cent. interest, to run 8 years, and be secured by land of twice the value of the loan or houses of three times that value. One-eighth of the loan was to be repaid each year, together with the interest. It was enacted that no one should borrow more than £100, it being desirable to guard against a control of the loan by the wealthy. It was also provided that the bills should be a full legal tender, and that refusal to receive them should cancel the debt. The bills would pay debts and taxes, but were not redeemable in gold or silver.

It was found that £15,000 was not sufficient for the needs of business, and further issues were made from time to time, partly on real estate and partly on tax redemption. The term of the loans was extended in subsequent issues so that it became 16 years instead of 8, which made the annual payment due from the borrower less than 12 per cent., including interest and the instalment of the principal. By 1764 there was about £500,000 of this "irredeemable" paper money in circulation, about £400,000 of it having been issued against taxes and the rest against realty.

This Pennsylvania money kept its value and did the work of the colony to the entire satisfaction of the people. Franklin said:[2] "The utility of this currency became by time and experience so evident that the principles on which it was founded were never afterwards much disputed. * * * In New York and Pennsylvania it has continued now nearly forty years without variation upon new emissions."

Some of the colonies, however, in the South and in New England, had, by over-issue, seriously depreciated their currency, and a movement took shape in England to restrain the emission of paper in America as legal tender. In February, 1764, the Board of Trade in England reported in favor of such a restraining law for the following reasons:

1. Such paper-credits carry the gold and silver out of the province and ruin the country.
2. Merchants trading in America have lost by this money.
3. Restriction upon it has had a good effect in New England.
4. That every medium of trade should have an intrinsic value which paper has not.
5. That debtors in the asemblies make paper money with fraudulent intent.
6. That the bills have never kept their nominal value in circulation, but have constantly depreciated to a certain degree whenever the quantity has been increased.

---

[1] Phillips, pp. 11, 12, 19, see also below citation from Franklin's works.
[2] See Franklin's Autobiography and Jared Sparks ed. of Franklin's Works, Vol. II., pp. 254 and 351.

Benjamin Franklin, then in England, replied to these objections as follows:

"1. The truth is that the balance of trade with Britain being greatly against the colonies, gold and silver is drawn out to pay that balance, and then the necessity for some medium of trade has induced the making of paper money, which could not be carried away. Thus, if the carrying out of the gold and silver ruins a country, every colony was ruined before it made paper money. But far from being ruined, the colonies have been and are in a flourishing condition.[1]

"Pennsylvania, before it made any paper money, was totally stripped of its gold and silver, tho they had from time to time, like the neighboring colonies, agreed to take gold and silver coins at higher nominal values, in hope of drawing money into and retaining it for the internal use of the province. During that weak practice, silver got up by degrees to 8s. 9d. per ounce * * * long before paper money was made. * * * The difficulties for want of cash were accordingly very great, the chief part of the trade being carried on by the extremely inconvenient method of barter, when in 1723, paper money was first made there (in Pennsylvania), which gave new life to business, promoted greatly the settlement of the new lands (by lending small sums to beginners, on easy interest to be paid by instalments) whereby the province has so greatly increased in inhabitants that the export from thence thither (to England) is now more than tenfold what it then was.[2]

"2. Merchants may have suffered loss by paper money in particular instances, as in New England and Virginia, when great sums were issued to pay the colony troops, or in South Carolina when she was thought in danger of being destroyed by the Indians and Spaniards, tho since that danger blew over their currency became fixed and has remained so to this day. But the merchants trading to the middle colonies (New York, New Jersey and Pennsylvania) have never suffered by any use of exchange.[3]

"3. The restraining of paper issues in New England has embarrassed the provinces for want of money to such extent that trade was under great discouragement.[4]

"4. Intrinsic value is not necessary. Bank bills and bankers notes are daily used here (in England) as a medium of trade, and in large dealings perhaps the greater part is transacted by their means; and yet they have no intrinsic value.

"Their being payable in cash on sight is indeed a circumstance that cannot attend the colony bills, their cash being drawn away by the balance of trade. But the legal tender, being substituted in its place, is rather a greater advantage to the possessor, since he need not go to a particular bank to get his money, finding (wherever he has occasion to pay out money in the province) a person that is obliged to take the bills.

"So that, even out of the province, the knowledge that every man within that province is obliged to take its money gives the bills a credit among its neighbors, nearly equal to what they have at home.

"At this very time even the silver money in England is obliged to be legal tender for part of its value, that part which is the difference between its real weight and its denomination. Great part of the shillings and sixpences now current are by wearing become 5, 10, 20 and some of the sixpences even 50 per cent. too light. For the difference between the real and the nominal you have no intrinsic value; you have not so much as paper; you have nothing.

---

[1] Franklin's works edited by Jared Sparks, Vol. II., p. 342.
[2] Ibid., pp. 343-4.
[3] Ibid., pp. 344-5.
[4] In substance, p. 346.

It is the legal tender, with the knowledge that it can easily be repassed for the same value, that makes 3 pennyworth of silver pass for sixpence.*

"On the whole, no method has hitherto been formed to establish a medium of trade in lieu of money, equal in all its advantages, to bills of credit, funded on sufficient taxes for discharging it, or on land security of double the value for repaying it at the end of the term, and in the meantime made a general legal tender. The experience of now near half a century in the middle colonies has convinced them of it among themselves, by the great increase of their settlements, numbers, buildings, improvements, agriculture, shipping and commerce, and the same experience has satisfied the British merchants who trade thither, that it has been greatly useful to them, and not in a single instance prejudicial.[1]

"5. To deprive all the colonies of the convenience of paper money because it has been charged on some of them that they made it an instrument of fraud, is as if all the India banks and other stock and trading companies were to be abolished because there have been Mississippi and South Sea schemes and bubbles.[2]

"6. The paper money of the middle colonies has kept its value. In New York and Pennsylvania it has continued now nearly forty years without variation upon new emissions, tho in Pennsylvania the paper currency has at times increased from £15,000 to £600,000, or near it.[3] Nor has any alteration been occasioned by the paper money in the price of the necessaries of life, when compared with silver. They have been for the greater part of the time no higher than before it was emitted, varying only by plenty and scarcity, according to the seasons, or by less or greater foreign demand.

"It is nothing to the purpose to object the wretched fall of the bills in New England and South Carolina, unless it might be made evident that their currency was emitted with the same prudence and on such good security as ours is, and it certainly was not.[4]

---

(*) Ibid., pp. 347-8.
([1]) Ibid., p. 354.
([2]) Ibid., p. 350.
([3]) Ibid., p. 351.
([4]) Ibid., p. 276. The reasons for the depreciation of colonial paper in Mass., R. I. and other New England colonies are very apparent. For example, in 1714 Mass. authorized an issue of £50,000 in bills to be put in the hands of five trustees and let out at 5 per cent. in safe mortgages on real estate, to be paid back in five annual instalments. This was like the Penna. plan except that the term was too short—a 25 per cent. payment per year was too great a burden and the debts were not paid back as agreed—on the contrary a clamour was raised for further issues, and paper was multiplied lavishly. Such is the account given by Bancroft in his History of the United States, Vol. II., pp. 262-3, and by Mr. Macfarlane in the article already referred to in the first chapter of this book.

For 1749, just before the close of the era of colonial paper in New England, Prof. Sumner states the paper of Mass. at £2,466,712, R. I. £550,000, and N. H. £450,000. While Phillips' data place the currency of Penna. at £85,000 in 1749 and that of N. J. at £76,000. Taking the population for 1749 from Mulhall's Dictionary of Statistics, we have the following contrasts:

| Colony. | Population 1749. | Currency 1749. | Per head. |
|---|---|---|---|
| Mass. | 220,000 | £2,466,712 | $60 |
| R. I. | 35,000 | 550,000 | 77 |
| N. H. | 30,000 | 450,000 | 75 |
| Penna. | 210,000 | 85,000 | 2 |
| N. J. | 60,000 | 76,000 | 6 |

New Jersey and Penna., whose bills were mutually honored over the boundary, had together a circulation of about $3 per head. Penna. started in 1723 with an issue of less than $1 per head and rose in 1749 to an average of $2 per head, while R. I. started in 1710 with an issue of $2.50 a head and rose by 1749 to an average of $77 per inhabitant. Even in 1775 the Pennsylvania paper outstanding was only $11 per capita.

It is no wonder that Pennsylvania paper kept its value, while the bills of New England sank to less than one tenth of their original purchasing

Adam Smith's "Wealth of Nations" appeared in 1776; on p. 262 of that great work, the author says:
"Pennsylvania was more moderate in the emission of paper money than the other colonies. Its paper currency accordingly is said never to have sunk below the value of the gold and silver which was current in the colony before the first emission of its paper money."

In the Annals of the American Academy of Political and Social Science, Vol. VIII., No. 1, July, 1896, Mr. C. W. Macfarlane tabulates at great length the prices current in Pennsylvania from 1723 to 1773 from contemporaneous newspaper data and old account books preserved by the Pennsylvania Historical Society. He finds (pp. 67-70) that up to the middle of the century (1749 according to his tables) there was no advance in prices either in the domestic or the export trade, but after that date there was a sharp and permanent advance in the prices of commodities that figured largely in the colony's exports, while those that were produced largely for home consumption or were imported into the province show no material advance in price, which shows clearly that the changes of price which did occur were not due to any depreciation of the currency (which would have affected home products and imports as well as exports), but were occasioned by a rising foreign market.

After citing Franklin[1] and Hume[2] to show the high degree of prosperity that existed in Pennsylvania during the period under consideration, the author concludes that the "irredeemable" paper money of Pennsylvania maintained its value thruout the fifty years of its existence.

"Our study of prices, together with the fact of this marvelous prosperity, seem to sustain Franklin's claim that this currency suffered no material depreciation for half a century.[3]

"The Pennsylvania currency maintained its value, because the amount issued was not in excess of their need[4] for a medium of

---

power. Neither is it to be wondered at that Parliament in 1751 restrained the Northern colonies from issuing legal tender bills and prohibited them from issuing any bills of credit of any sort except:

1. To cover expenses of the current year, the paper not to run over two **years, or,**
2. To provide for extraordinary emergencies (as in case of invasion) a fund to be established to sink such bills within five years.

Massachusetts led the way to a specie basis, which was restored in New England about the middle of the century and remained until the Revolution.

([1]) "Abundance reigned in Pennsylvania and there was peace in all her borders. A more happy and prosperous population could not perhaps be found on the globe. In every home there was comfort. The people generally were highly moral and knowledge was extensively diffused." Franklin.

([2]) "In Pennsylvania the land itself is coined. A planter immediately after purchasing land, can go to a public office and receive notes to the amount of half his land, which notes he employs in all payments. No more than a certain sum is issued to one planter, and he must pay back each year into the public treasury one-tenth of the notes. When they are all paid back he can repeat the operation. This caused a prosperity that Burke said was unparalleled." David Hume, historian of England, in a letter to Abbe Morellet.

([3]) Macfarlane, p. 71.

([4]) Hon. John Davis says (February Arena, '94):—"The paper money of Pennsylvania succeeded as long as it possessed the quality of legal tender. It failed when the British government forbade it having that quality. Coin money, being an exportable article, was always a fugitive in those colonial days. It was usually a failure when needed. It could not be relied upon as a circulating medium, nor could it even be trusted as a basis for paper. The Pennsylvania paper rested entirely on the quality of legal tender (backed by limited issue), and it remained good and sound money until that quality was withdrawn by the British government on purpose to destroy it, and thus to render the colony dependent for money on the usurers of England. The money did not depend on the land for its value as some suppose. The lands were merely security for the loans."

exchange, and had ample provision made for the redemption of the larger part of it by taxation."[1]

Gold and silver were among the articles which rose in value above the prices of 1723. The Journals of the Pennsylvania Assembly, and Phillips, p. 19, give the following figures:

|  | GOLD PER OZ. | SILVER PER OZ. |
|---|---|---|
| 1700 to 1709 | £7 | 9s. 2d. |
| 1709 to 1720 | 5, 10s. | 6s. 10½d. |
| 1720 to 1723 | 5, 10s. | 7s. 5d. |
| 1723 to 1726 | 6, 6s. 6d. | 8s. 3d. |
| 1726 to 1730 | 6, 3s. 9d. | 8s. 1d. |
| 1730 to 1738 | 6, 9s. 3d. | 8s. 9d. |

These data show a rise in the value of the precious metals of about 20 per cent. between 1723 and 1738, while commodity prices in currency remained at the level of the silver and paper prices of 1723. The exchange on London during the period under discussion is stated by Walker, Sumner and other authorities as 160 to 180. This was due to a rise in bullion as compared either with commodities in general or the home currency, and to the difficulty of transporting the bullion, or of obtaining bills on London. The rise of bullion was caused by the scarcity of it in the colonies and the necessity of obtaining it or exchange, which was also scarce, in order to pay rents, etc., in England.

In Massachusetts, where by over-issue the paper money greatly depreciated in reference to commodities, this depreciation together with the rise in bullion, produced an exchange of 500 in 1737 and 1100 in 1749.[2] That the rise of exchange to 160 or 180 in the middle colonies, New York, New Jersey and Pennsylvania, was not due to a depreciation of the paper was clearly shown by Franklin in his famous reductio ad absurdum.

"If the rising of the value of any particular commodity wanted for exportation is to be considered as a depreciation of whatever remains in the country, then the rising of silver above paper to that height which its capability (and need) of exportation only gave it, may be called a depreciation of the paper. Even here (in England where he was writing) as bullion has been wanted or not wanted, for exportation, its price has varied from 5s. 2d. to 5s. 8d. per oz. This is near 10 per cent. But was it ever said or thought on such an occasion that all the bank bills and all the coined silver and all the gold in the kingdom were depreciated 10 per cent.? Coined silver is now wanted here for change, and 1 per cent. is given for it by some bankers. Are gold and bank notes therefore depreciated?"[3]

The great philosopher then states that silver had risen because of the demand for it for exportation, and that exchange on London was at a still further premium, rising above bullion, since it saved the expense and risk of transporting gold or silver. In part his statement is as follows:

"It has, indeed, been usual with the adversaries of a paper currency to call every rise of exchange with London a depreciation of the paper; but this notion appears to be by no means just, for if the paper purchases everything but bills of exchange at the

---

Four-fifths of the currency did not rest upon land at all, but was issued against taxes in moderate volume and kept its value because it was a full legal tender, receivable for all dues public and private and was not issued in excessive quantities, but kept pace in its increase with the growing needs of business.

(1) Macfarlane, pp. 73-4.
(2) Walker on "Money," p. 321.
(3) Franklin's Works, Vol. II., p. 350.

former rate, and these bills are not above one-tenth of what is employed in purchases, then it may be more properly and truly said that the exchange has risen, than that the paper has depreciated. And as proof of this, it is a certain fact that whenever in those colonies (New York, New Jersey and Pennsylvania) bills of exchange have been dearer, the purchaser has been constantly obliged to give more in *silver*, as well as in paper, for them, the silver having gone hand in hand with the paper at the rate above mentioned.[1]

A diagram frequently serves to place in a very clear light the relations between two movements. Let us compare in this way the movements of money and prices. The Pennsylvania issues and circulation were as follows:[2]

| DATE. | ISSUES. | CIRCULATION. |
|---|---|---|
| 1723 | £15,000 | £15,000 |
| 1729 | 30,000 | 45,000 |
| 1739 | 35,000 | 80,000 |
| 1746 | 5,000 | 85,000 |
| 1749 | ..... | 85,000 |
| 1756 | 30,000 | 115,000 |
| 1757-9 | 300,855 | 415,855 |
| 1760-9 | 5,000 | 420,000 |
| 1771 | 15,000 | 435,000 |
| 1772 | 25,000 | 460,000 |
| 1773 | 11,000 | 471,000 |
| 1774 | 150,000 | 621,000 |
| 1775 | 158,000 | 779,000 |

As to the movement of prices, Mr. Macfarlane finds a "sharp and seemingly permanent rise" about 1749 in the prices of leading exports. Speaking of prices before 1723 and after 1749, he says:

"While those commodities that were produced largely for home consumption or were imported into the province show no material advance in price, those that figured largely in their exports had advanced 100 per cent."[3]

"Looking at the details of his data we find that some imports, as wine, increased in price, and that while the average prices of staple exports remained high after 1749, yet the price of any single article of export vibrated up and down, sometimes falling to the level of 1747 and 1748 or lower, but speaking generally Mr. Macfarlane's statements are borne out by his tabulated data. Putting these two sets of facts together we have the following results:

---

(1) Ibid., p. 351.
(2) Tabulated from Phillips Hist. and Penna. Laws and Records. The issues, or parts of issues used to replace former issues are omitted, as they did not affect the volume in circulation. In 1739 a committee of the Assembly reported the circulation as £80,000, and in 1745 this circulation was continued for 16 years. In 1753 a struggle began between the people and the English government in respect to further issues. Up to this time the issues had been on interest and payable in instalments, but subsequent issues were against taxes simply. From 1760 to 1769 inclusive £205,000 were issued and £200,000 withdrawn. The £150,000 issue was voted in 1773, dated October and issued mostly in 1774.
(3) Annals, etc., supra, p. 70.

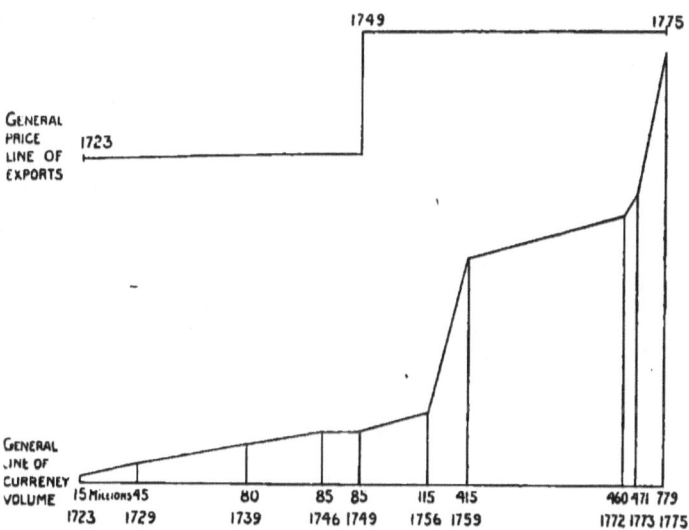

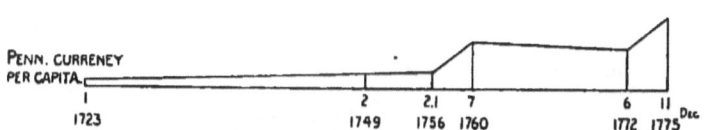

It is clear that the rise of prices in 1749 could not have been caused by an increase of currency in 1756 to 1759. At the time of the rise and for seven years after the currency was practically at a level, and when we come to the period of paper increase, 1756 to 1759, we find prices gliding smoothly along, showing some little ripples from year to year and from month to month, but on the whole quite level thruout the period under consideration. Taking an average of all the staples in Mr. Macfarlane's tables,[1] including exports and taking the prices of 1749 as a standard we have the following:

|  | GENERAL PRICE LEVELS. |
|---|---|
| 1749 | 100 |
| 1758 | 98 |
| 1759 | 106 |
| 1760 | 101 |
| 1773 | 112 |
| 1775 | 106 |

([1]) If, instead of summing the prices and dividing by the number of commodities, we find the quantity of each article that could be bought for $1 in 1749 and then ascertain the prices of the said quantities in subsequent years and sum the results, we shall discover that, by this method, the price level of 1775 was precisely the same as that of 1749, using the commodities listed by Macfarlane, p. 70, Annals, supra, so far as data are available.

## APPENDIX A.

It might be supposed that the increase of money had something to do with the rise from 1758 to 1759, but if so, the paper lost its effect in 1760, when the volume reached its height. Moreover, it is difficult to account, by means of the currency, for the drop between 1773 and 1775 in face of a great increase in the volume of circulation.

These averages vary much less from year to year than the prices of any one commodity in different years or even in different months of the same year; and if we had data for a hundred representative articles in place of the fifteen staples of Mr. Macfarlane's tables, we should probably find the average of prices practically identical every year from 1749 to 1775.

Whether the replacement of other forms of exchange and the rapid increase of business absorbed the issues of 1756-9, or the notes of Pennsylvania circulated more freely in other colonies than the bills of other colonies circulated in Pennsylvania, I do not know; but it seems reasonably certain that the notes of Pennsylvania did not depreciate from 1723 to 1775.

Phillips, speaking of the period from 1723 to 1738, says (p. 19):

"During all this time the notes, having ample provision made for their ultimate extinction, circulated freely at their value, superseding the bills of other colonies, which had until then constituted the chief part of the currency."

After summing up a longer time and looking back on the whole period before the Revolution, Phillips says (p. 30):

"The early notes of the colony seem to have kept their credit well, and had not the revolution intervened they would all have been redeemed at par," as ample provision was made by taxation, etc., for their extinction. But the battle of Lexington roused the colony, and the over-issues of the war together with British counterfeits, completed the work of destruction begun by Act of Parliament.

Franklin's wisdom and the success of paper money in Pennsylvania, New York and other colonies did not stop the English movement to deprive the colonies of the power of issuing paper, and in 1764 and 1773 Parliament passed acts restraining the issue of bills, and destroying the legal tender of the paper currency. The results were disastrous.

Peter Cooper, the great New York financier, was a deep student of the philosophy of money. His letters on the currency in pamphlet and newspaper form attracted wide attention.

In reference to the subject now before us, we note the following striking words from his pen:

"When Franklin was brought before the Parliament of Great Britain and questioned as to the cause of the wonderful prosperity growing up in the colonies, he plainly stated that the cause was the convenience they found in exchanging their various forms of labor one with another by paper money, which had been adopted; that *this paper money* was not only *used in the payment of taxes*, but in addition it had been *declared legal tender.* It rose two and three per cent. above the par of *gold and silver, as everybody preferred its use.* One of its advantages was its security against theft, as it could be easily carried and hidden on account of its having no bulk, as all kinds of specie must necessarily have. After Franklin explained this to the British Government as the real cause of prosperity they immediately passed laws forbidding the payment of taxes in that money. This produced such great inconvenience and misery to the people that it was the principal cause of the Revolution. A far greater reason for a general uprising than the tea and stamp act was the taking away of the paper money."

President Walker says that much of the force of the Revolutionary movement is attributed to "the chafing of the colonists under the restriction and final prohibition of paper money by the Crown."[1]

Rev. John Twells, of London, an able English writer, says of the colonial paper:

"This was the monetary system under which the American colonists prospered to such an extent that *Burke* said of them: '*Nothing* in the *history of the world is like their progress.*' It was a wise and beneficial system and its effects were most conducive to the happiness of the people. Half the value of his land was advanced to the head of the family in notes which circulated as money. With these notes he could hire labor and purchase implements of husbandry and cattle; and thus, where without these notes, one acre could be cleared and stocked in a year, ten would, by the assistance of the paper money advanced, be reclaimed from the forest and rendered productive. In an evil hour the British Government took away from America its 'representative money,' commanded that no more paper bills of credit should be issued, that they should cease to be legal tender; and collected the taxes in hard silver. This was in 1773. Now mark the consequences. This contraction of the circulating medium paralyzed all the industrial energies of the people. Ruin seized upon these once flourishing colonies; the most severe distress was brought home to every interest and every family; discontent was urged on to desperation, till, at last 'human nature' as Dr. Johnston phrases it, arose and asserted its rights." In 1775 the Congress first met in Philadelphia. In 1776 America became an independent State.[2]

[1] Money, p. 310. See also Professor Wm. G. Sumner's Hist. Amer. Currency, p. 30.

[2] Cited by Hon. John Davis, February Arena, 1894, p. 364.

## APPENDIX B.

### ENGLAND.
(See reference, page 20.)

In 1793 England went to war with France. Coin began to be hoarded and to go abroad. A financial stringency followed, and business was seriously affected. The Bank of England, unable to collect its loans, and fearing the drain of specie with so large a mass of its bills outstanding, began to contract its circulation. This embarrassed the country banks and they began also to contract. In 1796 a rumor of French invasion caused a run upon the country banks, and in consequence they made heavy demands on the Bank of England. The specie reserve was reduced to £1,000,000, when the bank was forbidden by order of Council to make further payments in specie, and in 1797 Parliament passed an act suspending specie payments. From that time on England carried on the war with Napoleon with inconvertible paper money, and during the first ten years at least, the issues being managed with prudence and firmness, so that the volume of money did not exceed the needs of business, the bills retained their value, and prices as a whole, after rising out of the depression caused by the flight of coin and the panic contraction of the circulation, remained substantially on a level with those that had obtained before the suspension of specie payments.[1]

In later years the bills were issued more heavily, and in 1809 the mint and the market price of bullion began rapidly to diverge. This may or may not have indicated a depreciation of the paper; it may have been a mere rise of gold. The true test of depreciation in time of war is the general rise of home products above their usual price level. There is reason to believe that these prices did rise decidedly in later years[2] but it is matter of common knowledge that for ten years or more after the suspension, while the bills were not issued in excess, England's independent "irredeemable" paper money did not depreciate, but retained substantially the same value that gold of equal stamp possessed before the war.[3]

At the opening of the war with France, the circulation of Great Britain, according to the estimate of the Lord's Committee of 1819, was as follows:

| | |
|---|---|
| Coin | £25,000,000 |
| Bank of England Notes | 10,500,000 |
| Country Bank Notes | 7,000,000 |
| Total | £42,500,000 |

As we have said there was in the first three years a contraction of the note circulation, which together with the retirement of large amounts of coin caused marked financial stringency and commercial distress. The Government gave relief by lending money to merchants and others.[4] On the suspension of specie payments

---

[1] Tooke's Hist. of Prices, showing that while war produced some fluctuations and carried the prices of certain articles to an extravagant height, yet exchanges were on the whole as favorable during the first 10 or 12 years of the suspension as they had been on an average of 96 years, or of any 10 consecutive years preceeding 1797. See also Walker on "Money," p. 351.

[2] According to Jevons' tables the price level of 1809 was 20 per cent. above the level of 1709.

[3] Professor Dunbar in Quarterly Journal of Economics, Vol. 6, p. 333.

[4] Pitt's government offered to lend on excellent terms. Over ten million dollars was loaned on personal security, and $936,000 on goods—the whole was faithfully repaid, much of it before maturity. (See Doubleday's "Financial Hist. of England., p. 137).

and issue of notes for Government expenses, the paper circulation of the Bank of England grew as follows:[1]

February, 1797 .................................. £9,674,780
February, 1800 .................................. 16,844,470
February, 1805 .................................. 17,871,170
February, 1810 .................................. 21,019,600
February, 1815 .................................. 27,261,650

That is, the notes of the Bank of England were tripled in 18 years. Considering the disappearance of coin and the increase of country bank bills, it seems probable that the total circulation was not much increased till after 1805, but by 1815 it may have been 80 to 100 per cent. greater than in 1797[2]—a per capita change from $14 per head in 1797 to about $21 per head in 1815.

The war ended in 1815. The average paper price of gold, which in 1814 stood at £5, 4s. per oz., fell to £4, 13s. 6d., where it remained through 1816, £3, 17s. 10½d. being the mint value. In 1817 the premium fell until, as Mr. Tooke says, there was "a spontaneous readjustment of the value between gold and paper to a perfect equality." This restoration of the value of the bank note coincided with an enlargement of the bank issues as compared with any previous period.[3] The "spontaneous readjustment" was due in this case to contraction of the currency, as we shall see in a moment.

Lord Liverpool became Prime Minister in 1812 and remained at the head of the Government until 1827. He was a firm believer in metallic money from hereditary attachment to the doctrines of his father, who (see his "Essay on Coins") was not only a metallist, but a believer in the gold standard for the reason that the richest country in the world should use the most costly metal.[4] Lord Liverpool's influence was one of the causes of the adoption of the contraction policy. It is said that another powerful cause of the change of policy was the great accumulation of capital in interest-bearing debts.[5] The wealthy holders favored a policy that would increase the value of these bonds and of all loans and mortgages, as well.[6]

The first contraction was by arrangement between the Government and the Bank in 1815 and 1816. The Bank of England and its country subordinates reduced their circulation—the country banks by nearly one-half—in 1816 and 1817.[7] "Gold fell almost to the mint price (i. e. almost to par). Wheat fell 64s. a quarter, and

[1] Doubleday, pp. 232-7.
[2] Financial Hist. Eng., pp. 234-7. The country banks were estimated at 200 in 1797, 702 in 1800, and 940 in 1814. High banking authority estimated the country bank notes in 1815 at 40 to 50 million pounds. The committee on the currency in 1819 at 30 million sterling. Mr. Sedgwick and Robert Mushet lower even this estimate somewhat.
[3] Tooke's Hist. Prices, ii., 52, 60-1. At this time the Bank of England offered to redeem their £1 and £2 notes, and as these notes were chiefly in the hands of the poorer classes, no inconvenience resulted, not more than £1,000,000 being paid out. In October the bank announced that it would pay gold for all its notes issued before 1817, but the demand for gold was so great that the banks had to recede from this position. (Walker on "Money," p. 355 et seq.)
[4] If it did it would not use gold; platinum and several other metals are more costly than gold.
[5] Brooks Adams, Fortnightly Review, August, 1894.
[6] The public debt, which was 1,200 million dollars in 1793 amounted to 4,200 millions in 1817. Pitt paid the interest in notes, believing that money which was good enough for the people was good enough for the bondholders. Not only had the debt increased enormously, but a large number of offices had been created, and these officials like the owners of bonds and mortgages were very favorable to specie payments and the "preservation of the public honor."
[7] "Resumption in Great Britain," by J. W. Schuckers, 1877.

such a scene both of agricultural and commercial distress ensued as this unhappy country had at that time never before witnessed."[0] In 1817 the Government relented for a time, and permitted an expansion amounting to 15 millions of dollars, which did much to restore confidence and prosperity. At the close of 1817, however, and thruout 1818 a crisis occurred which Mr. Tooke attributes to the contractional disturbance caused by large loans negotiated in England for the French and Russian Governments.

The second attempt by the Government to adopt the policy of contraction occurred in 1819 and was successful; i. e., the policy was adopted. "Peel's Bill," as it is called, providing for the resumption of specie payments at a specified date three years distant, was introduced into the Commons on May 24th and passed June 23d amid a pandemonium of excitement.[1]

The Directors of the Bank of England, true to the interests of their country, opposed the measure, declaring that the rapid contraction they would be compelled to make in self defense in order to resume at the required time would ruin the industrial interests of the nation. Eminent bankers and merchants of London and other cities also opposed the bill. Lord Liverpool admitted in his speech upon the bill that "the commercial world would always be against the return to specie payments." He also said that "there could be no doubt of the advantages which the paper system had produced during the war." It had enabled the country to make efforts to which its means could not otherwise have been equal, and he readily admitted that in peace also the system afforded facilities to commerce which it would not otherwise enjoy. But paper money had no intrinsic value; it did not accord with his father's theories, and it was not as good for the bondholders as gold and silver would be, and so the law was passed in 1819.

The contraction of the currency was pushed with vigor,[2] prices began to fall, merchants and manufacturers failed by the score, a terrific panic ensued in 1825, and for a whole generation the business of Great Britain was depressed by the evil consequences of the fall of prices that resulted from the contraction policy of 1818-9.

In 1829 prices were about one-half what they were in 1809, and in 1849 they were 60 per cent. below the level of 1809.[3] "With the first measures for resumption." says Robert Mushet, "the prosperity of the country seemed to vanish."

In 1839 Lord Brougham said that he had always regretted having supported Peel's Bill for resumption. Jean Baptiste Say, the great French economist, closes an extensive review of the resumption period in England by declaring that "the privileged classes, the public functionaries, the pensioners of the State, and the fundholders, profited by the enhancement in the value of money," consequent upon the resumption act, "but that it laid a burden upon the masses of the people and upon industry which so rich and industrious a nation could alone support."

We know that Mr. Tooke endeavors to persuade us that Peel's Bill and the consequent contraction did not produce the disasters of the following years; but Mr. Tooke was one of the projectors

---

[0] Ibid., quoting Sir James Graham.
[1] Corbett's Parliamentary History.
[2] The bank reduced its private discounts from 32 millions of dollars in August, 1819, to 13½ millions in August, 1821, and its paper circulation from 131 millions in August, 1818, to 88 millions in August, 1822, a reduction of 33 per cent., accompanying which there was a contraction of country bank circulation between January, 1819, and December, 1822, of more than 80 per cent. (Resumption in Great Britain, 1819-22; by J. W. Schuckers.)
[3] Jevons' Price-levels. See also Mulhall's Dictionary of Statistics, title "Prices."

and promoters of the bill, and his testimony on this point is of little weight against the limitless mass of evidence to the contrary, backed by the whole force of economic principles as expounded by all the leading writers, and by the analogies of every period of serious contraction of which we have any record since the world began.

If instead of adopting the policy of contraction, England had done as France did in 1870 and following years, and expanded the currency with easy loans on the slightest symptoms of business depression, the disasters of the period of falling prices might have been avoided. The condition of affairs in England under an expanding currency during the Napoleonic wars, and under contraction in the following decades, is so strikingly parallel to the state of things in this country during the war expansion of 1860 to 1865, and the epoch of contraction following it, and the story is told with so much power by Sir Archibald Alison, the great historian of Europe and of England, that we quote a few passages from his "England in 1815 and 1845." Speaking of the period from the suspension of specie payments to the beginning of contraction, he says:

"The next eighteen years of the war, from 1797 to 1815, were, as all the world knows, the most glorious, and taken as a whole, the most prosperous which Great Britain had ever known. Ushered in by a combination of circumstances the most calamitous, both with reference to external security and internal industry, it terminated in a blaze of glory and a flood of prosperity which have never since the beginning of the world descended upon any nation. \* \* \* *Agriculture, commerce, and manufacture had increased in unparalleled ratio; the landed proprietors were in affluence; wealth to an unheard-of extent had been created among the farmers.* \* \* \* In the years 1813 and 1814, being the twentieth and twenty-first of the war, Great Britain had above a million men in arms in Europe and Asia, and remitted £11,000,000 yearly in subsidies to continental powers. Yet was this prodigious and unheard-of expenditure so far from exhausting either the capital or resources of the country that the loan of 1814 was obtained at a lower rate than that paid at the commencement of the war."

Contrast this with what Mr. Alison says of the post-contraction period from 1819 to 1845, the year in which he wrote:

"Considered in one point of view, there never was a nation which in an equal space of time had made so extraordinary a progress; its population had advanced from 20 millions in 1819 to 28 millions in 1844; its imports from 30 million pounds to 70 millions; its exports from 44 million pounds to 130 millions; its shipping from 2,350,000 tons to 3,900,000. There never, perhaps, was such a growth in these great limbs of industry in so short a period in any other State. \* \* \*

"Considered in another view, there never was a period in which a greater amount of financial embarrassment has been experienced by the Government, or more widespread and acute suffering endured by the people. \* \* \* The government was brought to such a pass that it was extricated from absolute insolvency only by *the re-imposition, during European peace, of the war income tax.* \* \* \* The nation during the late years of the war prospered and experienced general well-being under an annual taxation of £72,000,000 drawn from 18 million souls; in the latter years of peace it has, with the utmost difficulty, drawn £50,000,000 from a population of 27 millions. Wages in the former period were high, employment abundant, the working classes prosperous, with an export of 45 to 50 million pounds annually; in the latter, wages were in many trades low, employment difficult, suffering general, with an annual export of 120 to 130 million pounds."

"But extraordinary and *apparently* inexplicable as these facts may seem, they are yet exceeded in marvel by the *details* of our social and economical state during this period of unparalleled increase in our material resources. It may safely be affirmed that the anxiety and distress which were felt during that brilliant period of National growth have never been surpassed, at least in a State possessing the external mark of prosperity. It is well known to what straits the Bank of England has been reduced on two different occasions in that period. In December, 1825, we were, as Mr. Huskisson said, 'within twenty-four hours of barter.' * * *

"'The distress among the mercantile classes for years after the dreadful crisis of December, 1825, of the agricultural interests during the low prices from 1825-1832, and of the whole community from 1837 to 1842, was extreme. *Wages* sank during these disastrous periods in the manufacturing districts so low that they barely sufficed with the great bulk of workers, especially females, for the support of existence. * * *

"While population was advancing with unparalleled strides in the manufacturing districts, pauperism even more than kept pace with it all, and the extraordinary fact has now been revealed by statistical researches that, in an age of unbounded wealth and general and long-continued peace, a seventh part of the whole inhabitants of the British Islands are in a state of destitution, or painfully supported by legal relief. * * * While 70 thousand persons have among them an annual income of 200 million pounds, or $14,000 each * * * frightful strikes among workmen, attended with boundless distress among, and hideous democratic tyranny over them invariably succeeded those periods of suffering, as pestilence stalks in the rear of famine; and popular insurrection has become so common that it is a rare thing to see two years pass over without martial law being of necessity practically enforced in some part of the empire. * * * And as if to bring this chaos of contradictions to a perfect climax, at the very time when unheard of exertions have been made for the education of the people in every part of the empire, and the newly aroused fervor of religion in all denominations of Christians has drawn forth unparalleled efforts for the diffusion of the gospel among the working classes, *crime* has made unexampled progress in every part of the empire; and the scandal has been exhibited of serious and detected offenses having multiplied sevenfold in a realm which, in the same period has not added more than 70 per cent. to its population; in other words, during a period of unparalleled growth of wealth and effort at instruction, crime has augmented ten times as fast as the numbers of the people. * * * What we do say is unparalleled is the co-existence of so much suffering in one portion of the people, with so much prosperity in another. * * * There is food enough in the land and to spare, the *surplus* of it produced by our cultivators is daily and rapidly on the increase. * * * Nor are our resources in any way approaching the natural limits. * * * Capital exists and to profusion, amply sufficient to give full and profitable employment to the whole community. Labor adequate to any possible expansion of industry is at hand. Above two millions of destitute persons are pining for employment in Ireland alone. Our colonies are increasing with unheard of rapidity. * * * Yet with all this, great and wide-spread distress generally exists among the working poor, and whole classes of society in the more affluent ranks are gradually slipping down to a state of insolvency. * * *

(The cause) A. "In investigating the cause of this extraordinary state of things, one fact of leading importance must at the very first glance strike the observer. It is that the *opulence which has* *flown into the nation has been very far indeed from being evenly distributed;* and that, generally speaking, the landed interests have been as much impoverished during that time as the commercial have been enriched. * * * The embarrassments of the landed proprietors are, with the exception of a few magnates, notorious and universal. This is decidedly proved by the prodigious extent to which commercial wealth is everywhere buying up the estates of the old gentry, and rooting them and their families out of the land. And what is very remarkable, this state of things is just the reverse of what it was during the war. Agricultural industry was then not only amply but splendidly remunerated; the farmers rapidly made fortunes, and laid the foundation of the whole subsequent agricultural progress of Great Britain; and the purchase of land with borrowed money was nearly as certain a mode of making a fortune as it has since become of losing one."

B. "*The next remarkable feature* in the social state of Great Britain for the last quarter of a century *has been that capital has daily acquired a greater advantage over industry, or rather, large capital over small.* * * * The colossal fortunes made by manufacturers and great capitalists, contrasted with the innumerable bankruptcies of lesser adventurers in the same perilous path, is a proof. * * * The common complaint that the money power has become all-powerful, that its sway is paramount in the legislature, and that it is able to set all other interests in the community at defiance, is another proof. And a most decisive proof of the universal sense of the overwhelming, and often despotic influence of capital, has been afforded within this period by the astonishing multiplication of joint stock companies. * * * Falling as they generally do under the entire guidance of one or two active and skilfull directors, they have in effect enormously augmented the influence, already preponderating, of accumulated capital; they often commit practically with impunity unbounded inroads on private property. The obligation of giving compensation for property injured or taken is often rendered almost illusory, from the results of trials to ascertain its value. Defying competition, such companies are often deaf to the cries of justice. *Industrial*, as the French say, *has come in place of territorial feudality;* and probably men have already discovered in many parts of the country, *that a joint stock railway company, with its patriotic professions, accumulated capital, legislatorial attorneys, skilled engineers, scientific witnesses, railway stockholding jurymen and judges, and legions of Irish laborers, is a more formidable neighbor than ever was feudal baron with his mailed men-at-arms, stout archers and strong castles.*"

C. "The third feature is the uprecedented growth of the city. Generally speaking, the city population has immensely increased, and the rural by no means in the same proportion. In some counties the latter appears from the late census to have actually declined. * * * Nor has the increase of opulence in cities been less remarkable than the augmentation in the number of their inhabitants. The daily display of wealth in the metropolis excites the astonishment of every beholder. * * * But there are by no means the same symptoms of growing prosperity in the rural districts. * * * The farmers are contented if they can live; to make fortunes has become so rare among them that it is scarce ever thought of. * * * Wealth is not accumulating in the hands of the cultivators of the soil. * * * The affluence of the towns is derived from manufacturing and commerce, from professional gains, or from capital rendered a burden on land in former times."

D. "The last feature, and it is a most distressing one, is *the extraordinary inequality in the condition of the working classes themselves.* * * * Wages differ in a remarkable and most distressing degree. \* \* \* *It is the condition of the poor of the lowest grade* which is the most extraordinary feature of the last 20 years, and which has now assumed such a magnitude as to have become in every point of view a national concern. \* \* \* In every great town in the empire there is a mass, about the twelfth or fifteenth of its number, who are generally in a state of almost total penury. In periods of commercial distress this destitute class rises to double, sometimes triple its average amount. It is from this frightful tribulation of poverty, intemperance, vice and destitution, that two-thirds of the physical contagion which ravages, and four-fifths of the convicted crime which burdens society, takes its rise. \* \* \* This desolate community consists of widows with large families, destitute old men, young thieves, abandoned drunkards, licentious prostitutes, shameless publicans, audacious receivers of stolen goods, and once virtuous families, brought into such hideous society by being thrown out of employment. And all this exists unnoticed, unrelieved, within a few hundred yards of the most unbounded opulence, amidst luxury unheard of, prosperity unexampled, and in a community making more rapid progress in material resources than any that ever appeared upon the earth."

E. It was said that this distress of the industrious classes was owing to the transition from the vast National expenditures of war times to the limited expenditures of peace. But Mr. Alison replied that it was "rather too late to speak of that as the cause when they were already in the thirtieth year of unbroken European peace." Then it was affirmed that protection was the cause of the aforesaid evils, and the tariff duties were repealed, but the condition of the English laborer continued to be most pitiable.

Having disposed of these false theories, Mr. Alison asks, "What was the real cause?" "The answer is: *It was the contraction of the currency which was unnecessarily made to accompany the resumption of cash payments by the bill of 1819, which has been the chief cause of all these effects.*"

"When the commercial transactions of a nation increase, the circulating medium should increase also. This is as necessary a step as that when a people increases, their subsistence should be augmented in a similar proportion. If twenty millions of men on an average of years and transactions require 40 millions of circulating medium to conduct their transactions, then if these men swell to 30 millions, they will require, other things being equal, 60 millions of money for their transactions. If a supply proportioned to the increase of men and the wants of their commercial intercourse is not afforded, the circulating medium will become scarce, it will rise in price from the scarcity and become accessible only to the more rich and affluent classes. The industrious poor, or those engaged in business with small capital, will be the first to suffer; they will find it impossible to get currency to carry on their business and will fail in consequence. To retain the circulating medium of a country at a stationary or declining amount, when the numbers are rapidly increasing and their transactions are daily augmenting in number and importance, is the same thing as to affix a limit to the issuing of rations to an army at a time when the number of soldiers it contained was constantly augmenting. The inevitable result would be that numbers would be famished."

Could there be a more vivid and lifelike picture of events in the United States since 1865 than this pen picture of Great Britain in 1845 by the great, clear-sighted, true-hearted historian of England? And not merely the post-bellum periods are of identical character in the two countries, but the prior period in each is also the same. Coin money fled when the war broke out. Paper was issued. Specie payments were suspended December 2ᵉ, 1861. The currency began to expand, prices rose, business was active. The war and expansion combined to employ all labor. Either cause would have been likely to produce that effect, but together they were sure to produce it. Manufactures, commerce, agriculture and labor flourished. Wages were high; capital well paid. Wealth increased at a marvelous rate in spite of the tremendous drain of the war. At the close of the war the people were nearly free from debt (except the National debt, and even that was far less that it was made in the process of contracting the currency); there were about two billions of money in circulation among 25 millions of people, trade was carried on for cash more largely than ever before; prosperity was intense and universal.

In 1866 the policy of contraction was inaugurated, and the cremation furnaces began to blaze. The National bonded debt was built up. In 1869 it was enacted that the bonds bought with depreciated greenbacks should be paid in coin. In 1873 silver was demonetized. In 1875 it was decreed that specie payments should be resumed January 1, 1879. The result was that in 10 years from the time contraction began, the currency had diminished one billion dollars, while the people using it had nearly doubled (25 millions of the North in 1865, 45 millions of the whole country in 1876), while their business had more than trebled. And the process of contraction has continued till now, for altho the absolute volume of money has been increased somewhat in the last few years, it has not increased as fast as population and business. Prices have gone down. Wages have fallen and are distressingly unequal in different places and employments. Small merchants have been ruined. Strikes and panics have devastated the country. Agriculture has come to be a struggle for subsistence. The farmers have petitioned for Government loans on land and agricultural produce, and have been told that the tariff question was the only issue in politics. Cities have grown abnormally, while rural districts have in some cases declined in population. Wealth has increased enormously. So have poverty and crime. The magnificence of the millionaire, and the squalor of the tramp, have both become too common to excite a moment's notice. Capital has acquired a tremendous power over labor, and large capital over small. Corporations and their abuses overflow the years. The condition of the poor of the lowest grade in the slums of our cities is frightful, and has become a matter of National concern. How exact and minute the parallel!

The grand fact is that in England and in the United States during the period of expansion, wealth was rapidly created, and *was well distributed*, whereby prosperity and happiness ensued. But during the subsequent period of contraction, tho wealth was still more rapidly created it was *not* well distributed, and misery was the result. *Contraction of the currency means false distribution, congestion of wealth, and that means tyranny, slavery, misery.*

If England and the United States would re-establish the splendors of the war time, *they must increase the currency as fast as business increases*, and they should also take possession of the monopolies that have grown so fast in later years, cut down the over-rapid growth of great fortunes by a graded income tax and a heavy inheritance fee, and make adequate preparations to employ in the construction of public improvements all workmen who at any time would otherwise be idle. Thus we should restore the great forces that produced a diffused prosperity in the periods of war. If these simple things were done, the embarrassments of our business would cease, and public works could be accomplished involving perhaps as vast a labor as that expended in war, not merely without impoverishing the country, but to its unexampled enrichment.

## NOTE ON THE REGULATION OF THE MONEY VOLUME.

The efficiency of government control over the money volume thru the purchase and sale of properties (p. 127) is perfectly clear, as is also the efficiency of the "call-bond" plan (p. 126), the governmental power to issue and recall bonds at its pleasure is the power to regulate at will the volume of money. All that is necessary is to provide for reasonable adjustment of interest and fair distribution of bonds, or purchases and sales, so as to ensure the application of the remedy at the points of special need.

One of the automatic methods spoken of on p. 127, the plan of government loans, is also sufficiently clear in its operation to make detailed discussion unnecessary, but the other automatic method operating thru government bonds payable on demand, needs some elucidation. The main likelihood of confusion arises from failing to note that to make the regulation completely automatic, the interest payable on the bonds must vary with the rise and fall of prices.

Suppose a large volume of demand bonds had been issued. If a scarcity of money occurs thru a shrinkage of credit or otherwise, interest on business loans would go up, and persons feeling the need of funds would soon find it more profitable to get money for the bonds they might possess, than to keep them for the low interest paid by the Government. So far automatic action would go even tho the interest on the demand bonds were fixed and constant. But to secure *automatic return* whether the bonds were in possession of embarrassed or unembarrassed persons in times of falling prices when men with funds are frequently willing to take or keep safe investments at very low interest, and to secure the taking of bonds in case of rising prices when interest on ordinary business loans sometimes rises and sometimes falls, it would be necessary to make the interest payable on the bonds a variable one, rising rapidly as the price level ascends, and falling fast as the price line descends.

If it were universally true that interest falls with a rising price level, and rises with a falling price level, a good volume of demand bonds at a moderate fixed interest would secure complete automatic regulation of the money volume. If prices rose and business interest went down, it would soon become profitable to buy bonds, thus diminishing the circulation by the amount of money paid the Government for the bonds, and so checking the rise of prices. On the other hand if prices fell and market interest went up it would soon become unprofitable to keep the bonds on the comparatively low interest paid by the Government so that bonds would be returned and the currency increased by the money received from the Government for them, so checking the fall of prices.

The rise and fall of interest in opposition to the rise and fall of the price line is however only a part truth. In times of rising prices, the abundance of money, lessened risk in lending, and comparatively small number who have severe need of borrowing, tend to lower interest, but the high profits often made on a rising market tend to lead men to borrow even at high interest to extend their business and enlarge their profits, and the demand for and absorption of capital in promising enterprises also tends to lift interest by reducing the loan fund. The result is that in times of rising prices interest sometimes falls and sometimes rises. In times of revulsion and falling prices "interest always rises inordinately, because while there is a most pressing need on the part of many persons to borrow, there is a general disinclination to lend." (Mill's Polit. Econ.; Bk. III, CXXIII, §3, see also §4.) The disinclination to lend or invest however does not extend to loans on Government bonds. The risks of production are great and owners of money are unwilling to loan and interest on business loans rises, but these same money owners are anxious at such times to put their money into Government bonds or other *safe* investment even at very low interest; and the more depressed business is, the less chance there is for capital in productive industry, the more the money owners call for bonds. (The American, vol. 29, p. 249.) Interest on loans to producers or on any ordinary business loans tends to rise in time of distress and falling prices, but the interest demanded on safe investments such as government bonds tends to fall at such times. Men seek to withdraw their money from the risks of production, and a large amount of money accumulates in financial centers eager to invest at low rates in anything *safe*.

So far, therefore, as demand bonds on constant interest might be held by unembarrassed persons or those having funds seeking safe investment, there would be no automatic return or monetization of the bonds in times of distress, but on the contrary there would be a demand for more bonds. On the other hand so far as the bonds were held by embarrassed parties or men in need of money, they would be turned into money either by demand on the Government or sale to aforesaid capitalists who had withdrawn or withheld their funds from ordinary investment and circulation, and in either case the result would be an increase in the available circulation, and a corresponding relief from financial pressure and stringency.

It is evident from this that in order to make the automatic action of demand bonds certain and sufficient under all circumstances the *rate of interest* payable on the bonds must be made *a variable quantity*. The law must provide (1) that as prices rise the rate of interest that will be paid by the Government on the bonds shall grow rapidly larger so as to create a demand for the bonds that will at once bleed the plethoric currency and restore a wholesome circulation, and (2) that as prices fall the rate of interest that will be paid by the Government on the bonds shall go down a steep incline so that it shall fall below the rate at which money is willingly lent on such security, whereby the bonds will flow toward the Government and the tide of money flowing out in return for them shall lift the price line again to its normal level.

It must not be forgotten that, if the reasoning of this book is valid, after the Multiple Standard System is once in operation times of serious depression and withdrawal of money from ordinary investment will no longer occur, and the hoarding of money unwilling to venture on productive circulation will become a thing of the past, and a factor that need not be reckoned with in the problem under discussion.

It must be noted further that provision should be made to avoid the massing of the bonds in the hands of moneyed syndicates whereby the issue and return of the bonds might be prevented from having its due effect on the general circulation. This could be guarded against by limiting the amount of bonds to be held by one individual or company, and by provisions securing the fair distribution of the securities in different sections of the country and among the various states and cities and counties.

The third and fourth methods of regulating the money volume (p. 127) are not subject to the difficulties above considered. They are proof against interference from the variations of market interest, (the interest being adjusted by *law* in the 4th plan, and the properties dealt with by the 3d plan, including some that fall with a falling price level and some that *may* rise with a falling price level, and vice versa), and adequate distribution or application of the remedy in any required amount at the precise points where the cure is needed, is easy and natural,—with the fourth plan in fact the distribution will be automatic since the demand for Government loans will arise at the points where money is stringent and funds are needed, and loans will be returned where rising prices lift the Government interest to an uncomfortable height. The loans could be made thru existing banks and monetary agencies, but might be much more advantageously made thru postal banks.*

There is then one automatic plan of regulation the entire efficiency of which is as clear as anything can be made by reasoning in the absence of actual experiment, and another which could probably be made completely efficient by careful provisions as to interest and distribution. And entirely aside from automatic regulation of any kind the Government has at least two methods of regulation, the "call-bond" plan (p. 126) and the purchase and sale of properties (p. 127), which are easily capable of being operated with complete efficiency.

*Postal banks are not *necessary* to the success of the Multiple Standard System, but they would add greatly to the ease, economy and certainty of the Government's transactions, not only with reference to the regulation of the money volume, but in reference to various other monetary affairs, and would afford the people an absolutely safe deposit for their savings, a cheap financial agency for the collection of claims,&c., an extra guard against bank monopoly and a powerful aid for the accumulation of funds for purchase and nationalization of railways, telegraphs, etc. A complete system of national finance must include postal banks as well as National Multiple Standard currency.

www.ingramcontent.com/pod-product-compliance
Lightning Source LLC
Chambersburg PA
CBHW032137160426
43197CB00008B/680